Warman's
Fenton Glass
2nd Edition

Mark F. Moran

Identification and Price Guide

©2007 Krause Publications

Published by

700 East State Street • Iola, WI 54990-0001
715-445-2214 • 888-457-2873
www.krausebooks.com

Our toll-free number to place an order or obtain
a free catalog is (800) 258-0929.

Library of Congress Control Number: 2007924539

ISBN 13: 978-0-89689-571-3
ISBN 10: 0-89689-571-8

Designed by David Jensen
Edited by Kristine Manty

Printed in China

Contents

Introduction

The Fenton Art Glass Co. once prospered because of a century of innovation and responsiveness to public tastes. But 100 years ago, the vision of two Fenton brothers was just one small venture in the industrial landscape of an American economy grappling with competing forces at the end of the Victorian era.

The last years of the 19th century and the first decade of the 20th century witnessed the arrival of dozens of American glass-making operations, the result of years of development after the process of pressing glass into molds was refined in the mid-1820s.

Manufacturers included such familiar names as A.H. Heisey of Newark, Ohio; Anchor-Hocking Glass Co. of Lancaster, Ohio; Cambridge Glass Co. of Cambridge, Ohio; Consolidated Lamp & Glass of Fostoria, Ohio; Dugan & Diamond Glass of Indiana, Pa.; H. Northwood Co. of Wheeling, W.V.; Imperial Glass Co. of Bellaire, Ohio; Jeannette-McKee Glass Co. of Jeanette, Pa.; U.S. Glass Co. of Pittsburgh; and Westmoreland Glass Co. of Grapeville, Pa.

Prominent among these glass houses was Fenton.

The Fenton Art Glass Co. was founded in 1905 by Frank L. Fenton and his brother, John W., in an old glass factory building in Martins Ferry, Ohio. They initially sold hand-painted glass made by other manufacturers, but it wasn't long before they decided to produce their own glass. The new Fenton factory in

Frank L. Fenton, founder of the Fenton Art Glass Co.

Williamstown, W.V., opened on Jan. 2, 1907. From that point on, the company expanded by developing unusual colors (custard and chocolate, just to name two) and continued to decorate glassware in innovative ways.

Two more brothers, James and Robert, joined the firm. But despite the company's initial success, John W. left to establish the Millersburg Glass Co. of Millersburg, Ohio, in 1909. The first months of the new operation were devoted to the production of crystal glass only. Later iridized glass was called "Radium Glass."

After only two years, Millersburg filed for bankruptcy. (See more about Millersburg in the Carnival Glass section.)

Fenton's iridescent glass had a metallic luster over a colored, pressed pattern, and was sold in dime stores. It was only after the sales of this glass decreased and it was sold in bulk as carnival prizes that it came to be known as carnival glass.

Fenton became the top producer of carnival glass, with more than 150 patterns. The quality of the glass, and its popularity with the public, enabled the new company to be profitable through the late 1920s. As interest in carnival was subsiding, Fenton moved on to stretch glass and opalescent patterns. A line of colorful blown glass (called "off-hand" by Fenton) was also produced in the mid-1920s.

During the Great Depression, Fenton survived by producing functional colored glass tableware and other household items, including water sets, table sets, bowls, mugs, plates, perfume bottles and vases. The company also did subcontracting work for other retailers. In fact, some sources believe it was a single account to provide bowls and creamers in the early 1930s that saved the company from going under.

Restrictions on European imports during World War II ushered in the arrival of Fenton's opaque colored glass, and the lines of "Crest" pieces soon followed. A solid-colored (usually white) glass with ruffled edges was used to form the base of these items, with a clear or colored border around the ruffled edge.

In the 1950s, production continued to diversify with a focus on Milk-glass, particularly in Hobnail patterns.

In the third quarter of Fenton's history, the company returned to themes that had proved popular to preceding generations, and began adding special lines, like the Bicentennial series.

Innovations included the line of Colonial colors that debuted in 1963, including Amber, Blue, Green, Orange and Ruby.

Based on a special order for an Ohio museum, Fenton in 1969 revisited its early success with "Original Formula Carnival Glass."

The 1960s also wouldn't have been complete without Vasa Murrhina ("Vessel of Gems"), in Autumn Orange, Blue Mist and "Aventurine."

Fenton also started marking its glass in the molds for the first time.

Early Fenton production used various forms of paper labels to mark the glass. After 1969, an oval mark with "Fenton" inside it was introduced. Over a period of about five years, the logo was added to almost all Fenton glass. With the coming of the '80s, the mark was altered to reflect a new decade with an "8" placed

The "Decorating Room" of Fenton glass in 1907.

beneath Fenton in the oval; in the 1990s, a "9" was added. (For more details on marks, see Fenton Logos on Page 11.)

Opalescent patterns that were given new life included Cactus, and Satin finishes also developed a strong following. But the star of the 1970s was the yellow and blushing pink creation known as Burmese, which remains popular today. This was followed closely by a menagerie of animals, birds, and children.

In 1975, Robert Barber, an award-winning glass artist, was hired by Fenton to begin an artist-in-residence program with some of Fenton's most skilled craftsmen, producing a limited line of art-glass vases in a return to the off-hand, blown-glass creations of the mid-1920s.

The last chapter of the Fenton story was as much about technology as changing public taste.

Shopping at home via television was a recent phenomenon in the late 1980s when the "Birthstone Bears" became the first Fenton product to appear on QVC (established in 1986 by Joseph Segel, founder of The Franklin Mint). More than 1,400 different Fenton pieces have been sold on QVC.

Fenton established a Web site—www.fentonartglass.com—as a user-friendly online experience where collectors could learn about catalog and gift shop sales, upcoming events and the history of the company.

The site featured the Fenton Forum, a community of Fenton Art Glass enthusiasts who post messages and discuss topics; the *Glass Messenger*, Fenton's quarterly publication; and information on factory tours, and the company gift shop.

But Fenton's 102-year run came to an end in August of 2007.

The "Selecting Room" of Fenton glass in 1907.

Employees pose in Fenton's press shop in this 1910 photo.

The new Fenton factory in 1907.

The rose garden behind the company, with its creative landscaping.

1905: Frank L. Fenton and John W. start the Fenton Art Glass Company in Martins Ferry, Ohio, selling glass made by other companies.

1906-07: Fenton builds a new factory in Williamstown, West Virginia, which opens on Jan. 2, 1907. The company produces its own glass.

1909: John W. Fenton leaves the company to establish Millersburg Glass Co. of Millersburg, Ohio. The company goes bankrupt in 1911.

1920s: Fenton becomes the leading producer of carnival glass, with more than 150 patterns.

1925: Frank Fenton's brother, Robert C. Fenton Sr., is appointed vice president, secretary and sales manager.

1930s: The company begins to produce cranberry glass, baskets, crested ware and the Hobnail pattern.

1948: Frank M. Fenton becomes president after Frank L. and Robert C. Fenton die. Wilmer C. "Bill" Fenton becomes vice president.

1950s: Milk-glass, particularly in Hobnail pattern, is a focal point for the company.

1969: Fenton enters a business relationship with Cracker Barrel. The company also revives Original Formula Carnival Glass.

1970s: The Bicentennial series celebrates the nation's 200th anniversary.

1975: Robert Barber begins an artist-in-residence program and produces a line of art glass vases.

1978: Frank M. Fenton becomes chairman and Bill Fenton is named president of the company.

1980s: The Connoisseur Collection joins Milk-glass, Burmese and Rosalene as popular Fenton lines.

1986: George M. Fenton becomes president, his current position, and Bill Fenton becomes chairman, with Frank M. Fenton retiring to be the company historian.

1988: Bill Fenton offers the first of about 1,400 Fenton products to be sold on the QVC TV network.

1994: Fenton starts a Showcase Dealer Program with 235 dealers, which at its peak numbered more than 1,000.

1996: Fenton begins publication of the *Glass Messenger* quarterly newsletter for Fenton collectors.

2000: Fenton launches its Web site, www.fentonartglass.com.

2005: Fenton observes its 100th anniversary on May 4 and hosts a Fenton Centennial Celebration in Williamstown from July 31-Aug. 2.

2007: Company president George M. Fenton announces that the company will lay off its remaining workforce and close before the end of the year.

It's rare to find a company still in family hands after a century in business, but despite the involvement of four generations of the Fenton family, economic realities won out.

More than a 100 years of glass production drew to a close with the announcement that Fenton Art Glass Company was going out of business. Company president and CEO George M. Fenton blamed foreign competition, rising fuel prices and changing tastes of the middle class.

Fenton announced on Aug. 9, 2007, that the 102-year-old company would immediately lay off 25 of its 150 employees and cease taking orders at the end of the month. Glassmaking operations were to end in September and the company expected to close by the end of October.

"Certainly competition plays a role ... the cost of natural gas," said Fenton, whose grandfather started the plant in 1905. At the time of the announcement, nine family members still worked for the company. "I believe the discretionary income for the middle class, where our major market is, is part of the trend."

The company had been trying to restructure the business and develop plans to move forward, but it finally exhausted its options, Fenton said.

In a 2006 interview, Scott Fenton, vice president of sales, talked about the challenges facing the company.

"We are always looking ahead, but for the

Scott Fenton

past four years we've been in react mode," said Scott. "We've been reacting to economic issues that have directly affected the gift and collectible industry. We sold to twice as many storefronts a few years ago.

"Last year we looked at the floral market and jewelers. The mom-and-pop antique and gifts shops—although still out there and we were doing well with many of them—there just aren't as many as before."

Scott grew up on the manufacturing side of the business. His father, Thomas K. Fenton (George's brother), retired in 2006 from his post as vice president of manufacturing. Scott's grandfather was Frank M. Fenton, past company president and chairman of the board. Scott's great-grandfather was Frank L. Fenton, co-founder of the firm.

Dr. Chuck Bingham, a respected Fenton collector from Altoona, Wis., offered these thoughts on the demise of the company:

"Upon learning that Fenton would be

9

closing its doors, I felt a sense of personal loss—never again would I experience the joy of opening up the latest catalog and seeing what wonderful new items would need to be added to my collection. With further reflection, I sensed the loss of a large part of American art glass history—not only the glass output itself, but the cadre of highly skilled glass artisans, the proprietary knowledge of how to manufacture hundreds of different colors and types of glass, and the collection of historic glass molds amassed by the Fenton Art Glass Company. With more than a century of glassmaking under its belt, it seemed unfathomable that after surviving the Great Depression, two World Wars, and countless economic ups and downs, this great company had succumbed to the very pressures that have caused most other American glass companies to cease operations.

"But what a 102-year run it has been! Fenton is known for a vast variety of art glass produced over the years, from the iridescent glass made in its early decades, through its famous hobnail and crested glass, to its rebirth of hand-decorated glass and innovative colors and designs. One of the most exciting developments to come out of Fenton was the recreation of Burmese glass in 1970s, followed by what Fenton called Blue Burmese in the 1980s, and the unprecedented and stunning Lotus Mist Burmese in the 1990s. Happily, even in what proved to be its final year, Fenton was celebrating its glassmaking heritage as well as pushing the envelope in the manufacture of new types of glass. The year 2007 saw the remake of the stunning off-hand mosaic glass, originally produced in the 1920s, as well as the introduction of exquisitely sand-carved art glass designed by renowned artist Kelsey Murphy. These works of art surely epitomize the high quality of art glass made at Fenton.

"The Fenton Art Glass Company was not, however, just a manufacturer of glass—it was the quintessential family-run company. For those who had the pleasure of corresponding or conversing with historian extraordinaire Frank Fenton, meeting the younger Fenton family members at one of their many glass-signing events throughout the country, or simply enjoying Bill Fenton's witty repartee on QVC, the dedication of each member of the Fenton family was readily apparent. That personal touch added greatly to the experience of collecting Fenton glass.

"Though the furnaces in Williamstown may go cold, the astonishing variety of Fenton glass produced over the years will live on. As collectors, we will necessarily refocus our collections away from new items and toward those must-have "old" items, whether they are recent pieces we wished we had purchased, or a cherished item from the early decades of the company. The mission of our collectors' clubs will become even more important in keeping the history of Fenton art glass alive. Written documentation of Fenton's output, including this comprehensive volume, will attain even more importance in our studies.

"Farewell, Fenton! May your unparalleled legacy of fine American art glass be enjoyed for generations to come."

The Fenton oval was put into Carnival Glass only in 1970. Between 1972 and 1973, it was added to Hobnail and other wares. By 1975, almost all glass had the logo.

75th—Added to the 75th Anniversary collection in 1980.

In 1980, along with the Fenton oval, a small "8" was added to molds to denote the decade of the Eighties.

The Fenton "Script F" without oval has been inscribed on some blown ware or used as a special decal when the logo in the mold was not readable.

FENTON 80th—Added to the 80th Anniversary collection in 1985.

Beginning in 1983, the "Script F" inside an oval appears in molds acquired from McKee or other glass companies (Verlys, Paden City, and U.S. Glass are exceptions). An "8" to denote the 1980s or a "9" to denote the 1990s may also appear. The "0" was added beginning in 2000.

In 1990, along with the Fenton oval, a small "9" indicates glass produced in the decade of the Nineties. This appears in Fenton molds and also in all Verlys, Paden City and U.S. Glass molds used at Fenton.

"90th"—Added to the company's 90th Anniversary 1995 Historic Collection.

"95" in a circle—Added to the two 1995 Historic Collections in 2000 (Lotus Mist Burmese and Willow Green Opalescent).

The "Fenton" logo is sandblasted onto pieces in which the mold logo may not show well. This logo is only used in molds from Fenton, Verlys, Paden City, and U.S. Glass. An "8" to denote the 1980s or a "9" to denote the 1990s may also appear. The "0" was added beginning in 2000.

Early in the 1990s, seconds were marked with a "flame" that resembles a calligraphy-style S.

A solid or open single star may be found sandblasted on the bottom or sides of "preferred seconds" sold primarily in the Fenton Gift Shop (June 1996 to July 1998). A double star was put on ware donated to Williamstown, West Virginia, organizations for fund-raising activities.

A simple "F" replaced the star in August 1998 on the bottom of "preferred seconds" sold primarily in the Fenton Gift Shop.

Cautions About Dating Fenton Glass

By Mark Chervenka

Although Fenton Glass hasn't been deliberately reproduced with the intention to mislead collectors, Fenton buyers still need to be somewhat wary. The biggest problem is not fake or spurious copies, but incorrectly dating pieces of legitimate Fenton. Many inexperienced sellers, especially in online auctions, often describe modern Fenton pieces as vintage items. Understanding Fenton's marking system, Fenton's private mold work and a few technical details of glass production will help most buyers sort through the questionable items.

Fenton Glass, founded in 1905, never consistently marked all of its standard production glass until 1974. In that year, the word "Fenton" in cursive, or script, lettering inside an oval began to be molded into Fenton glass. The letters of "Fenton" were the only characters to appear within the oval until 1980. At that time, a dating code also began to appear within the oval. The dating code is a single digit, or number, which represents the decade in which the glass is made. The first date code was the number "8" for the decade of the 1980s; the number 9 was for the decade

Basic raised molded script Fenton mark in pressed glass since 1974.

Beginning in 1980, a single digit representing the decade of production was added to the molded mark. An "8" designates the 1980s; a "9" the 1990s, and so on.

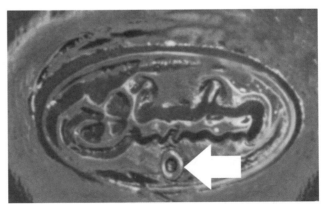

Fenton marks in blown-molded wares are often blurred. This mark is from the bottom of a blown-molded pickle castor insert. Note the decade digit 0, indicating production in the first decade of the 21st century.

of the 1990s and so on. The date code using a "0" represents the first decade of the 21st century. As a general guideline, except for new carnival glass, all pieces marked "Fenton" in the mold, then, could be no earlier than 1974 when the oval mark was introduced.

While Fenton's policy of permanent, date-coded markings should be applauded, there are several potential problems of which collectors should be aware. The most significant is that private mold work—glass made by Fenton for other companies for sale under different names—is excepted from the marking policy. Whether permanent Fenton marks appeared on private mold work was decided by the customer; it is therefore possible for private mold work made in a Fenton mold after 1974 to appear in the market without the molded Fenton mark. In that case, it would be necessary to refer to a collector's book like this one or a catalog reprint and use color to determine when, if ever, the piece was a part of the official Fenton product line. Some beginning collectors find these unmarked privately made pieces and immediately conclude they have a "rare unlisted" pre-1974 item. Carefully checking production records will prevent making that mistake.

The other problem with Fenton marks is related to technical aspects of glass manufacturing. The majority of Fenton pieces, for example, were made by pressing. With pressed glass, a metal plunger, or mirror-image mold section, forces glass against a design in the mold including any marks. Once the mold is filled, the glass mass does not change size. Any design imparted by the mold, including marks, retains its shape after it leaves the mold. Marks on pressed Fenton are almost always quite legible and easy to recognize.

Producing permanent marks in blown glass, though, is considerably more difficult. Unlike pressed glass, which essentially doesn't change size when it comes out of the mold, blown pieces generally require additional shaping and handling which alter the size and surface of the glass. Marks on mold-blown Fenton can often be very difficult to locate and in many cases almost invisible to the average buyer.

Spot molds, for example, like the ones used to create the patterns in almost all opalescent glass, only created a pattern on the glass gather. The gather was then blown out into a shape mold (vase, tumbler, etc.) for its final form. If the mold slug with the mark was in the spot mold, the mark expanded as the gather was blown into the shape mold. As it expanded, the mark distorted and became less distinct. Rotating the glass in the shape mold, running over the glass surface with smoothing paddles or reheating the glass further blurred any marks. By the time the finished piece left the shop for the annealing oven, the mark may be difficult to find and almost impossible to read.

It's important to understand how marks on Fenton blown glass may be affected during production because some of the most

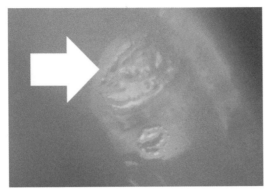

The Fenton mark in a blown-molded jadite rolling pin. It's so blurred, the mark is all but illegible even assuming that it could be located.

Another Fenton mark in a blown-molded vaseline glass rolling pin. Even under strong light from behind, the mark is difficult to recognize as a Fenton date mark.

desirable and highest priced pre-1974 Fenton was made by blowing. If you don't understand how these marks are made, it's not uncommon to mistake later blown glass for pre-1974 unmarked Fenton or even Victorian-era glass.

This became particularly important as Fenton increased the number of pieces it made by blowing. In 1999, for example, Fenton was a major buyer at the auction of LG Wright Glass Co. molds. Most collectors are aware that although Wright owned the molds, actual production was jobbed out to Fenton and other glass companies. Of

the approximately 700 molds auctioned, Fenton bought 202, many of which were spot molds, which require blowing. Fenton had been reworking those molds and bringing them back into production. By late 2000 and continuing into 2001, Fenton began using the Wright spot molds to make a number of opalescent patterns including Spanish Lace, Fern, Dot Optic and others. These patterns were made as pickle castor inserts, lamp fonts, shakers and other forms. Although these new pieces began the production process with a permanent Fenton mark, many marks were all but invisible by the time the glass was finished and offered for sale.

Around 2000, Fenton also bought at least one mold originally used by McKee Glass, the mold used to make the rare so-called "double-ring" blown jadite rolling pin. Fenton first used the mold to make new rolling pins for Martha Stewart's catalog and online sales divisions in two colors, pale green opaque glass, or jadite, and a pink opaque glass. In 2002, Fenton used the McKee mold again to produce more pins in jadite, vaseline, and other colors for other distributors. The Stewart pins, as far as can be determined, were not originally marked at the time of production. The later pins made from the McKee mold in 2002 were marked at the time of production but the finishing process has made the marks difficult to find.

Another important caution about marks is to be sure you inspect the complete object, especially items made of two or more pieces,

Two new blown-molded pickle castor inserts made by Fenton. The marks on the bases are located on the bases. Blowing and finishing the glass can frequently cause the marks to almost disappear.

A new vaseline glass rolling pin made from the original McKee mold which Fenton now owns. The rolling pin is made by blowing glass into the mold, which blurs the Fenton mark.

like covered dishes, jars with lids and similar shapes. Most two-piece objects made after 1974 are only marked on one of the pieces. An example of these potentially confusing Fenton shapes is the massive two-piece covered dish originally sold in the 1950s under the catalog name "Chickenserver." The bottom half of the Chickenserver is a huge 11-inch by 13-inch platter-like base. Molded scallops around the outer rim of the base are for serving deviled eggs. Molded in the center of the base is an 8-inch "nest" covered by the lid, a figural 8-inch-long hen.

The Chickenserver was first made by Fenton from 1953 to 1954 in solid Milk-glass, catalog #5188. A slight variation with colored-glass heads on a Milk-glass body, #5189, was made from 1955 to 1956. Known

authentic variations include Milk-glass bases with colored glass covers. Both of the 1950s originals, #5189 and #5188, were unmarked.

After 1956, the Chickenserver was dropped from regular production until 1996 when it was brought back into the Fenton line as a limited edition and sold through 1997. The Fenton pieces were made of decorated Milk-glass, marked in the lid (only) and limited to 950 pieces. About this same time, 1997 or early 1998, Fenton began making the Chickenserver in jadite, and possibly other colors, for Martha Stewart's mail-order and online catalogs. The 1990s versions by Fenton and Stewart are both marked in the lid with Fenton in an oval alongside the number 9. Original 1950s Chickenservers can sell for more than $300 in the collectors' market depending on the particular color combination. The Fenton 1996-97 limited-edition version retailed for $112; the Stewart jadite version retailed for $98.

Even though all Chickenservers were pressed, not blown, the mark may still be difficult to find because of its size and location. Marks in the lids of the 1990s versions are unusually small, much smaller than the regular molded Fenton mark. If the mark is overlooked, the post-1974 examples could be mistaken for pieces of earlier production. There is also the potential for mixing old unmarked lids with new unmarked bases.

While deliberate fakes and reproductions of Fenton aren't a problem now, that doesn't mean you shouldn't have a healthy skepticism when considering a purchase, especially when buying online without a first-hand examination. Don't assume because a date mark is not readily apparent that a piece was automatically made before 1974. Look twice and consider how the piece was made. If it was blown in a mold, be especially careful. When in doubt, check the original production colors. Keep in mind that Fenton also owned many of the LG Wright molds. Glass that Fenton made with those molds might be confused with pre-1974 Fenton or Wright products, especially if the glass was private work, which may be unmarked.

Mark Chervenka is America's most recognized expert on antique fakes and reproductions. He is the publisher of the Internet-based Antiques and Collectors Reproduction News, www.repronews.com.

The jadite Chickenserver Fenton made for Martha Stewart in 1998 is marked in the lid only. Original 1950s chickenservers are not marked on lid or base.

This is a Fenton look-alike piece made by LE Smith glass. Both Fenton and LE Smith pieces, first introduced in the 1950s, have been reproduced.

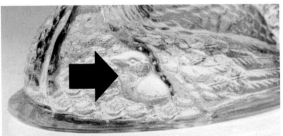

Neither the 1950s version or the modern reproduction of the Smith piece is marked. The LE Smith piece has a chick peeping out from under the hen's left wing.

How to Use This Book

Warman's Fenton Glass is divided into five eras: 1905 to 1930 (this includes vintage carnival glass), 1930 to 1955, 1955 to 1980, 1980 to 2007 and Post-2007. Each section lists glass colors and patterns alphabetically, and includes a brief summary of glass characteristics and/or times of production.

Prices

The prices in this book have been established with the help of more than a dozen seasoned collectors and dealers in Fenton. These values reflect not only current collector trends, but also the wider economy. The adage that "an antique (or collectible) is worth what someone will pay for it" also holds true for Fenton. A price guide measures value, but it also captures a moment in time, and sometimes that moment can pass very quickly.

Beginners should follow the same advice that all seasoned collectors have learned: Make mistakes and learn from them; talk with other collectors and dealers; find reputable resources (including books and Web sites), and learn to invest wisely, buying the best examples you can afford. Unlike most other collecting areas, Fenton has not been plagued with reproductions, and when the company reissued pieces based on earlier designs, the company logo often helps determine age and authenticity.

Words of Thanks

The gathering of information for this guide was greatly assisted by these generous folks:

Sharon and Alan Fenner

Bev and Jon Spencer

Steve Duncan

Bob Grissom

Richard and Sara Speaight

Dick and Marilyn Trierweiler

Randy and Peg Bradshaw

Diane Rohow

Chuck Bingham

Doug Horton

James Langer

Mel and Lynn Bausch, Susan McLaughlin
and the other members of the Fenton Finders
of Southeastern Wisconsin

Fenton by Era

Fenton's early production was not limited to carnival glass.

Water sets (also called lemonade or iced tea sets)—made up of a pitcher or tankard and matching tumblers—came in clear ("crystal") and colored versions, the earliest examples (1907) with enameled floral decoration. A few were later made in carnival glass.

Chocolate glass resembles coffee to which cream has been added, with lighter and darker swirls accenting a range of tableware, novelties, utilitarian pieces and vases. It was made until about 1910, and some collectors call it "caramel slag." It was reintroduced from the mid-1970s to mid-1980s, including a line of Bicentennial pieces.

The Water Lily and Cattails pattern, introduced in 1907, included bowls, butter dishes, comports, covered sugars, creamers, pitchers, plates, spooners and tumblers; they are found in crystal and frosted (satin). Patterns that followed from 1908 to about 1911 included No. 65 Northern Star, No. 100 Honeycomb and Clover, No. 400 Crystal "Sunburst," Beaded Stars, and Holly. These patterns also featured bonbon dishes, nappies and vases.

Opalescent glass colors introduced in this era include amethyst, blue, crystal (called "French opalescent" in the 1930s) and green. Patterns include Basket Weave with Open Edge, Beaded Stars, Blackberry Spray (sometimes referred to as having "Goofus" decoration), Buttons and Braids, Coin Spot, Fenton Drapery, Honeycomb and Clover, Stag and Holly, and Water Lily and Cattails.

The most common examples of wheel-cut crystal (1912)—usually with floral or fruit motifs—are bud vases, bowls, pitchers, tumblers

Chocolate glass footed bowl in Vintage, circa 1908, 6" diameter, $125+.

and larger vases are also numerous. Pieces in this group are among the most affordable examples of Fenton glass. Peak production occurred in the years just prior to World War I, and production eventually halted during the Great Depression.

Early custard glass (circa 1915) ranges in color from pale ivory to a creamy yellow, and can be found with green highlights, and a rusty tan or pink applied decoration sometimes called nutmeg or "peach blow." The most common pattern is Cherry and Scale (called "Fentonia" when made in carnival glass), but there are several other known patterns. Custard glass is also found with hand-painted decoration in several colors.

Custard glass was made using uranium salts, which were also a common ingredient in producing brightly colored yellow and green glass for more than a hundred years. In custard glass, uranium is what gives the glass its deep cream color. Restrictions on the use of uranium during World War II marked the end of custard glass made this way.

Custard glass made after 1972 may have a satin finish, and bears the Fenton name in raised letters, a practice that began in 1970.

Persian Blue (circa 1915) is commonly found with a hand-applied Banded Laurel motif, in either white (enamel) or gold, and with other floral motifs, often on tableware.

A rare line introduced about 1916, the Vertical Ribbed pattern came plain (No. 250), and with deep amber horizontal trim lines (No. 580). It featured covered butter dishes and sugar bowls, creamers, jugs (pitchers), nappies (bowls), spooners, and tumblers. Prices are only slightly higher for examples with amber trim.

Stretch glass is iridized glass that has been re-heated after the mehic sprays that cause the iridescence have been applied. This causes the external surface, which has bonded to the spray, to expand less then the glass beneath it, and so to split and produce fine striations on the surface of the glass. These give the glass a shiny matte appearance, unlike carnival glass, which is not re-heated after spraying and is usually shiny.

Stretch glass was introduced in the U.S. in about 1916, was very popular in the 1920s and continued to be made until the mid-1930s. The name was applied by glass collectors in a much later period, and was not used by the manufacturers of this glass.

Most stretch glass is produced from plain designs, usually without surface decoration or pattern, unlike carnival glass, which usually has a pattern pressed in the glass. Some stretch glass is mold blown and quite often, it is mistaken for art glass produced by such contemporary companies as Steuben and Tiffany. Their glass, however, has an iridescence that was produced by chemicals in the glass, not sprays applied to the glass, even if a stretch-glass effect was sometimes added later.

Fenton by Era

The pale blue transparent glass called Aquamarine was also known as azure early in its production. Dolphin handles and a Diamond Optic pattern are frequently found. Pieces in "Mermaid Blue" were not made until 1933.

Aquamarine, two pieces, circa 1927, from left: crimped bonbon, handled, 6" diameter, **$30**; crimped comport in Diamond Optic, dolphin handles, 5" h, **$45**.

Amethyst Opalescent flared bowl in Water Lily and Cattails, 1920s, 8-1/2" diameter, **$55+**.

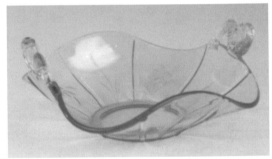

Aquamarine dolphin-handle bonbon with wheel-cut flowers, late 1920s, 5-1/2" square, **$20+**.

Though it originated about 1910, Black glass was not put into wide production until the late 1920s, and early examples—beginning about 1915—also used carnival glass molds. Some pieces may be found paired with Moonstone. Ebony is generally used to describe glass made after the 1930s.

Black (Ebony) comport with dolphin handles and silver overlay, late 1920s, 5" h, rare, **$150**.

Two candlesticks with Black (Ebony) bases, 1920s: blue, 8" h; Grecian Gold, 10" h, **$120+** each.

Black (Ebony) bud vases in Prayer Rug, circa 1916, one flared and one tulip crimped, each 6" h, **$30+** each.

Black (Ebony) shaker in Lincoln Inn, pewter top, late 1920s, 4-1/2" h, **$200+.**

Black (Ebony) fan vase, 1926, with thistles in an encrusted pattern done by Lotus Glass Decorating Co., Barnsville, Ohio, 8" h, rare, **250+.**

Black (Ebony) flared vase with an etched floral pattern, 1920s, 10" h, $95.

Fenton by Era

Early opalescent colors include amethyst, blue and green. It was not until the 1930s that Crystal examples became known as French Opalescent.

Blue Opalescent bowl in Northern Star, circa 1910, 8-1/2" diameter, **$45+.**

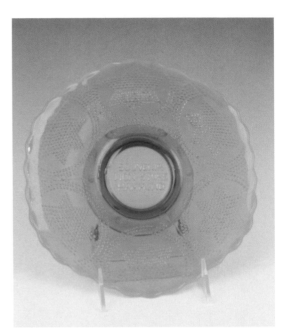

Blue Opalescent footed advertising plate in Beaded Stars, marked "Souvenir Lyon Store Hammond" (Ind.), circa 1910, 8-1/2" diameter, **$50+.**

Blue Opalescent covered jug and tumbler in Rib Optic with cobalt handles, part of a lemonade set that would have included six tumblers, 1920s; jug, 10" h; tumbler, 5" h, **$700+** for complete set.

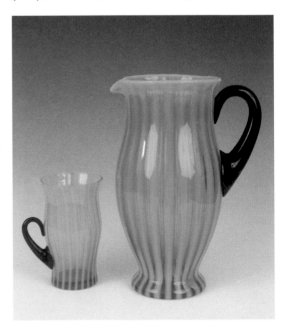

Blue Opalescent jug and tumbler in Rib Optic with cobalt handles, part of a lemonade set that would have included six tumblers, 1920s; jug, 10" h; tumbler, 5" h, **$800+** for complete set.

Blue Opalescent swung vase in Fenton Drapery, circa 1910, 14" h, **$45+.**

Cameo Opalescent covered candy jars, 3/4 pound and one pound, 1926-27, 9-1/4" h and 10" h, **$55+** each.

Cameo Opalescent was put into wide production only for a short time in 1926-27, although pieces with a hexagonal form are known to be at least a decade earlier. For later examples of Cameo Opalescent, see 1955 to 1980.

Celeste Blue stretch-glass covered jug and tumbler with cobalt handles, base and coaster, part of a lemonade set that would have included six tumblers, 1920s; jug, 11-1/4" h with base; tumbler, 5" h not including coaster, which is 3-1/4" diameter; **$700+** for complete set.

Celeste Blue stretch-glass candleholders and footed console bowl (also called an "orange bowl"), circa 1920; candleholders, 8-1/2" h, **$80+** pair; bowl, 11" diameter, **$275+**.

Celeste Blue stretch glass was made in dozens of shapes beginning in 1917, and is rarely found with an engraved design in shallow bowls and plates. A few examples may be found without iridescence. Reintroduced as part of the company's 90th anniversary celebration, these pieces bear the Fenton logo.

fenton by Era

Three candleholders, all 1920s to mid-1930s, from left: Dolphin in Ruby, 3-1/2" h, **$40+**; Velva Rose and Celeste Blue, 2-3/4" h, **$35+** each.

Two candlesticks in Grecian Gold and Celeste Blue, mid-1920s, 8" to 8-1/2" h, **$65+** each.

Celeste Blue bud vase, 1920s, 11-1/2" h, **$55+**.

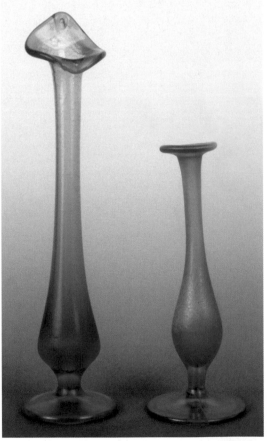

Celeste Blue stretch-glass bud vases in two sizes, circa 1917: 12" h, **$65**; 8" h, **$45**.

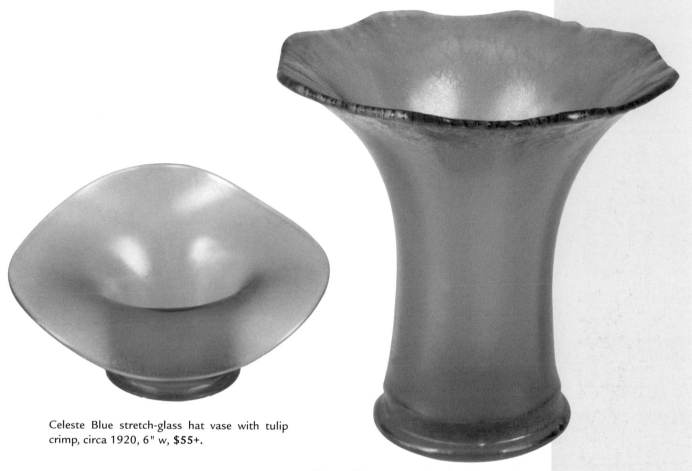

Celeste Blue stretch-glass hat vase with tulip crimp, circa 1920, 6" w, **$55+.**

Celeste Blue stretch-glass flared vase, circa 1920, 6-1/2" h, **$70+.**

Celeste Blue stretch-glass guest set including jug with cobalt handle and tumbler, mid-1920s; jug, 7" h; tumbler (which fits inside jug), 3-3/4" h, **$500+** set.

Fenton by Era

Though made into the 1930s, Chinese Yellow was introduced about 1922. For examples in the Dancing Ladies pattern, see 1930 to 1955.

Three candlesticks, mid-1920s, 8" and 10" h: Florentine Green, **$120**; Chinese Yellow and Cameo, **$150** each.

Chinese Yellow flared bowl with rolled rim, with Ebony base, mid-1920s, 11" diameter, **$125+** set.

Chinese Yellow flared vase with Ebony base, mid-1920s, 7-1/4" h overall, **$125+** set.

With few exceptions, Crystal pieces can often be dated by pattern. They are among the most affordable of all Fenton glass.

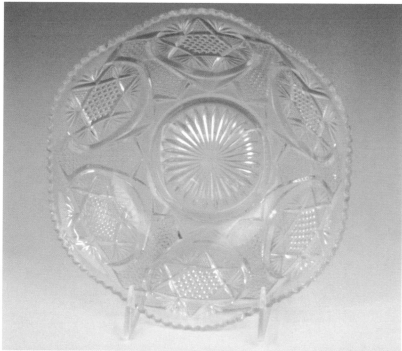

Crystal flared bowl in Northern Star, circa 1908, 8-3/4" diameter, **$25+.**

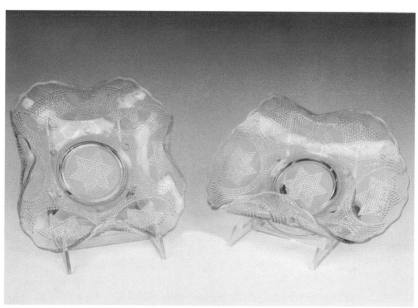

Crystal pieces in Beaded Stars, circa 1910, from left: square crimp bonbon and banana boat, each 8-1/2" w, **$45+ each.**

Crystal bud vase, wheel-cut floral decoration, 1914, 8" h, **$20+.**

Fenton by Era

Crystal Opalescent pieces in Beaded Stars, circa 1910, from left: square crimp bonbon, 6-1/2" w; bowl, 7-1/2" diameter; **$45+** each.

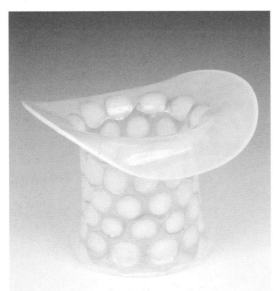

Crystal cupped bowl in Beaded Stars, left, circa 1910, 6" diameter; Crystal Opalescent lipped plate in Beaded Stars, right, circa 1910, 8" diameter; **$45+** each.

Crystal Opalescent hat vase in Coin Spot, circa 1915, 8-1/4" w, 6" h, **$150+.** In Coin Dot, the "coins" are clear; in Coin Spot, the coins are opaque.

Crystal and Jade Green shakers in Diamond Optic (the pattern is on the inside of the Jade Green shaker), late 1920s, 4-1/2" h; Crystal, **$30-$40**; Jade Green, **$50-$75.**

Early Opalescent handled bonbon in Blackberry Spray, 1911, with "Goofus" decoration, 6" diameter, **$20.**

"Goofus glass" is a generic term for pressed glass with "cold painted" decoration that was not fired on to the surface. Cold paint tends to wear easily. The most common kind of Goofus glass has red or green paint on flowers or berries, and a mehic background, usually gold or silver. Made in large quantities from the turn of the 19th century until the 1920s, it was popular for its bright colors, and because it could be cheaply made.

Florentine Green stretch-glass candleholders, circa 1920, 3-3/4" h, **$90+ pair.**

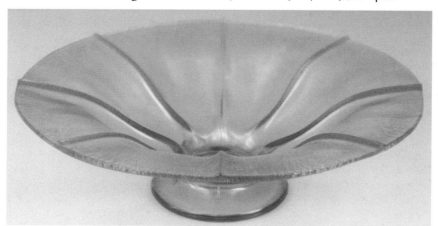

Florentine Green stretch-glass flared bowl, circa 1920, 11" diameter, **$75+.**

Florentine Green stretch-glass was made for just over a decade, from 1917 to about 1928, when it apparently lost ground to the less-expensive Green Transparent, which many beginning collectors think of as Depression Glass.

Fenton by Era

Green Opalescent plate in Northern Star, circa 1910, 10-1/2" diameter, **$50+.**

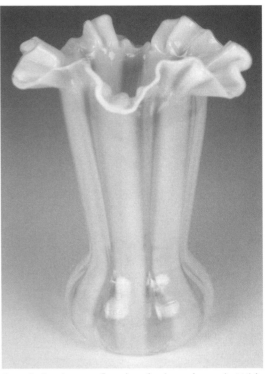

French Opalescent flared and crimped vase in Wide Rib Optic, 1920s, 9-1/2" h, **$275+.**

Green Opalescent covered jug and tumbler with cobalt handles in Rib Optic, part of a lemonade set that would have included six tumblers, 1920s; jug, 10" h; tumbler, 5" h, **$700+** for complete set.

Green Opalescent tumblers in Rib Optic, with cobalt handles, 1920s, 4-1/2" h, **$65+** each.

Green Opalescent pieces in Beaded Stars, circa 1910, showing variations in color and opalescence: square crimp bonbon, left, and hexagonal bowl, each about 8-1/2" w, **$45+** each.

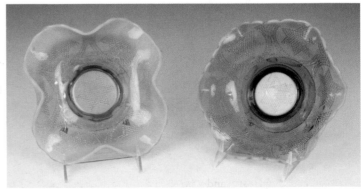

Green Transparent comport in Ribbed Holly Sprig, early 1920s, 4" h, **$20+**.

Green Transparent dolphin-handle bonbon with ruffled edge and wheel-cut flowers, late 1920s, 7-1/2" w at handles, **$20+**.

Hanging Hearts and Vines off-hand footed bowl, mid-1920s, 10" diameter, **$2,800+**.

Green Transparent glassware varies considerably in intensity of color. Made from about 1923 to the late 1930s, examples with wheel-cut decoration are especially prized, but because it was made in such large numbers, it is still among the most affordable of all early Fenton glass. (See 1930 to 1955.)

Early off-hand glass—made without molds—was produced for only one year, in 1925-26. The experiment didn't last because of the high cost of production, and because it was such a dramatic departure from the cheap carnival glass that had made Fenton famous. In addition to Hanging Hearts, see Karnak and Mosaic. The process was briefly revived in the mid-1970s in what has come to be called the "Robert Barber era" (see 1955 to 1980).

Fenton by Era

Jade Green was a phenomenally successful color introduced in 1921. Many more examples of Jade Green can be found in 1930 to 1955. Fenton reintroduced Jade Green in 1980.

Jade Green pieces, late 1920s, from left: footed ashtray, 4-1/2" diameter, **$40+**; footed candleholder in Basket Weave with open edge, 5" diameter, **$45+**.

Table lamp made with Karnak Red off-hand vase in Hanging Hearts and Vines, with a bronze leaf-form base, mid-1920s; vase, 14" h; lamp, 28" h with base and fitting, no established value.

Mosaic off-hand candlestick, mid-1920s, 5" h, **$900+**.

Mandarin Red candleholder No. 318, mid-1920s, 3" h, **$65**.

Introduced in 1927 and in production for little more than a year, Orchid is frequently found in the Diamond Optic pattern.

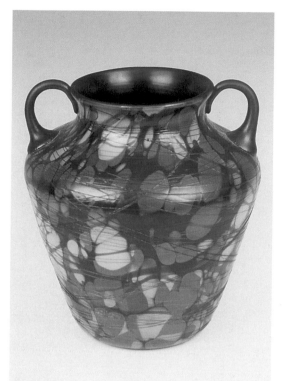

Mosaic off-hand handled vase, mid-1920s, 7" h, **$1,800+.**

Mosaic off-hand vase, mid-1920s, 8" h, **$1,500+.**

Peach Blow custard-glass vase in Butterfly and Berry, left, 1915, 8" h, **$50**; custard-glass mug in Rose No. 2, 1915, 3-1/2" h, **$30+.**

Orchid dolphin-handle tidbit or sandwich tray in Diamond Optic, late 1920s, 10" diameter, **$100+.**

Pekin Blue and Royal Blue candleholders, style No. 318, late 1920s to early '30s, 3" h, **$40-$50** each.

Fenton by Era

Persian Blue pieces, 1915, showing the variations in color intensity; handled bonbon, left, and shallow bowl, both in Pond Lily and Leaf, about 6" diameter, **$30** each. (Fenton revived Persian Blue in 1980, but the later pieces are all marked.)

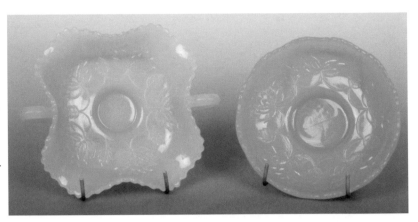

Persian Blue pieces, 1915, in Laurel Leaf: vase, 8" h, **$40**; nappy, 4-1/2" diameter, **$20**.

Persian Blue handled bonbon, 1915, in Pond Lily with enamel decoration, 7" diameter, **$35**.

Persian Blue rose bowl, 1915, in Persian Medallion, with enamel decoration, 3-1/4" h, **$55**.

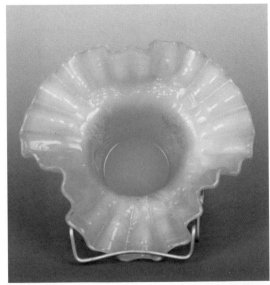

Persian Blue violet vase, 1915, in Flowering Dill interior, tri-crimp with ruffled edge, enamel decoration, 6" diameter, **$30**.

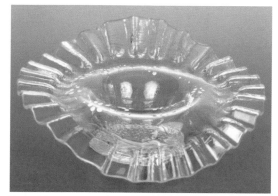

Rose Transparent hat vase with Blackberry Spray, enamel decoration, late 1920s, 7" diameter, **$30.**

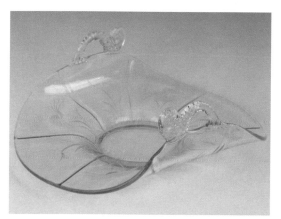

Rose Transparent dolphin-handle bonbon with wheel-cut flowers, late 1920s, 9-1/2" w, **$35+.**

Bud vases in Rose and Green Transparent, wheel-cut floral decoration, late 1920s, 8" and 9" h, **$15+ each.**

The transparent version of Rose was introduced at about the same time (1927) as the stretch-glass variety, which was called Velva Rose (1926). For more examples of Rose, see 1930 to 1955.

Rose Transparent elephant-form flower bowl, late 1920s, 7" h, **$500+.**

Fenton by Era

Ruby made its debut in 1921, and pieces may also be found with dolphin handles and in the Diamond Optic pattern. Some forms may have a gold tinge around rims and bases. For more examples of Ruby, see 1930 to 1955.

Ruby bonbon with Dolphin handles, late 1920s, 6-1/2" w, **$50+**.

Ruby dolphin-handle comport in Diamond Optic, late 1920s, 6" h, **$110+**.

Ruby candlestick No. 549 with Black (Ebony) base, 1925, 8" h, **$150+**.

Ruby flared vase with wheel-cut decoration, ribbed, late 1920s, 6" h, **$200+**.

Ruby flared vase with etched flowers, 1920s, 11-1/2" h, **$150+**.

Tangerine stretch-glass comport with dolphin handles, late 1920s, 5" h, **$160+.**

Tangerine stretch-glass tidbit tray in Diamond Optic, late 1920s, 10" diameter, **$125+.**

Tangerine stretch-glass flared bowl, late 1920s, 10" diameter, **$150+.**

Tangerine stretch glass was made from 1927 to 1929. It is valued considerably higher than the non-iridescent Tangerine made at the same time. Again, pieces may also be found with dolphin handles and in the Diamond Optic pattern.

Tangerine stretch-glass dolphin-handle comport in Diamond Optic, and a pair of Tangerine stretch-glass candleholders in Diamond Optic, late 1920s. Comport, 5" h, **$100+**; candleholders, 3" h, **$100+** pair.

Tangerine stretch-glass candleholders and fan vase, late 1920s; vase, 5-1/2" h, **$100+**; candleholders, each 3-1/2" h, **$150+** pair.

37

Fenton by Era

Topaz glass made in this era is commonly the stretch variety, introduced in 1921. But some attributed examples have been found without iridescence and with what has been called a "shiny" surface. For Topaz Opalescent glass, see 1930 to 1955. The exception is Victoria Topaz, an opalescent variety made at the same time as the stretch colors.

Topaz stretch-glass covered candy jar with dolphin handles, early 1920s, 8" h, **$110+**.

Topaz (shiny) jug and tumbler with cobalt handles and etched floral pattern, mid-1920s; jug, 10" h, **$250+**; tumbler, 5" h, **$75+**.

Topaz coasters used under tumblers in a lemonade set, 1920s, 3-1/4" diameter, **$125+** for set of six.

Topaz stretch-glass lemon server with hand-decorated exterior, circa 1921, 5" diameter, **$50**.

Topaz cut candlestick with notched profile, 1920s (?), 10-1/2" h, **$100+**.

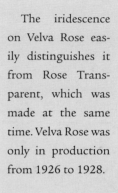

The iridescence on Velva Rose easily distinguishes it from Rose Transparent, which was made at the same time. Velva Rose was only in production from 1926 to 1928.

Topaz stretch-glass pitcher and tumbler with cobalt handles, part of a lemonade set that would have included six tumblers, 1920s; pitcher, 10" h; tumbler, 5" h, **$800+** for complete set.

Topaz Stretch pitcher (part of a guest set), 7" h, and tumbler, 4-1/2" h, with cobalt handles, 1921, pitcher, **$200+**; tumbler, **$90+**.

Pair of Velva Rose candleholders in style No. 316, 1926 33, 3-1/2" h, **$75+** pair.

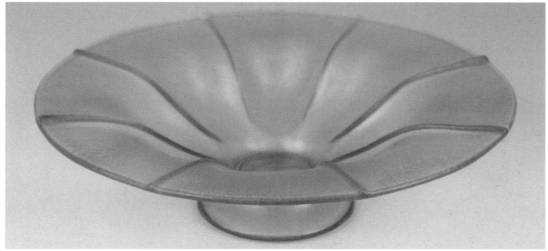

Velva Rose stretch-glass flared bowl, late 1920s, 11-1/4" diameter, **$75+**.

Fenton by Era

Velva Rose stretch-glass fan vase, circa 1926, 5-1/2" h, **$50+**.

Velva Rose lemon server, 1926, 4-1/2" diameter, **$50+**.

Venetian Red is often confused with Mandarin Red, but Venetian was made a decade earlier, starting in about 1924. Mandarin Red also typically has golden marbling, but it can be bold or subtle (see 1930 to 1955). Also, this color was revived for the Bicentennial as "Patriot Red."

Venetian Red flared and scalloped vase, mid-1920s, 5-1/2" h, **$75+**.

Venetian Red ginger jar with Ebony lid and stepped base, late 1920s, 8 1/2" h overall, **$250+**.

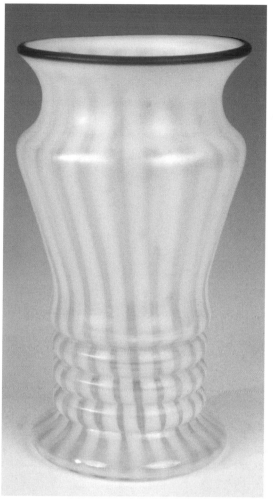

Whether in Rib Optic or a drape pattern, Victoria Topaz is rare. The same form of vase seen here can also be found in a drape pattern, without the cobalt rim. Jugs and pitchers may be found with topaz or cobalt handles.

Witch Hazel bottle in Clam Broth, with transfer lettering and made to accept a cork, 1915-20, 7" h, **$80+.**

Victoria Topaz stretch-glass vase in Rib Optic with cobalt rim, circa 1925, 8" h, **$800+.**

The rich purple color of Wisteria stretch glass was also introduced in 1921, but production halted before the end of the decade. Don't confuse the name with "Wistaria," which was a satin-glass line from the late 1930s. Some collectors also use Wisteria to describe Amethyst glass made later.

Wisteria stretch-glass cupped bowl, circa 1921, 5" diameter, **$90+.**

Carnival Glass

The golden era of carnival glass was from about 1905 to the mid-1920s, and all of the pieces included here fall into those two decades.

The iridescent luster on this patterned, pressed glass is achieved by spraying the hot surface of the glass with metallic salt solutions and then re-firing to set the iridescence.

During the 1880s, hand-operated press molds were perfected by American glass houses, which enabled them to produce domestic glassware in large quantities much more cheaply than the traditional methods allowed.

Two molds were used. The molten glass was poured into the outer mold, and then the inner mold (or "plunger") was forced in, using intense pressure. Sometimes the molds were in two or more parts, and so a trickle of the molten glass would seep through the gaps. Later, these seam lines could be polished out if they weren't hidden in the intricate designs. At first the products were made from clear glass, but gradually colors were introduced.

Though the United States was the home of carnival glass, no one is absolutely certain when the various manufacturers first developed their products. It is believed that by 1906 the first cheap, iridized glass to rival the expensive Tiffany creations was in production.

Carnival glass was originally made to bridge a gap in the market by providing ornamental wares for those who couldn't afford to buy the fashionable, iridized pieces popular at the height of the art nouveau era.

It wasn't until much later that it acquired the name "carnival glass." When it fell from favor, it was sold off cheaply to carnivals and offered as prizes. The term is generally credited to collectors Rose Presznick and Marion Hartung.

A key figure in the history of carnival glass is English-born Harry Northwood, son of a talented glass manufacturer. Northwood left England to work in America in 1880, when he was 20 years old, and founded his own factory in 1887 in Ohio, before moving to Wheeling, W.V. Some researchers believe that it was Northwood who brought the technique of making the iridized glass to the U.S., having seen it at his father's glassworks.

The first known mention of Fenton carnival glass was in a trade magazine in October 1907. The glass was called "Iridill."

Fenton made about 150 patterns of carnival glass. Most Fenton glass was pressed by hand and hand finished, often using molds designed by Frank Fenton. It was sold by the large retail stores of the period, such as Woolworths.

In 1908, with the Fenton Art Glass Company now going strong, brothers Frank and John Fenton reportedly clashed over company policy. John left to establish his own plant in Millersburg, Ohio.

On May 20, 1909, the first glass was poured. The initial molds were designed by John Fenton and were Ohio Star and Hob-star and Feather, both crystal patterns, not carnival. Carnival was also produced in the first month in amethyst, green and a soft marigold.

The Millersburg plant flourished briefly, but John Fenton found himself in financial straits and he eventually filed for bankruptcy. The factory was sold in late 1911 and renamed the Radium Glass Company. The Jefferson Glass Company reused many of the molds when it bought the plant. Jefferson used the factory for a short time and again it was sold, this time to a tire company.

To tell the true color of a piece of carnival glass, hold it up to a strong light source. The base color is often the most important feature of carnival glass and is sometimes the most difficult to classify. Not all pieces come in all colors. Marigold is by the far the most common.

Here are some of the basic colors:

Amethyst: A purple color ranging from quite light to quite dark

Aqua opalescent: Ice blue with a milky (white or colored) edge

Black amethyst: Very dark purple or black in color

Clam broth: Pale ginger ale color, sometimes milky

Cobalt blue (sometimes called royal blue): A dark, rich blue

Green: A true green, not pastel

Marigold: A soft, golden yellow

Pastel colors: A satin treatment in white, ice blue, ice green

Peach opalescent: Marigold with a milky (white or colored) edge

Red: A rich red, rare

Vaseline (Fenton called it topaz): Clear yellow/yellow-green glass

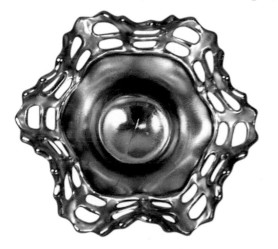

Amberina basket in Open Edge, **$75.**

Amethyst banana boat in Thistle, **$185.**

Amethyst advertising card tray, "Utah Liquor Co.," 6" l, **$800-$1,000.**

Amethyst advertising plate, "Seasons Greetings, Eat Paradise Sodas," 6" d, **$500-$800.**

Amethyst bowl in Feathered Serpent, candy-ribbon edge, **$150.**

Amethyst bowl with 3-in-1 edge, Peacock Tail, 9-1/2" d, **$70.**

Amethyst turned-up punch bowl in Wreath of Roses, base, six cups, Vintage interior, **$650.**

Amethyst opalescent vase in April Showers, 11-1/4" h, **$1,450.**

Amethyst water pitcher and six tumblers in Butterfly and Fern, **$1,050.**

Electric amethyst bowl with 3-in-1 edge in Ribbon Tie, 8-1/2" d, **$125.**

Aqua bowl with 3-in-1 edge, Holly, rare, 8-1/2" d, **$200-$350.**

Amethyst water pitcher in Butterfly and Berry, **$3,000.**

Black amethyst flat plate in Persian Medallion, 6-1/4" d, **$250-$400.**

Black amethyst vase in April Showers, 12" h, **$80- $150.**

Amethyst water pitcher and six tumblers in Fluffy Peacock, **$1,050.**

Aqua opalescent ruffled bowl in Dragon and Lotus, 9" d, **$2,200.**

Aqua opalescent ruffled bowl in Peacock and Grape, 8-3/4" d, **$5,000+.**

Dark aqua bowl in Acorn, ice cream shape, **$20.**

Blue bowl in Bird and Cherries, candy ribbon edge, **$750.**

Blue ice cream shape bowl in Fantail, 9" d, **$250-$350.**

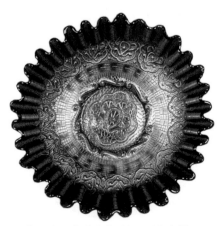

Blue bowl in Persian Medallion, candy-ribbon edge, **$85.**

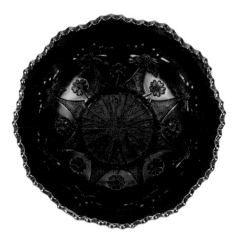

Blue bowl in Little Flowers, 8" d, **$150.**

Blue bowl in Dragon and Strawberry, 8-3/4" d, **$650.**

Blue flat plate in Leaf Chain, 9" d, **$700-$1,200.**

Blue flat plate in Captive Rose, 9" d, **$400-$700.**

Blue bowl with 3-in-1 edge, Ten Mums, 9-1/2", **$350.**

Blue sauce in Persian Medallion, six ruffles, 6" d, **$50-$80.**

Blue ruffled-top tankard in Blackberry Block, 11" h, **$1,500-$1,800.**

Blue tankard in Floral and Grape Variant, candy-ribbon edge, 9-1/2" h, normally **$300-$500**; outstanding example, **$900.**

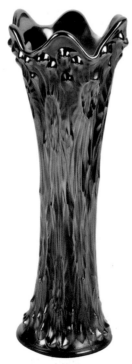

Blue vase in Bullseye and Beads, 11-1/4" h, **$350.**

Blue whimsy vase in Blackberry Open Edge, Two Row, 7" h, **$2,000.**

Blue whimsy vase in Paneled Dandelion, no handle, made from a water pitcher, **$16,000.**

Blue jardinière vase with pinched in mid-section in Rustic, 5-2/8" base, 7-1/2" h, **$1,500.**

Blue water pitcher and tumbler in Fentonia, **$875.**

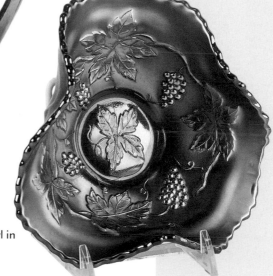

Blue tri-fold bowl in Vintage, 6", **$100-$150.**

Blue vase in Target, 6-1/2", **$100.**

Blue water pitcher and six tumblers in Orange Tree Orchard, **$750.**

Cobalt Blue footed bowl with ruffled edge in Holly, 1911, 7" d, **$45+.**

Cobalt Blue footed bowl with ruffled edge in Orange Tree, 1911, 10" d, **$125+.**

Cobalt Blue shallow comport or sherbet in Miniature Blackberry, 4-1/2" d, **$125-$150.**

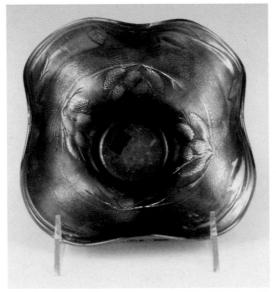

Cobalt Blue square-crimp bowl in Briar Patch, with paneled back, 6-1/2" d, **$100+.**

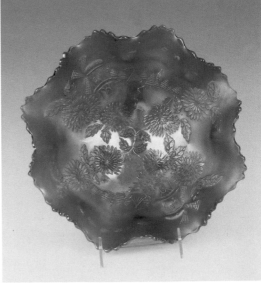

Cobalt Blue footed bowl with ruffled edge in Windmill and Mums, with wide-panel back, 11" d, **$500+.**

Electric blue bowl in Chrysanthemum, large, footed, **$250.**

Persian blue ice-cream shape bowl in Lotus and Grape, **$575.**

Green bowl in Cherry Chain, 3-in-1 edge, large, **$200.**

Green ruffled bowl in Blackberry, **$75.**

Green bonbon in Stippled Rays with Scale Band exterior, 1908, 7" w, **$50+.**

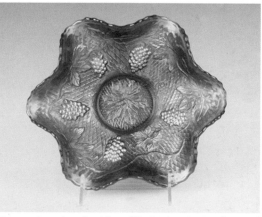

Green deep bowl with ruffled edge in Lattice and Grape, with paneled back, 9" d, **$400+.**

Carnival Glass

Green flat plate in Holly,
9-1/2" d, **$700-$900.**

Green flat plate in Peter Rabbit,
9" d, **$4,000-$6,000.**

Green whimsy vase in Diamond
and Rib, pinched in, **$1,350.**

Green vase in Plume
Panels, 12" h, **$190.**

Green water pitcher and tumbler in
Blackberry Block, **$4,000.**

Green lady's spittoon in
Feathered Serpent, 3-3/4" w,
2-1/4" h, **$7,500.**

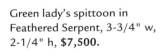

Green table set in Butterfly and Berry, including creamer, covered sugar, covered butter dish and spooner; butter, 6" h; creamer, 5" h; spooner, 4-1/4" h; sugar, 6-1/2" h, **$2,500+**/set. Also found in marigold and cobalt blue, and rarely in amethyst.

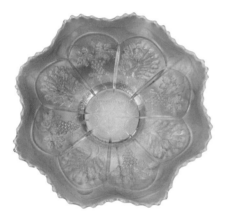

Lime green opalescent bowl in Peacock and Grape, **$600.**

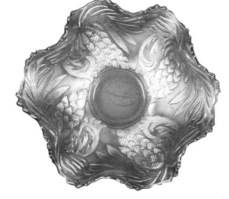

Marigold ruffled bowl in Pine Cone, 7" d, **$20.**

Marigold basket in Open Edge, with "Miller's Furniture" advertising, **$25.**

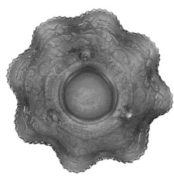

Marigold ruffled bowl in Little Fishes, 10" d, **$165.**

Lime green opalescent vase in Rustic, 9-1/4" h, **$1,250.**

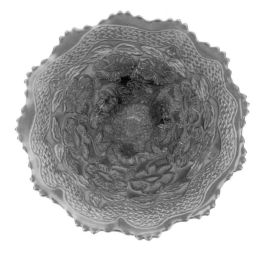

Dark marigold chop plate in Two Flowers, chip on rim, 11", **$750.**

Marigold sawtooth chop plate in Stag and Holly, 11-1/2", **$1,200.**

Marigold cup and saucer in Kittens, **$200.**

Marigold covered sugar and creamer in Leaf Tiers, **$200.**

Marigold jardinière in Diamond and Rib, 6-1/2" h, **$1,500-$1,800.**

Marigold plate in Coral, **$1,100.**

Marigold flat plate in Holly, 9-1/2" d, **$200-$300.**

Marigold flat plate in Persian Medallion, 6-1/4" d, **$50-$80.**

Marigold spittoon in Blackberry Wreath, whimsy, **$700.**

Marigold Butterfly ornament, 3" w, **$1,200-$1,500.**

Marigold water pitcher and tumbler in Bouquet, **$265** pair.

Marigold funeral vase with plunger base in Diamond and Rib, 21-1/2" h, **$1,100.**

Marigold tankard in Lattice and Grape, **$100.**

Marigold water pitcher and six tumblers in Field Flower, **$450.**

Marigold over moonstone bowl in Dragon and Lotus, **$1,000.**

Marigold water pitcher and six tumblers in Strawberry Scroll, **$2,500.**

Marigold tumblers in Lattice and Grape, **$60.**

Marigold over moonstone bowl with ice-cream edge in Orange Tree, **$1,500.**

Marigold table set (creamer missing) in Fentonia; covered butter, 6" h; spooner, 4-1/4" h; sugar, 6-1/2" h. Partial set seen here, **$400**; complete, **$750+.**

Marigold over moonstone ruffled bowl in Peacock and Grape, 9", **$500.**

Peach Opalescent ruffled bowl in Dragon and Lotus, 8-1/2" d, **$100+.**

Peach opalescent bowl in Kittens, ruffled, **$150.**

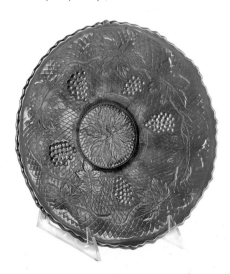

Purple flat plate in Concord, 9" d, **$2,000-$3,000.**

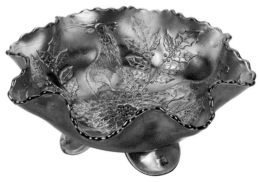

Purple banana shape in Vintage, 7-1/2", **$500-$700.**

Red ruffled bowl in Stag and Holly, spatula feet, 6-1/2" d, **$1,500.**

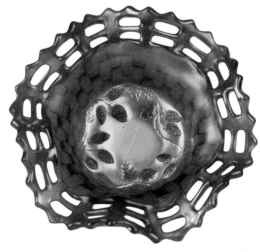

Red-slag bowl in Grape and Cable, ice-cream shape, 6", **$225.**

Red bowl in Basket Weave with two-row open edge, and Blackberry Spray interior, 6-1/4" d, **$250+.**

Red bowl in Plaid, 8-1/2" d, **$2,500.**

Red ruffled bowl in Holly, 9" d, **$1,200.**

Red bonbon with two handles in Persian Medallion, **$700.**

Red large bonbon in Cherry Chain, **$5,000.**

Red/amberina ruffled bowl in Little Flowers, 9-1/2", **$2,000.**

Red bowl with six ruffles in Panther, footed, 6", **$800-$1,200.**

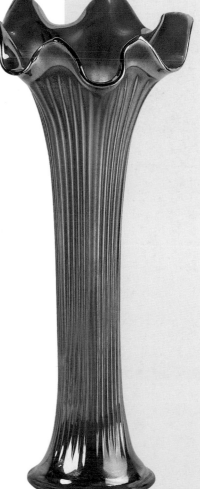

Red bowl with ruffled edge in Peacock and Grape, 9" d, **$2,000+.**

Red opalescent ruffled hat in Blackberry Spray, **$650.**

Red vase in Fine Rib, 10" h, **$300-$500.**

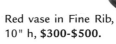

Dark red bowl in Acorn, ruffled, 6-1/2" d, **$400.**

Dark red bowl in Dragon and Lotus, ruffled collar, 8-1/2" d, **$1,800.**

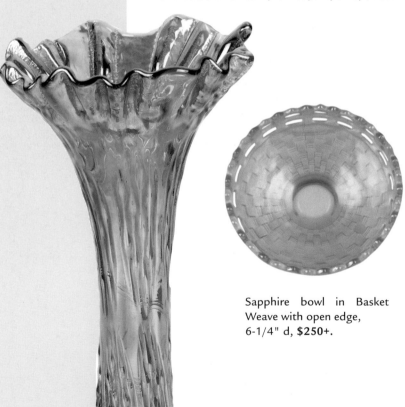

Sapphire opal hat in Blackberry Spray, jack in the pulpit, **$1,700.**

Sapphire bowl in Basket Weave with open edge, 6-1/4" d, **$250+.**

Sapphire vase in Knotted Beads, **$450.**

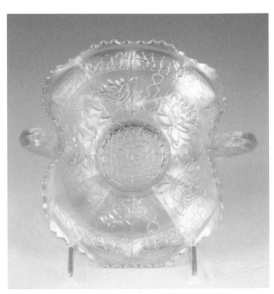

White handled bonbon in Pond Lily, 7-1/4" w, **$60+.**

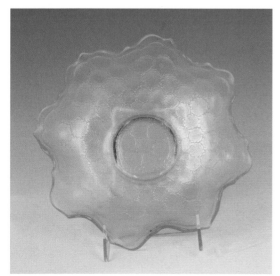

White plate in Leaf Chain, 9-1/2" d, **$500+.**

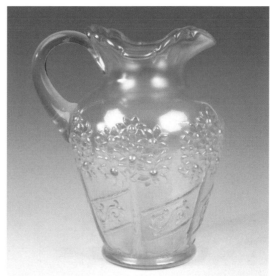

White jug in Orange Tree Orchard, 10" h, **$500+.**

White hatpin holder in Orange Tree, 6-3/4" h, **$3,000+.**

White covered butter dish in Orange Tree, with traces of gilding on lid, 6-1/2" h, **$500+.**

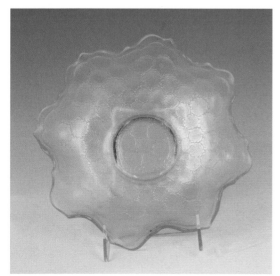

White bowl with ruffled edge in Feather Stitch, 9" d, rare, **$500+.**

White swung vase in Hobnail, 6-1/2" h, **$75+.** Vases in this style that are about 6" are called Rustic.

Fenton by Era

The second quarter of Fenton's history saw dramatic changes in style and production techniques, as the colors and shapes of the art deco era gave way to mid-century design influences.

While the opalescent patterns in Rib and Spiral Optic remained, Hobnail grew in popularity. The Crest lines presented special challenges and, though they were initially made in all the colors of the rainbow, only a handful stayed in production for more than a few years.

The most significant contrast in this 25-year span? The Dancing Ladies popular in the 1930s had waltzed away, replaced by the stark simplicity of the Milk-glass patterns that represented Fenton's biggest success since carnival glass arrived at the beginning of the century.

Amber cupped footed bowl in Silvertone, 1937, 5" diameter, **$30+**.

Though it was introduced in the mid-1920s, most examples of Amber found today date from after 1930. Made in several patterns, the veined design known as Silvertone is among the easier to find.

Amber turtle-form aquarium base, left, shown with Crystal flower frog, 1930s, 9" l, **$200+**. Right: amethyst turtle-form candleholder, 1930s, 4" l, **$100+**.

Amber console bowl, 10" diameter, and footed candleholder, 4-1/2" diameter, both in Silvertone, 1937. Bowl, **$35+**; candleholder, **$22+**.

Amethyst and Milk-glass Chick on Nest, early 1950s, 4" h, scarce, **$100.**

Amethyst Snow Crest four-horn epergne in Threaded Optic, 1940s, made for L.G. Wright, 17" h, **$800+.**

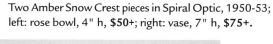

Two Amber Snow Crest pieces in Spiral Optic, 1950-53; left: rose bowl, 4" h, **$50+**; right: vase, 7" h, **$75+.**

Though Fenton made glass in amethyst and Wisteria earlier in its history, the pieces here are later examples, and were not made in large numbers at this time.

Left: Amethyst and Milk-glass footed ivy ball with unusual flared lip, 1950s, 8-1/2" h, **$100**; center: Cranberry ivy ball in Coin Dot, 1950s, 5" h, **$55**; right: Amber and Milk-glass footed ivy ball in Coin Dot, 1950s, 8-1/2" h, **$50.**

Fenton by Era

Though some sources indicate that the Crest lines were not firmly established until 1940, research shows that some pieces are believed to have been produced in the late 1930s. Aqua Crest was made briefly in 1941-42, and again in the late 1940s up to about 1953. It returned for two years in the early 1960s as Blue Crest. Though it isn't an infallible test, the density of the Milk-glass can help to date the pieces. Milk-glass made prior to the late 1950s frequently has greater opalescence (what Fenton collectors call "fire") than later examples. Also, the intensity of the blue crests varies considerably.

Aqua Crest square-crimp bowl, early 1940s, 7" diameter, **$25+**.

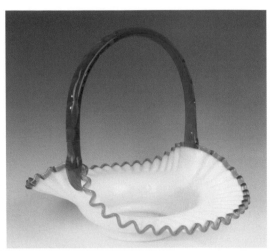

Aqua Crest large basket, 1940s, 14-1/2" w, 13" h, **$500+**.

Aqua Crest tri-crimp vase, 1940s, 4-1/2" h, **$25+**.

Aqua Crest sherbet with piecrust edge, late 1940s, 5-1/2" diameter, **$20+**.

Aqua Crest dresser set, melon form, including two squat perfumes and powder box, early 1940s; perfumes, 4-1/2" h; powder box, 3-3/4" h, **$250+** set.

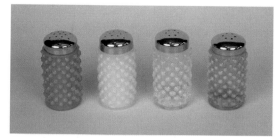

Turquoise, "Skim" Milk-glass, French Opalescent and Blue Opalescent shakers in "5 & 6" Hobnail, 1940s, 3-1/2" h; Milk-glass, **$15**; others, **$30+** each.

Aquarium, Jade turtle with Green Opalescent bowl in Rib Optic, 1930s, 7" h overall, **$800+** set.

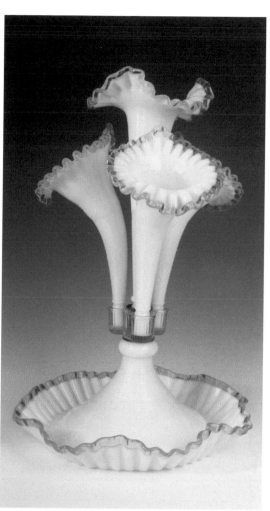

Aqua Crest four-horn epergne in Threaded Optic, 1950s, made for L.G. Wright, 16-1/2" h, **$700+**.

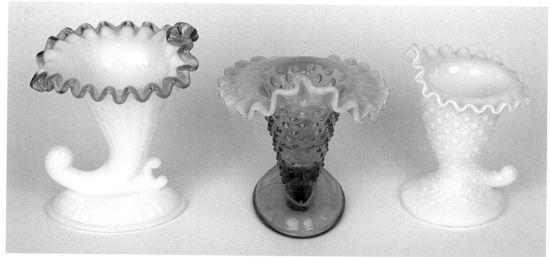

Three cornucopia candleholders from left: Aqua Crest ribbed, Blue Opalescent in Hobnail and Milk-glass in Diamond Lace, 1940s, 5-1/2" to 6-1/2" h, **$35+** each.

Fenton by Era

Though it originated about 1910, Black glass was not put into wide production until the late 1920s, and early examples—beginning about 1915—also used carnival glass molds. Some pieces may be found paired with Moonstone. Ebony is generally used to describe glass made after the 1930s.

Black (Ebony) batter jug and syrup, with serving tray, circa 1938; jug (lid missing), 7-1/2" h (with lid); syrup, 4-3/4" h; tray, 9-1/2" w, **$350+** if complete.

Black (Ebony) candleholders, 1930s, footed petal, style No. 848, 5" diameter, **$20+**, and a double in style No. 2318, sometimes called Pineapple, 6" h, **$65+**.

Black (Ebony) covered candy dish with flower finial, 1931, 6-1/2" h, **$250+**.

Black (Ebony) basket in Ribbon Band, rattan handle, 1930s, 9-1/2" w, **$200+**.

Black (Ebony) and Cobalt footed candleholders in Basket Weave with open edge, late 1930s, 5" diameter, **$30+** each.

Black (Ebony) Empress vase, 1935, 7-1/2" h, **$110+.**

Black (Ebony) crimped vase in Hobnail, 1950, 5" h (not in the regular line, perhaps made for the Randall Co.), **$35+.**

Black Rose basket, 1953-54, 8" h, **$175+.**

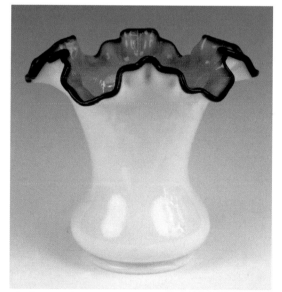

Black Rose flared and crimped vase, 1953-54, 6-1/2" h, **$85+.**

Black Rose was a short-lived experiment in the Crest lines from 1953-54.

Black (Ebony), Milk-glass and Ruby Overlay shakers in a swirl pattern, 1950s, 2-1/2" h, Black (Ebony), **$25**; Milk-glass, **$15+**; Ruby Overlay, **$50+.**

Fenton by Era

Black Rose vase with tulip crimp, 1953-54, 8" h, **$110+**.

Black Rose pieces, early 1950s; left and right, a pair of hurricane lamps in Hobnail (also found with Ebony bases), each 8" h, no established value; center, hand vase, 10" h, **$400+**.

Blue Opalescent glass has been produced throughout Fenton's history. Examples in Hobnail often date from about 1940 to 1954. It made a brief reappearance in 1960-61, and again in the early 1980s. Blue Opalescent glass in a Spiral Optic pattern dates from about 1938-39. The pattern known as Coin Spot had wide production in the late 1930s and early 1940s. Pieces in Coin Dot were made primarily from 1947 to 1955. (In Coin Dot, the "coins" are clear; in Coin Spot, the coins are opaque.) Also see 1955 to 1980.

Blue Opalescent biscuit jar in Hobnail, 1940s, 7-1/2" h, **$900+**.

Blue Opalescent rose bowl in Spiral Optic, late 1930s, 5" h, **$85+**.

Blue Opalescent special rose bowl in Hobnail, 1940s, 7" diameter (also made 1959-61, and in other colors), **$75**.

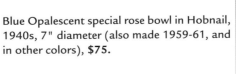

Blue Opalescent and French Opalescent candleholders in Diamond Lace, 1949-54, 4-1/2" diameter, **$25+** each.

Blue Opalescent, French Opalescent and Cranberry Opalescent candlesticks in Spiral Optic, with and without crimping, circa 1940, 4" h. Blue, **$50+**; French, **$40+**; Cranberry, **$75+**.

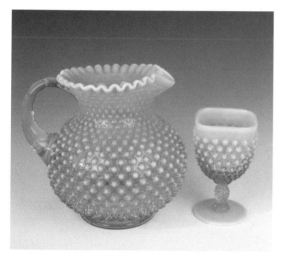

Blue Opalescent jug and square-top goblet in Hobnail, part of a lemonade set that would have included six tumblers, 1950s; jug, 8" h; goblet, 5-1/2" h, **$500+** for complete set.

Blue Opalescent hat novelty in Coin Dot, circa 1950, 3" h, **$100+**.

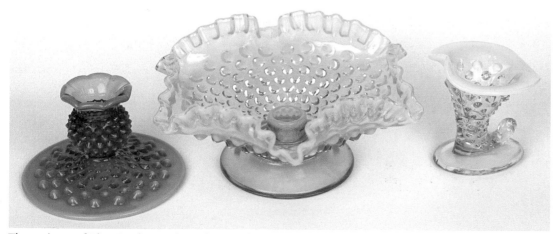

Three pieces of Blue Opalescent in Hobnail from left: candleholder in style No. 3974, low Hobnail, **$30+**; candle bowl, **$65+**; miniature cornucopia candleholder, style No. 3971, 1940-57, 3-1/2" h, **$25+**.

Fenton by Era

Blue Opalescent footed vase in Diamond Lace, early 1940s, 5" h, **$80+.**

Blue Opalescent, French Opalescent and Topaz Opalescent shakers in footed Hobnail, 1940s, 3-1/2" h, Blue and French, **$40+** each; Topaz, **$60+.**

Blue Opalescent toothpick holders or novelties, each with different crimping, early 1940s, each 2" h, **$75** each.

Blue Opalescent vase in Rib Optic with tulip crimp, 1930s, 8" h, **$200+.**

Blue Opalescent mayonnaise bowl and under-plate in Basket Weave with Open Edge, mid-1930s; bowl, 5-1/2" diameter; plate, 8" diameter, **$60+** set.

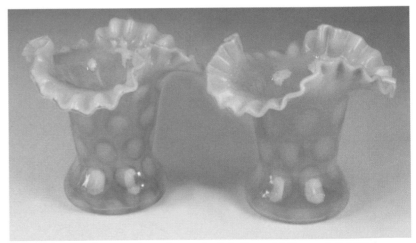

Pair of Blue Opalescent crimped vases in Coin Spot, 1940s, each 5-1/2" h, **$45+** each.

Fenton by Era 1930-1955

Introduced in 1943, Blue Overlay was made until 1953, and included both the plain melon forms and beaded melon. The latter was part of the Tiara Line from 1951.

Blue Overlay tri-crimp vase, mid-1940s, 7-1/2" h, **$65+**.

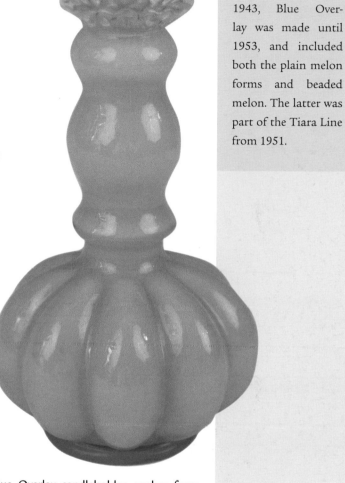

Blue Overlay candleholder, melon form (same form as perfume), mid-1940s, 7" h, **$50+**.

Blue Overlay shakers in Floral Sprig, made for L.G. Wright, 1940s, 3-1/2" h, **$75+** pair.

Blue pastel and Green Pastel footed covered candy jars in Hobnail, 1950s, 8-1/2" h, **$85** each.

Fenton by Era

Blue Ridge made a brief appearance in 1938-39. It is a line that features French Opalescent glass and a Spiral Optic pattern, with cobalt trim on ruffled edges. It was revived for Fenton's 80th anniversary in 1985.

Blue Ridge hat vase, 1939, 7" h, **$300+**.

Blue Ridge hat basket/vase, 1939, 13" h, **$500+**.

Though made into the 1930s, Chinese Yellow was introduced about 1922. See other examples in the Dancing Ladies pattern.

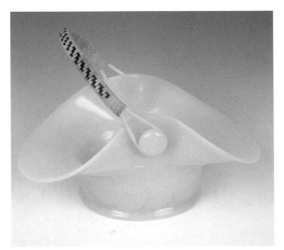

Chinese Yellow basket in Big Cookies, with rattan handle, 1930s, 11" w, **$200+**.

Two Blue Snow Crest vases in Spiral Optic, 1950-51, 9" h, **$180+**, and 11" h, **$250+**.

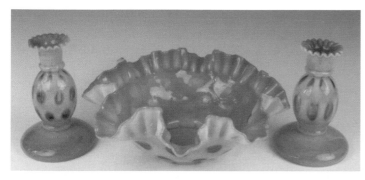

Cranberry Coin Dot console set including ruffled bowl and candleholders, circa 1950; bowl, 10" diameter; candleholders, 5-1/2" h, **$400+** set.

Cranberry Opalescent is another color combination made by Fenton for decades in various patterns. Examples in Spiral Optic arrived in the late 1930s. The Hobnail alone was produced for almost four decades from 1940 until the late 1970s (also see 1955 to 1980). Coin Dot was made for just under two decades, from the late 1940s to the mid-1960s. Two interesting subsections of this color include pieces from the New World line, 1953-54, and Polka Dot, 1955.

New World shakers, two sizes, in Cranberry Opalescent Rib Optic, 1953, 5" h and 4" h, **$175** pair.

Cranberry Coin Dot vase, 1950s, 7-1/2" h, **$110+.**

Cranberry Opalescent low basket in Hobnail, early 1950s, 5-1/2" widest point, **$150+.**

Cranberry Coin Dot bowl, flared and crimped, circa 1950, 7" diameter, **$55+.**

Fenton by Era

Cranberry Opalescent basket in Hobnail, 1940s,
4-1/2" h, **$65+.**

Cranberry Opalescent and Blue Opalescent Coin
Dot candlesticks, 1950, 5-1/2" h; Cranberry, **110+;**
Blue, **$95+.**

Cranberry Opalescent bowl in Coin Dot, 1950s,
7" w, **$60+.**

Cranberry Opalescent cruet in Hobnail, introduced
in 1942 and made through the late 1970s, 6" h,
$125+.

Cranberry Opalescent bowl, flared and crimped, in
Spiral Optic, 1930s, 10-1/4" w, **$150+.**

Cranberry Opalescent covered candy in Hobnail,
with clear lid, 1940s, 5-1/2" diameter, **$300+.**

Cranberry Opalescent lamp in Hobnail, with onyx base, 1940s, 12" h, no established value. Also shown, Cranberry Opalescent cruet in Hobnail, used to make lamp body, stopper may be replaced, no established value.

Cranberry Opalescent 70-ounce jug in Coin Spot, mid-1930s, 8-1/2" h, **$200+.**

Cranberry Opalescent pieces in Hobnail, left: rose bowl, 1953, 3" h, **$250+;** right: crimped vase, early 1950s, 7" h, **$90.**

Two pairs of New World shakers in Cranberry Opalescent and Green Opalescent Rib Optic, 1950s, sold in pairs of two sizes, 4" h and 5" h. Cranberry, **$175** pair; Green, rare, **$300** pair.

Cranberry Opalescent and Topaz Opalescent (1940s) and Plum Opalescent (1990s) shakers in "5 & 5" Hobnail, 3-1/2" h, Cranberry, **$60+,** Topaz and Plum, **$75+** each.

Left: "5 & 6" Hobnail; right: "5 & 5" Hobnail.

Fenton by Era

Cranberry Polka Dot footed ivy bowl, 1955, 8-1/2" h, **$225.**

Cranberry Opalescent vase in Coin Dot, 1940s, 10-3/4" h, **$175+.**

Cranberry Opalescent vase in Spiral Optic, late 1930s, 6-1/2" h, **$85.**

Cranberry Opalescent pieces in Coin Dot, 1940s, left: flared and crimped vase, 8" h, **$125+**; right: hat novelty, 3" h, **$70+.**

Cranberry Opalescent 4" fan vases, 1940s, smooth top, **$45+**; crimped top, **$90+.**

Three ivy vases in Cranberry Opalescent Spiral Optic and Coin Dot, and Topaz Opalescent Coin Dot, 1950s, 5" h, Cranberry Spiral, **$100**; Topaz, **$75**; Cranberry Coin Dot, **$85.**

Crystal bonbon in Pineapple, 1937, 7" diameter, **$35+.**

Crystal candleholders in Santoy Etched, from left: cornucopia, 1936, 5-1/2" h; style No. 349, 1937, 3" h, **$40+** each.

Three candleholders, all mid-1930s, left: Swan in Crystal Satin, 5-1/2" h, **$85+**; center: Dolphin in Crystal, 3-1/2" h, **$35+**; right: Pineapple in Crystal, 5-1/2" h, **$75+.**

Two Crystal wine glasses in Flower Window, late 1930s, each 4" h, **$30+** each.

Crystal crimped bonbon in Pineapple, 1938, 6-1/2" diameter (unusual to find without satin finish), **$45.**

Crystal candleholder with acid-etched decoration, dolphin-handle, part of a console set, mid-1930s, 6" diameter, **$25.**

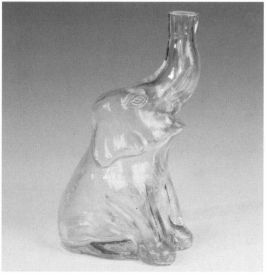

Crystal elephant-form liquor bottle, stopper missing, mid-1930s, 8" h, **$150+** as is.

With few exceptions, Crystal pieces can often be dated by pattern. They are among the most affordable of all Fenton glass.

Fenton by Era

Ming is an acid-etched pattern from 1935-36 that some collectors group under the heading of satin glass. Crystal, Green, and Rose are the predominant colors, and examples can be found later in this section. Other Crystal variations include a satin finish and patterns like Silvertone.

Crystal Ming dolphin-handled bonbon with Silvertone decoration, mid-1930s, 7" diameter, **$40.**

Crystal Ming fan vase with applied metal decoration and base, mid-1930s, 9" h, **$125+.**

Crystal Ming cocktail shaker with chrome top, mid-1930s, 11" h, **$125+.**

Crystal Ming "Plymouth" ice bucket with chrome handle, mid-1930s, 6" h without handle, **$150+.**

Crystal Ming flared vase, mid-1930s, 10" h, **$100+.**

Crystal Satin plate with acid-etched Poinsettia decoration, late 1930s, 8" diameter, rare, **$75.**

Crystal Satin ashtrays, set of four in Dragonfly, 1935, 3" diameter, found in other colors, **$60+ set.**

Crystal console set in Silvertone Etch, late 1930s: cornucopia candleholders, 5-1/2" h; console bowl, 10-1/2" w, **$125+ set.**

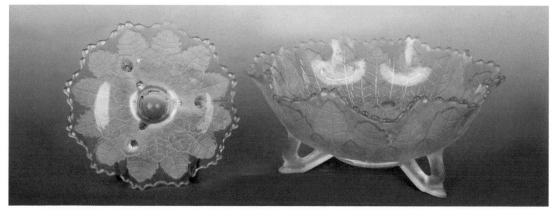

Crystal Satin pieces in Leaf Tiers, mid-1930s: left, footed plate, 6" diameter, **$30+**; right, footed crimped bowl, 10" diameter, **$40+.**

Fenton by Era

Of all the Crest lines, Crystal Crest posed the most production problems, and this explains why it was made for only about six months in 1942. Its edge of alternating white and clear glass proved too difficult to produce efficiently.

Crystal Crest basket, 7" w, **$80+.**

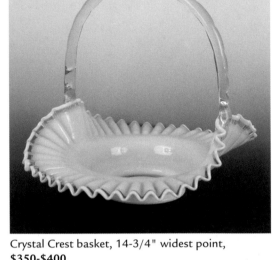

Crystal Crest basket, 14-3/4" widest point, **$350-$400.**

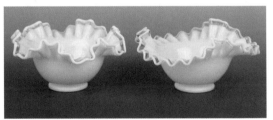

Crystal Crest bowls with standard and tri-crimps, 7" diameter each, **$50+ each.**

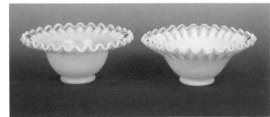

Crystal Crest bowls, one with flattened rim, one flared, 7" diameter each, **$50+ each.**

Crystal Crest bonbons, 6" diameter each, **$35+ each;** melon bowl, 10" diameter, **$75+.**

Crystal Crest bowls, one with square crimp and one with tri-crimp, 7" diameter each, **$100+ each.**

Crystal Crest rose bowls with different rim treatments, and two cone vases, one with standard crimp and one with tri-crimp, 4" h to 5" h each, **$35-$50** each.

Crystal Crest covered candy dishes. Left: 3-7/8" h, lid is 5" diameter inner lip; right: 3-5/8" h, lost its outer ring; covers for both examples. Also note the difference in the opacity and opalescence of the glass; less opaque Milk-glass is sometimes called "skim milk," **$150+** each.

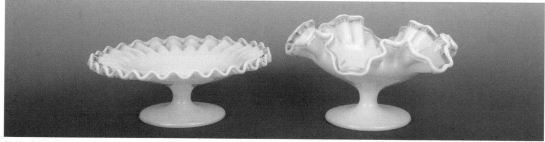

Crystal Crest comports or candy dishes (same molds, different treatments), 7-1/2" diameter each, **$80-$90** each.

Crystal Crest console bowl, 13-3/4" diameter, **$200+**.

Crystal Crest epergne with flower frog, four pieces, 7-1/2" h, 11" diameter, **$200+**.

Fenton by Era

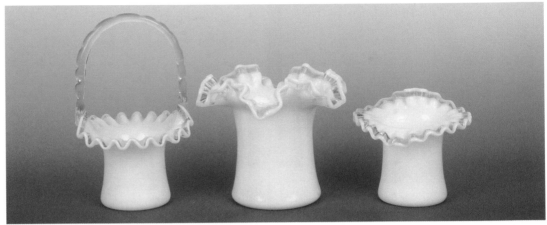

Crystal Crest hat basket, 3-1/2" h without handle, **$150+**; hat vase, standard crimp, 6" h, **$60+**; hat vase, tulip crimp, 3-1/2" h, **$60+**.

Crystal Crest melon jug, left, with tri-crimp, 6-3/4" h; right: Crystal Crest melon-form squat jug, 5-1/2" h, **$100+** each.

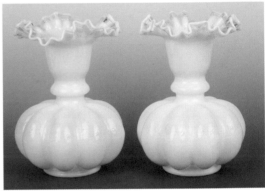

Crystal Crest melon vases with variations in crimping, approximately 8" h, **$100+** each.

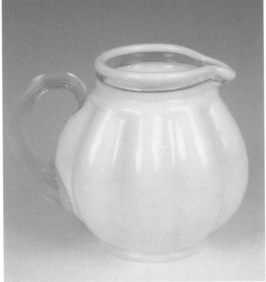

Early Crystal Crest squat jug, melon form, without crimped top, 5-1/2" h, **$100+**.

Crystal Crest 70-ounce jug with original label, 9-1/2" h, **$450+**.

Crystal Crest toothpick holders (also called mini-vases), with different rim treatments, and varying opalescence, each up to 2-1/2" h, **$250** each. Milk-glass made prior to the late 1950s frequently has greater opalescence (what Fenton collectors call "fire") than later examples.

Crystal Crest melon vases, approximately 6" h, with variations in crimping (center example has tulip crimp—also called "Jack-in-the-Pulpit"), **$100+** each.

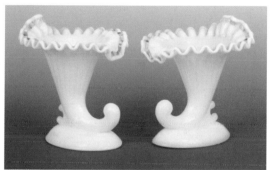

Crystal Crest fan vases, two sizes, 6-1/2" h, **$60+**; 4-1/2" h, **$35-$50**.

Crystal Crest ribbed cornucopia vases with tulip crimps, 6" h each, **$175+** pair.

Crystal Crest 6" vases, one with a tri-crimp, one with standard crimp, one with tulip crimp (also called "Jack-in-the-Pulpit"), **$45+** each.

Crystal Crest vases with tri-, standard, and basket crimps, the center with melon profile, 5-1/2" h each, **$100+** each.

Fenton by Era

The Dancing Ladies represent an entire collecting area for Fenton enthusiasts, with pieces in nearly 20 known colors. They were made in 1932 to 1935.

Crystal Crest 8" vases with standard crimp and tricrimp, **$50+** each.

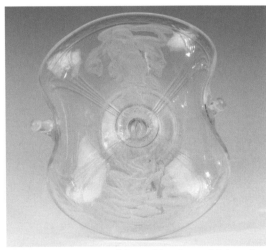

Dancing Ladies Chinese Yellow bowl, oval footed, early 1930s, 11" w, 4-1/2" h, **$250+**.

Dancing Ladies Chinese Yellow small urn, cover missing, 1930s, 5" h, **$500+** as is; with cover, **$1,200+**.

Dancing Ladies Crystal footed bonbon with handles, and with unusual satin finish on figures, early 1930s, 4-1/4" h, 6-1/2" w, **$160+**.

Dancing Ladies Crystal cone vase (unusual form), early 1930s, 8-1/2" h, **$200+**.

Dancing Ladies French Opalescent square-top vase, mid-1930s, 9" h, **$800+**.

Dancing Ladies Mongolian Green vase, flared and ruffled, mid-1930s, 8-1/2" h, **$650+.**

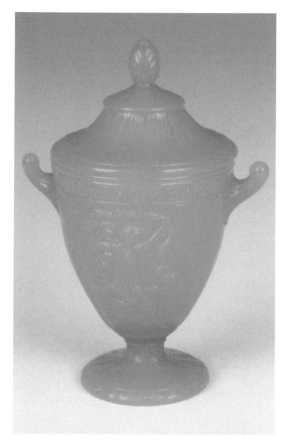

Dancing Ladies Jade Green covered urn, mid-1930s, 7" h, **$400+.**

Dancing Ladies Ruby flared vase, mid-1930s, 8-1/2" h, **$450+.**

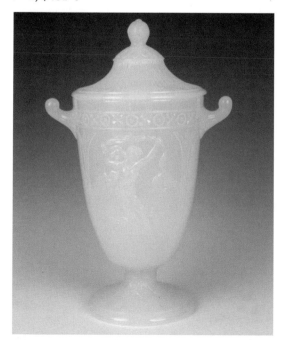

Dancing Ladies Moonstone covered urn, early 1930s, 12" h, **$450+.**

Dancing Ladies Topaz Opalescent footed bowl, mid-1930s, 8-1/2" w, **$750+.**

Fenton by Era

Most collectors associate Milk-glass with the 1950s, but pieces first appeared in Fenton records as early as the mid-1920s.

Emerald Crest and Emerald Green Snow Crest were in production at the same time, starting in the late 1940s and continuing through 1953. The time also marked the appearance of the Priscilla pattern in colors also found in some Crest lines.

Early Milk-glass flared vase in Basket Weave with Open Edge, circa 1933, 4" h, **$35+**.

Early Milk-glass vases (ware No. 107), circa 1933, in flared, tulip and cupped flared styles, each about 6" h, **$50** each.

Emerald Crest bonbon dish, 1950s, 6" w, **$40+**.

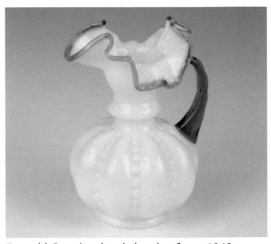

Emerald Crest jug, beaded-melon form, 1940s, 6" h, **$75+**.

Emerald Crest three-horn epergne in Diamond lace, late 1940s, 10-1/2" h, **$350+**.

Emerald Green platter in Priscilla, early 1950s, 12" diameter, **$40+**.

Emerald Green Snow Crest hats in Spiral Optic, early 1950s, 7" h, **$250+.**; and 4-1/2" h, **$100+.**

Three Emerald Green Snow Crest pieces, 1950-53, from left: Spiral Optic vase, 9-1/2" h, **$150+**; planter with attached underplate, **$75+**; Spiral Optic vase, 11-1/2" h, **$200+.**

Emerald Green Snow Crest hurricane lampshade, early 1950s, 11" h, **$225+.**

Emerald Green Snow Crest vase in Spiral Optic, early 1950s, 4-1/2" h, **$60+.**

Emerald Green and Milk-glass footed ivy ball, 1950s, in an unknown pattern, perhaps one of a kind, 8-1/2" h, **$150.**

Fenton dealer sign, plastic, mid-1950s, 6-3/4" w, **$35.**

Fenton by Era

Two "flip" vases in Pekin Blue and Mandarin Red, early 1930s, each 8" h, **$150+**.

Two "flip" vases in Jade Green and Chinese Yellow (pale), early 1930s, each 8" h, **$150+**.

In the 1930s, Crystal Opalescent became known as French Opalescent and Fenton used this glass in a variety of patterns, including Coin Dot, Hobnail, and Rib and Spiral Optic. Rarely seen patterns include Ring Optic and wide Rib Optic, and a hybrid called Block Optic. Production of French Opalescent continued well into the 1950s.

French Opalescent cruet in Coin Dot, late 1940s, 8" h, **$150+**.

Florentine Green, Celeste Blue and Jade Green candleholders in style No. 316, mid-1930s, 3-1/2" h, **$35-$50** each.

From left: French Opalescent candleholder in Sheffield, 1930s, 4-1/2" h, **$35+**; Cameo Opalescent candleholder, style No. 318, late 1920s to '30s, **$45+**.

French Opalescent pieces in Hobnail, early 1940s, from left: ashtray, 4" l; hat-form novelty or cigarette holder, 2-1/2" h; hat-form toothpick holder, 1-3/4" h; card tray, 4-1/2" l, **$25** each.

French Opalescent petite epergne in Hobnail (the horn sits in a shallow ring rather than a hole), with original label, early 1950s, 4-1/2" h, **$90.**

French Opalescent three-horn epergne in Emerald Crest/Diamond Lace, 1949-55, 11" h, **$250+.**

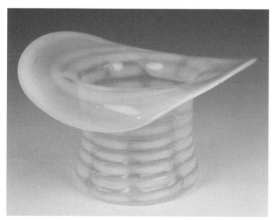

Large French Opalescent hat in Block Optic, late 1930s, 12" w, **$500+.**

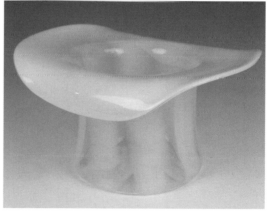

Large French Opalescent hat in wide Rib Optic, late 1930s, 12" w, **$500+.**

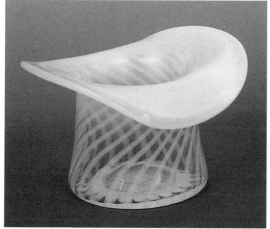

French Opalescent hat novelty in Spiral Optic, late 1930s, 3" h, **$60.**

French Opalescent single-horn epergne in Diamond Lace, with metal base in the form of cupids done by Henry Turim Co., Brooklyn, N.Y., 1950s, 11-1/2" h, **$175+.**

Fenton by Era

French Opalescent jug in Ring Optic with Ebony handle (also found with clear and opaque handles, and matching tumblers), late 1930s, 6-3/4" h, **$175+**.

French Opalescent jug and tumbler in Ring Optic, part of a lemonade set that would have included six tumblers, late 1930s; jug, 7-1/4" h, **$175+**; tumbler, 5" h, **$60+**.

From left: French Opalescent hurricane lamp in Spiral Optic, two pieces, 1930s, 11" h, **$110+**; Silver Turquoise hurricane lamp, two pieces, made for only six months in 1956, 8-1/2" h, **$150-$175**.

French Opalescent perfume bottles or squat candleholders in Rib Optic, late 1930s, 3-1/2" h, **$35+** each. Not found in the regular line. Perhaps a special order?

French Opalescent "pancake" lamp in Coin Spot, early 1930s, 10" h, **$325+**.

French Opalescent perfume bottle in Hobnail, with original wood stopper (often found with glass stoppers, which were made by Anchor Hocking), 1939, 6" h, **$25+**. This bottle was made with a six-part mold. Four-part molds indicate manufacture by Anchor Hocking.

Two French Opalescent martini glasses in Hobnail, circa 1940, with significant difference in opalescence, each 3-1/2" h, not made for the regular line, **$75** each.

French Opalescent flared vase in Hobnail, circa 1940, 5" h, **$35+**.

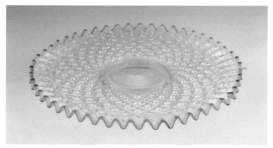

French Opalescent low cake plate in Emerald Crest/ Diamond Lace, 1949-55, 13" diameter, **$150+**.

French Opalescent vase in Spiral Optic, with pierced metal band on base, late 1930s, 7" h, **$25+**.

French Opalescent tray/dish in Hobnail, early 1940s, 10-1/2" w, **$35+**.

Two ivy balls with hard-to-find diamond-shaped bases: Green Opalescent Rib Optic, 1955, and Crystal Satin in etched Wisteria, 1938, 5" h and bases 8" l; green, **$125**; crystal, **$60**.

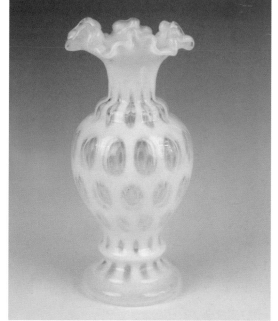

French Opalescent vase in Coin Dot, late 1940s, 9" h, **$65+**.

Fenton by Era

Gold Crest made its debut in 1943, but only lasted until 1945. It was revived for two years in 1963-64 (see 1955 to 1980). Since neither incarnation is marked, remember that old-formula Milk-glass from the 1940s is less opaque (called "skim milk" by collectors), while glass made after the late 1950s is usually a solid, shiny white.

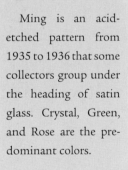

Ming is an acid-etched pattern from 1935 to 1936 that some collectors group under the heading of satin glass. Crystal, Green, and Rose are the predominant colors.

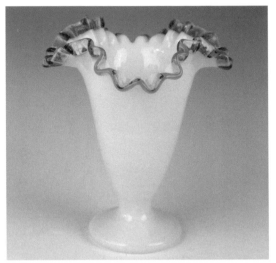

Gold Crest flared and crimped vase, 1940s, 6-1/2" h, **$35+.**

Green Ming paneled bowl and underplate, mid-1930s: bowl, 10" diameter; plate, 15" diameter, **$125+** set.

Green Ming ginger jar with Ebony lid and base, mid-1930s, 8-1/2" h, **$325+** set.

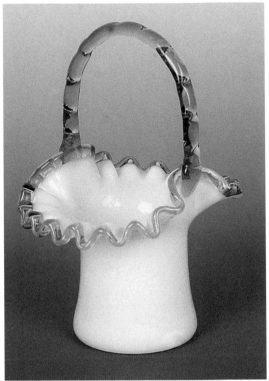

Gold Crest hat basket with gold handle, mid-1940s, 6-1/2" h, **$50+.**

Gold Crest fan vase, mid-1940s, 6-1/2" h, **$45+.**

Green Pastel and Rose Pastel shakers in Lamb's Tongue, 1954-55, 3-1/2" h, **$40+** each.

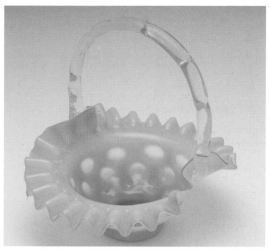

Green Overlay basket in Coin Dot, early 1940s, 7-1/2" h and 7" w, **$500+**.

Green Pastel, Milk-glass and Blue Pastel candleholders in a swirl pattern, 1954-56, 2-1/2" h; pastels, **$40+** each; Milk-glass, **$20+**.

Green Transparent and Green Opalescent candleholders, low Hobnail, style No. 3974, 1950s; transparent, **$20+**; opalescent, **$30+**.

Green Transparent glassware varies considerably in intensity of color. Made from about 1923 to the late 1930s, examples with wheel-cut decoration are especially prized. But because it was made in such large numbers, it is still among the most affordable of all early Fenton glass.

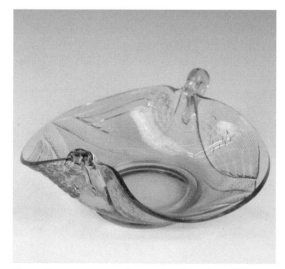

Green Transparent oval swan bonbon, late 1930s, 7-1/2" w, **$35+**.

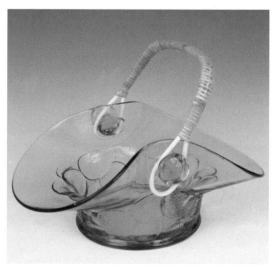

Green Transparent basket in Big Cookies, with rattan handle, 1930s, 11" w, **$125+**.

Fenton by Era

Hand vases, 6" h; far left and right: Topaz and Blue Opalescent in Hobnail, early 1940s; center left and center right: Wisteria (Amethyst?) and Aqua in Daisy and Button, late 1930s, **$50+** each.

Made in 1948 and 1949, all examples of Honeysuckle are elusive.

Honeysuckle Opalescent lamp in Coin Dot, late 1940s, 16" h, **$250+**.

Mini hand vases in Opal, Topaz Opalescent, Blue Opalescent, Milk-glass, and French Opalescent, early 1940s, between 3-1/2" and 4" h, **$45-$65** each. Topaz Opalescent is in the higher value range.

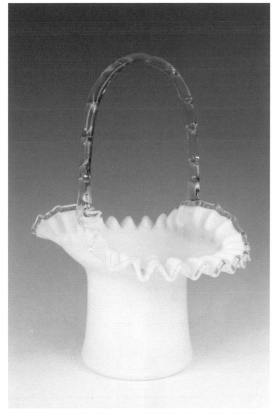

Ivory Crest hat basket/vase, 1940-41, 14" h, **250+.**

Ivory Crest pieces, early 1940s, left: hat vase with tulip crimp, 5" h, **$30+**; right: vase with tulip crimp and irregular swirl pattern, 8" h, **$50+.**

Ivy Overlay vase with applied Charleton Ivory Leaves and Needles decoration, early 1950s, 5" h, **$85.**

Like custard glass, Ivory Crest from 1940 to 1941 was made using uranium salts, which were also a common ingredient in producing brightly colored yellow and green glass for more than 100 years. The uranium is what gives the glass its deep cream color. Restrictions on the use of uranium during World War II marked the end of custard glass and Ivory Crest.

Ivy Overlay vase, tulip crimp, 1949-52, 7" h, **$85+.**

Ivy Overlay vase, 1950s, 8" h, **$90+.**

Like other overlay designs made by Fenton in the middle of the 20th century, Ivy dates from 1950-53. Decorated examples like the one seen above are not common.

Fenton by Era

Jade Green was a phenomenally successful color introduced in 1921. The Wide Rib pattern pieces here are tough to find. Other examples of Jade Green can be found in 1905 to 1930. Fenton reintroduced Jade Green in 1980.

Jade Green covered candy jar, 1/2-pound size, early 1930s, 9-1/2" h, **$65+**.

Jade Green pieces in Wide Rib, early 1930s, left: creamer and sugar, each 3-3/4" h, **$80+** pair; center and right: jug with crimped ice lip, 7-1/2" h, and tumbler, 4-1/4" h, **$125+** pair.

Jade Green bonbon with small handles in Diamond Optic, early 1930s, 7-1/2" w, **$45+**.

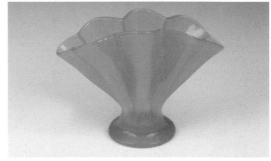

Jade Green fan vase, early 1930s, 6" h, **$30+**.

Jade Green flower-form console bowl, flared, early 1930s, 9" diameter, **$45+**.

Jade Green fan vase with dolphin handles, 1931, 6" h, **$55+**.

Jade Green candle vase, 1930s, 7" h, **$80+**.

Lilac dates from about 1933. It varies in opaque color from whitish lavender to pale mauve depending on how light hits it.

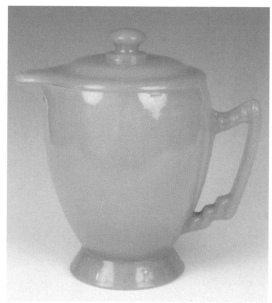

Lilac batter jug with cover (also found with Ebony lid), 1930s, 8-1/2" h, **$550+**.

Lilac cookie jar in Big Cookies, with original rattan handle, 1933, 7" h without handle, rare, **$400+**.

Lilac footed deep oval bowl with dolphin handles, 1930s, 6" h, 9-1/2" w, **$225+**.

Lilac cupped bowl with three dolphin handles on Ebony base, early 1930s, 6" diameter, **$150+**.

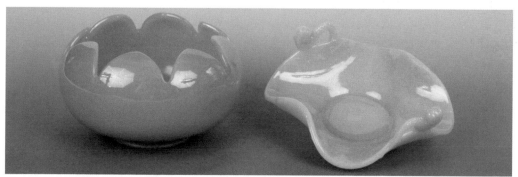

Lilac pieces, 1933, showing variations in color intensity, from left: cupped petal bowl, 4" h, **$100+**; dolphin-handled bonbon, 6" diameter, **$75+**.

Fenton by Era

Not a common color, Lime Green Opalescent was made from 1952-54.

Mandarin Red is often confused with Venetian Red, but Venetian was made a decade earlier, starting in about 1924. Mandarin Red (1933-35) also typically has golden marbling, but it can be bold or subtle (see 1930 to 1955). Also, this color was revived for the Bicentennial as "Patriot Red."

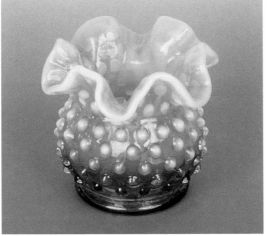

Lime Green Opalescent vase in Hobnail, early 1950s, 3", **$65.**

Mandarin Red flared bowl, mid-1930s, 8-1/2" diameter, **$50+.**

Mandarin Red cupped and lobed bowl, mid-1930s, 6" diameter, **$55+.**

Mandarin Red cupped bowl with five-legged Ebony base, 1933, 6" h overall, **$200+** set.

Mandarin Red bowl, mid-1930s, 10", **$85+.**

Mandarin Red flared bowl with applied gold decoration and Ebony base, mid-1930s, 8" diameter, **$200+** pair.

Mandarin Red candlesticks, mid-1930s, in cornucopia, 5" h, **$75+**; faceted, 8-1/2" h, **$75+**.

Mandarin Red cigarette box and two ashtrays with intaglio flower pattern, mid-1930s; box, 4-1/2" l; ashtrays, 4" diameter, **$250+** set.

Mandarin Red flared vases, mid-1930s, from left: footed Dancing Ladies, 8-1/2" h, **$700+**; Peacock, 7-1/2" h, **$200+**.

Mandarin Red flared vase, early 1930s, 11-1/2" h, **$150+**.

Fenton by Era

Mandarin Red pieces with applied gold decoration, mid-1930s, from left: fan vase, 5" h; cupped and lobed bowl, 3-1/2" h, **$150+** each.

Mandarin Red fan vase, two views, showing the strong golden swirls sometimes found in these pieces, mid-1930s, possibly a lunch-hour piece, ex-Harry Rosenthal collection with serial numbers on base, 5" h, 8-1/2" w, **$275+**.

This rare experimental vase is made of what collectors call "Kitchen Green," similar to Fire-King's Jadeite Green made by Anchor Hocking.

"Milady" vase in Kitchen Green, 1942, 11" h, **$500+**.

Milk-glass console bowl in Daisy and Button (originally called Cape Cod in the 1930s), this example mid-1950s, 11" w, **$25+**.

Milk-glass candleholders in Block and Star, one with finger ring, 1955, square 5" diagonal, round 4" diameter not including ring, **$15+** each.

What carnival glass was for the first quarter of Fenton's history, Milk-glass was for the second. Millions of pieces found their way into kitchen cupboards, sideboards, and china shelves. What began in the middle of the 19th century as a cheap alternative to porcelain was now a staple of American glass making. For more Milk-glass, see 1955 to 1980.

Milk-glass cupped and footed low bowl in Hobnail, 1950s, 3-1/2" h and 6" diameter, no established value.

Milk-glass console set of bowl and candleholders in Block and Star, mid-1950s: bowl, 8-1/2" diameter; candleholders, 4" diameter not including handles, **$75** set.

Fenton by Era

Milk-glass Tulip swan bowl with raised wing pattern on underside, circa 1938, 14" l, **$85.**

Three Milk-glass candleholders in Hobnail, 1950s, from left: cupped bowl in style No. 3770, 3-1/2" h, **$50+**; two-piece in style No. 3745, 9-1/2" h, **$65+**; style No. 3870, 3-1/2" h, **$25+.**

Milk-glass three-horn epergne in Diamond Lace, 1955, 9" h, **$75+.**

Milk-glass, Plum and French Opalescent miniature cornucopia candleholders, style No. 3971, 1940-57, 3-1/2" h, **$20+** each.

Milk-glass lacy-edge plate in "Backwards C" pattern, mid-1950s, 9" diameter, **$15+.**

Milk-glass lacy-edge plate, reverse in "Backwards C" pattern, mid-1950s, 9" diameter, with metal wall pocket made especially for Fenton, **$40+.**

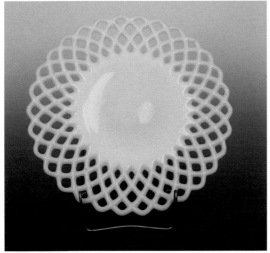

Milk-glass lacy-edge plate, mid-1950s, 12" diameter, **$40+.**

Milk-glass lacy-edge plate with hand-painted apple, mid-1950s, 8" diameter, **$25+.**

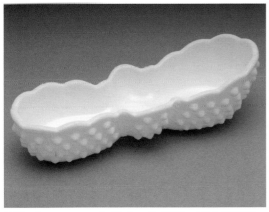

Milk-glass spooner in Hobnail, 1950s, 7" l, **$100+.**

Milk-glass, French Opalescent and Black (Ebony) shakers in "5 & 5" Hobnail, 1940s, 3-1/2" h, Milk-glass, **$15**; French and Black, **$30** each.

Milk-glass, Green Pastel and Rose Pastel shakers in a swirl pattern, mid-1950s, 3-1/2" h; Milk-glass, **$15+**; pastels, **$25+** each.

Milk-glass leaf plate, mid-1950s, 8" diameter (also found in 11" size), **$25.**

Fenton by Era

Milk-glass pieces from left: bottle vase, 1950s, 7-1/2" h, **$15+**; crimped flowerpot with attached under-plate and drain hole, 1950s, 4" h, **$45.**

Milk-glass vase in Apple Tree, mid-1930s, 10" h, **$95.**

Milk-glass swirl vase, mid-1950s, 6" h, **$15.**

Pink, Crystal and Amber cornucopia candleholders in Ming, mid-1930s, 5-1/2" h; Pink, **$75+**; Crystal and Amber, **$50+** each.

Mongolian Green macaroon jar in Ribbon Band, mid-1930s, 6-1/4" h, **$225+**.

Mongolian Green fan vase, mid-1930s, 5-1/2" h, **$55+**.

Though only made for a short time in 1934-35, Mongolian Green is still readily available in bowls and vases, though the vase in the Dancing Ladies pattern seen on P. 85 is a prize for any collector.

Mongolian Green pieces, mid-1930s, from left: flared vase, 5-1/2" h, **$70+**; "Flip" vase, 6-1/4" h, **$85+**; cupped and lobed bowl, 4-1/4" h, **$55+**.

Mongolian Green console set with flared bowl and cornucopia candleholders, mid-1930s; candleholders, each 5" h; console bowl, 12" w, **$275+** set.

Fenton by Era

Moonstone was another short-lived line, made in 1932-34. Pieces with covers or stoppers may have contrasting colors of Black or Jade Green.

Moonstone double candleholders, 1930s, each 6" h, **$125+** pair.

Moonstone three-footed base, used for a variety of bowls and vases, early 1930s, 6" diameter, **$25.**

Moonstone shaving mug, early 1930s, with a period shaving brush, mug 3-1/2" h, **$40** pair.

Moonstone and Ebony vanity set (found in other colors), two perfumes, powder box and rectangular tray (not pictured), early 1930s; perfumes, each 5" h; box, 4-1/4" diameter, **$600+** set.

Mulberry pieces in Diamond Optic, 1942, showing the typical color variations from blue to purple; left: hat novelty, 2-3/4" h, **$100+**; right: squat jug, melon form, clear handle, 5-1/4" h, **$250+**.

Mulberry crimped bowl in Diamond Optic, 1942, 10" diameter, **$125+**.

Production snags doomed the original Mulberry to less than a year of output. Look closely to make sure an "early" example doesn't have the Fenton logo, which appeared when the color was reissued in 1989.

Mulberry pieces in Diamond Optic, 1942, left: square-crimp melon vase, 5" h, **$95+**; right: small hat vase or novelty, 3-1/4" h, **$80+**.

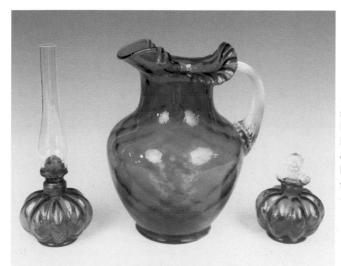

Mulberry pieces in Diamond Optic, 1942, showing the typical color variations from blue to purple, from left: small kerosene lamp, melon form, 4-1/4" h without chimney, **$150+**; 70-ounce jug with clear handle, 9" h, **$325+**; perfume, melon form, 4" h, **$110+**.

Fenton by Era

Sometimes called "September Morn," the Nymph sets first appeared in the late 1920s, with other colors added through the early 1940s. They are found with a variety of flared and cupped bowls, and often include a flower frog and base. Newer examples were made in special colors with the Fenton logo.

Nymph Ruby console set including figurine in flower frog, flared petal bowl, Ebony base and footed candleholders, early 1930s; Nymph, frog, bowl and stand, 9" h; candleholders, 4-1/2" diameter, **$225+.**

Nymph Figure with flower frog, cupped petal bowl and Milk-glass base in swirl pattern, a specialty item in Milk-glass, found in a range of colors, 1930s; figure and frog, 7-1/4" h; bowl and stand, 6-1/2" h, depending on color, a wide range of values, **$225.**

Nymph Figure with flower frog, cupped petal bowl and five-legged base, a specialty item in Black (Ebony), found in a range of colors, 1930s; figure and frog, 7-1/4" h; bowl and stand, 6-1/2" h, depending on color, a wide range of values, **$350.**

Nymph in footed bowl in Green Transparent, 1930s, 7-1/2" h, **$275+** set.

Nymph, flower frog and footed bowl in Rose Transparent, early 1930s; figure and frog, 7" h; bowl, 10" diameter, **$300+** set.

While plain Peach Blow was a brief entry from 1939, it was quickly followed by Peach Crest in 1940, and production continued into the late 1960s. Peach Blow Hobnail didn't arrive until the early 1950s.

Peach Blow basket in Hobnail, early 1950s, 9" h, **$150+.**

Peach Blow jug and tumbler in Beaded Curtain, made for L.G. Wright, part of a lemonade set that would have included six tumblers, 1940s; jug, 12-1/2" h, **$500+**; tumbler, 4" h, **$90+.**

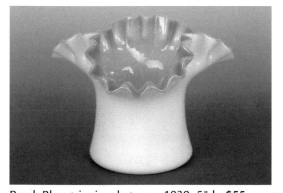

Peach Blow tri-crimp hat vase, 1939, 5" h, **$55.**

Peach Blow crimped vase in Hobnail, mid-1950s, 5" h, **$65+.**

Peach Blow (1952-55) and Milk-glass (1950s) hurricane lamps in Hobnail, two pieces, 8" h; Peach Blow, **$125+**; Milk-glass, **$65+.**

Fenton by Era

Peach Crest double-crimp bowl, 1940s, 13" diameter, **$120+.**

Peach Crest perfume bottle, melon form, with Charleton decoration, 1940s, 6" h, **$75+.**

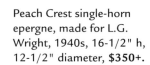

Peach Crest single-horn epergne, made for L.G. Wright, 1940s, 16-1/2" h, 12-1/2" diameter, **$350+.**

Peach Crest melon-form vase with Charleton decoration by Abels, Wasserberg of New York, mid-1950s, 5-1/2" h, **$75+.**

Peach Crest hat basket, late 1940s, 15" h, **$300+.**

Peach Crest hurricane lamps with spiral bases, 1940-41, each 11" h, **$300+** pair.

Peach Crest vase, melon form, with Charleton decoration, mid-1950s, 8" h, **$90+.**

Peach Crest double-crimped vases with Charleton decoration, 1940s, each 8" h, **$100+ each.**

Peacock vases were made at the same time as the Dancing Ladies, and also come in a variety of colors. Note in the Milk-glass collection that smaller sizes can have larger values.

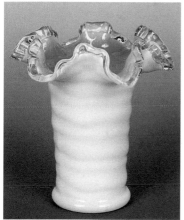

Peach Crest double-crimp vase with irregular swirl pattern, early 1940s, 5-1/2" h, **$45+.**

Peacock vases in Milk-glass, including one with gilt trim on the lip and base, early 1930s; 9-1/2" cupped and flared, **$300+**; 7-1/2" flared, **$125+**; 5-1/2" flared, **$150+**; two 4" vases, one flared, one cupped and flared, **$200+.**

Peacock vases, early 1930s, from left: Crystal, 7-1/2" cupped and flared, **$100+**; 7-3/4" flared, possibly pale Orchid, no established value.

Peacock Periwinkle Blue flared vase, mid-1930s, 7-1/2" h, **$150+.**

Fenton by Era

Periwinkle Blue is another of the slag-glass products from 1933-35. Later examples made as specialty items will bear the Fenton logo.

Periwinkle Blue scalloped bowl, early 1930s, 8" diameter, **$50+**.

Periwinkle Blue fan vase, mid-1930s, 5-1/2" h, **$85+**.

Periwinkle Blue pieces, early 1930s, from left: cupped bowl, 5-1/2" diameter, **$85+**; macaroon jar in Ribbon Band with rattan handle, 6-1/4" h, **$135+**; fan vase, 6" h, **$85+**.

The transparent version of Rose was introduced at about the same time (1927) as the stretch-glass variety, which was called Velva Rose (1926). For more examples of Rose, see 1905 to 1930.

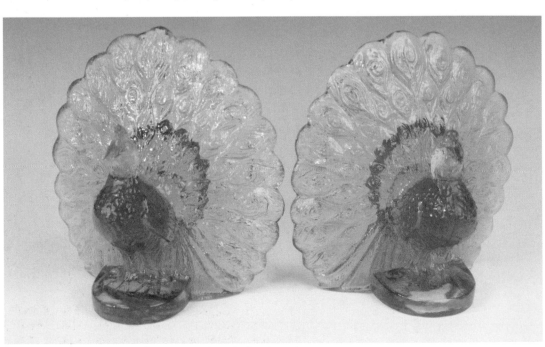

Rose peacock-form bookends, 1935, each 6" h, **$500+** pair.

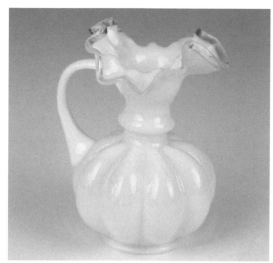

Rose Crest (pale) jug, melon form, 1940s, 6" h, **$75+.**

Rose Crest (1950s) and Ivory Crest (1942) cornucopia candleholders, style No. 951, 6-1/2" h, **$35-$40** each.

Rose Crest was made from 1944 to 1947. It is one of the more difficult Crest lines to find.

Rose Ming two-piece baby reamer, mid-1930s, 4-1/2" h, **$700+.**

Rose Ming covered ginger jar and base, mid-1930s, 8-1/2" h, **$250+.**

Ming is an acid-etched pattern from 1935-36 that some collectors group under the heading of satin glass. Crystal, Green, and Rose are the predominant colors.

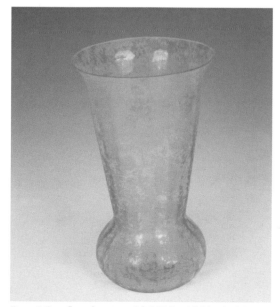

Rose Ming flared vase, mid-1930s, 10" h, **$100+.**

Rose Ming jug and tumbler, mid-1930s, part of a lemonade set that would have included six tumblers; jug with crimped ice lip and Ebony handle, 10" h; tumbler, 5-1/4" h, **$600+** for complete set.

Fenton by Era

Complete lemonade or iced tea set in Rose Ming, including jug with crimped ice lip and Ebony handle, six tumblers, and seven coasters (rare), mid- to late 1930s; jug, 9-1/2" h; tumblers, 5-1/4" h; tumbler coasters, 4" diameter; jug coaster, 6-1/2" diameter, no established value.

Rose Overlay basket, mid-1940s, 7" h, **$85+**.

Unlike Blue Overlay, which was in production for a decade, Rose Overlay was made from 1943 to about 1948. It is not found in beaded-melon form, which was introduced in 1951 as the Tiara line.

Rose Overlay pieces on Opal, mid-1940s, from left: crimped jug, 5-1/2" h, **$50**; small hat basket, 4" h, **$50+**.

Rose Overlay pieces, melon form, mid- to late 1940s; left: small jug, 4-3/4" h, **$35+**; center: vase, 8-1/2" h, **$85+**; right: vase, 4-3/4" h, **$35+**.

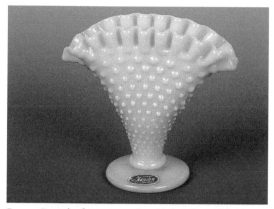

Rose Pastel fan vase in Hobnail, mid-1950s, 4" h, **$40+**.

Rose Satin flared and crimped vase in Diamond Optic, early 1950s, 6-1/2" h, **$110+**.

The Pastel line of Milk-glass included Blue, Green, and Rose, made from 1954-56. It is often found in Daisy and Button.

Royal Blue oval footed bowl and cornucopia candleholders, 1930s: bowl, 11" w, **$100+**; candleholders, each 5-1/2" h, **$175+** pair.

Satin patterns made in 1953-54 also included Blue and White (French) Opalescence.

Royal Blue flower-form footed candleholder, mid-1930s, 4-1/2" diameter, **$30+**.

Royal Blue flower-form console bowl, flared, mid-1930s, 9" diameter, **$45+**.

Royal Blue footed whimsy with tri-crimp in Georgian, early 1930s, 4-1/2" diameter, **$25+**.

Some collectors use "Royal Blue" to describe carnival glass items made of cobalt glass, but this line that originated in the mid-1920s borrowed only sparingly from carnival molds, and remained in production until the late 1930s.

Fenton by Era

Ruby made its debut in 1921, and pieces may also be found with dolphin handles and in the Diamond Optic pattern. Some forms may have a gold tinge around rims and bases. For more examples of Ruby, see 1905 to 1930.

Ruby slipper ashtray in Daisy and Button, late 1930s, found in many other colors, 6" l, **$25.**

Ruby basket in Big Cookies, original rattan handle, 1930s, 10-1/2" w, **$175+.**

Ruby footed bowl in Basket Weave with Open Edge (three-holes), mid-1930s, 8-1/2" diameter, **$55+.**

Ruby basket in Hobnail, circa 1950, 12", **$100+.**

Left: Ruby candleholder in style No. 316, 1930s, 3-1/2" h, **$75+**; right: Ruby Stretch candleholder similar to style No. 316, 2003, 4" h, **$35+.**

Ruby square bowl in Sheffield, 1950s, 9-1/2" w, **$85+.** This bowl, with the same pattern, dimensions and era, was also produced by Imperial Glass Corp., Bellaire, Ohio.

Ruby console set with petal bowl and footed candleholders, 1930s; bowl, 9" w; candleholders, 4-1/2" w, **$125+** set.

Ruby comport in Georgian, a whimsy, not a production piece in this form, early 1930s, 7" diameter, no established value.

Ruby jug and tumbler in Georgian, part of a lemonade set that would have included six tumblers, 1930s; jug, 7-1/2" h; tumbler, 4" h, **$150+** for complete set.

Decanters in Ruby and Royal Blue, with flower-form stoppers (each part of a set that included small cordial glasses), mid-1930s, each 9" h, **$175+** each.

Ruby and Crystal footed candleholders in Basket Weave with Open Edge, late 1930s, 5" diameter; Crystal, **$25+**; Ruby, **$35+.**

Ruby salt and pepper shakers in Diamond Optic, pewter tops, 1930s, 4-1/2" h, **$200+** pair.

Ruby and Amber footed shakers in Georgian (found in eight colors), 1931-39; Ruby, **$65+**; Amber, **$35+.**

Fenton by Era

Ruby candle vase, 1930s, 7" h, **$80+.**

Ruby flared vase in Apple Tree, with raised circle where handle could have been attached to side, 1930s, 9" h, rare in this color, **$300+.**

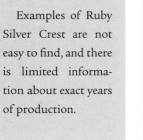

Examples of Ruby Silver Crest are not easy to find, and there is limited information about exact years of production.

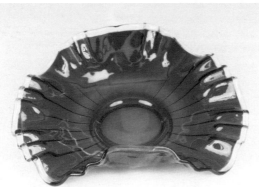

Ruby Silver Crest ribbed shallow bowl with irregular crimp, 1940s, 10" diameter, **$150+.**

Ruby Silver Crest ribbed shallow bowl with standard crimp (most common form found), 1940s, 10" diameter, **$75+.**

Ruby Silver Crest ribbed shallow bowl with smooth edge, 1940s, 10" w, **$150+.**

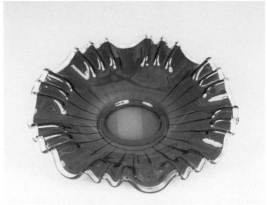

Ruby Silver Crest ribbed shallow bowl with irregular crimp, 1940s, 10" diameter, **$150+.**

Ruby Silver Crest ribbed cornucopia candleholders with smooth tulip crimp, 1940s, each 6" h, **$180-$200+** pair.

Ruby Silver Crest pieces, 1940s, left: crimped vase with hexagonal base, 6" h; right: ribbed cornucopia candleholder with tulip crimp, 6" h, **$100+** each.

Three Ruby pieces in Plymouth, mid-1930s: water goblet, 5-1/2" h, **$35+**; tumbler, 6" h, **$40+**; wine glass, 4" h, **$20+**.

Ruby Silver Crest crimped vases with hexagonal bases, 1940s, each 6" h, **$120+** each.

Santoy Etched decanter, 1936, 9" h, **$150+**.

Ruby Snow Crest hats in Spiral Optic, early 1950s, 7" h, **$300+**; 4-1/2" h, **$100+**.

Ruby Snow Crest appears to have been introduced in 1950, but sources vary on exactly how long it was made.

Three Ruby Snow Crest vases in Spiral Optic, early 1950s, from left: pinched, 8-1/2" h, **$150+**; 11" h, **$225+**; 9" h, **$140+**.

Fenton by Era

Some collectors believe that the avalanche of Silver Crest glass production actually began in the late 1930s, but it's certain that in the early 1940s, Fenton knew it had a winner. As other Crest lines fell away (only to be revived later), Silver Crest numbers continued to mount, and pieces were being made generations after its introduction. For more Silver Crest, see 1955 to 1980.

Silver Crest bowls, smooth crimps, 8" and 10" diameter, rare, **$40-$60** each.

Silver Crest bowls, all about 5" diameter, from left: soup, 2-1/2" h, **$35+**; low dessert, 1-3/4" h, **$15+**; deep dessert, 3" h, **$15+.**

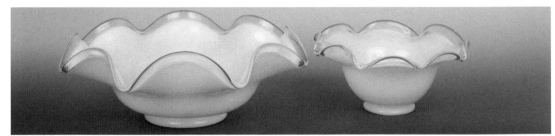

Silver Crest bowls, smooth crimps, 7" and 11" diameter, **$40-$60** each.

Silver Crest ivy bowl, with hand-painted decoration, 1950s, 5" w at crimp and 3-1/2" h, **$40+.**

Silver Crest salad bowls, 10-3/4" and 7" diameter, **$40-$60** each.

Silver Crest ribbed bowl, two views, 9" diameter, rare form, **$300+**.

Silver Crest pieces, 1940s, in old-formula Milk-glass, left: serving bowl, 6" diameter, **$90+**; right: double-crimp bonbon, 6-1/2" diameter, **$35+**.

Silver Crest covered boxes, melon form: 4" h powder box, **$40+**; 6" h candy box, **$60+**.

Silver Crest tall cake plate, unusual variation, with symmetrical peaked profile, purchased from the "special room" at the Fenton factory, probably one of a kind, 7-1/2" h, 12" diameter, no established value.

Silver Crest tall cake plate, 5" h, 13" diameter, **$45+**.

121

Fenton by Era

Silver Crest, Ivory Crest and Peach Blow candlesticks, 1940s and '50s, 4-1/2" to 5" h; Silver, **$30+**; Ivory and Peach, **$45+** each.

Silver Crest, Ruby Overlay and Gold Crest melon-form candleholders, 1942-49, 3-1/2" to 4" h; Crests, **$25+** each; Ruby overlay, **$45+.**

Silver Crest candleholders with Silvertone pattern, 3" h each, **$200+** pair.

Silver Crest chip and dip, 1950s; 13-1/2" bowl, dip 3-1/2" h, **$100+** set.

Silver Crest covered candy dishes showing base variations, 1940s, 9-1/2" h, **$75+** each.

Silver Crest candy dish in old-formula Milk-glass (called "skim milk" by collectors), and with clear ring attached to base rather than lid, late 1930s, 6-1/4" h, **$200+.**

Silver Crest pieces, left: melon-form squat jug, opaque handle, 6" h, **$100+**; right: Silver Crest syrup pitcher, clear handle, 5-1/2" h, **$60+**.

Silver Crest cupped comport or footed bowl, ribbed, unusual, possibly one of a kind, 4" h, 8-1/2" diameter, no established value.

Silver Crest plain creamer and sugar (each about 3-1/2" h), **$75+** pair; cup and saucer (6" diameter, other variations found), **$60+** pair.

Silver Crest cruets, 5" h, **$250+** pair.

Silver Crest comport or footed bowl, ribbed, 4-3/4" h, 10" diameter, **$65+**.

Silver Crest pieces, from left: Silver Crest creamer (hard-to-find form), 3" h, **$125+**; Silver Crest beaded-melon squat jug, 3-1/2" h, **$100+**; Silver Crest plain syrup pitcher, 3-5/8" h, **$75+**.

fenton by Era

Silver Crest single-horn epergne, 10" h, **$75+.**

Silver Crest single-horn epergne, 14" h, **$150+.**

Silver Crest four-piece epergne: horn, flower frog, bowl, and stand, 8-1/2" h, **$200+.**

Silver Crest three-horn epergne with original label, 11" h, **$100+.**

Silver Crest 70-ounce jug, 8-1/2" h, **$250+.** Silver Crest goblets (also called footed tumblers), each 6" h, **$70+** each.

Silver Crest 70-ounce jug with unusual ice lip, 1940s, 10" h, very rare, **$850+.**

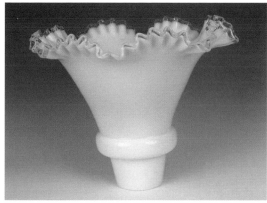

Silver Crest lampshade, double crimped, 1950s, 10" h, 12" diameter, **$350+**.

Silver Crest Apple Tree jug and vase, each 10" h, **$100-$130** each.

Silver Crest lampshade, called the No. 2 torchiere, early 1950s, only one known, 8" h, no established value. According to Frank M. Fenton, the shade was made for the Rembrandt Co. of Chicago, and in a 2004 letter, he wrote, "We sold a good many of them."

Silver Crest melon-form perfume bottle or candleholder (inside of neck is not ground), 1940s, 6" h, **$50+**.

Silver Crest hurricane lamp, 8-1/2" h, **$250+**.

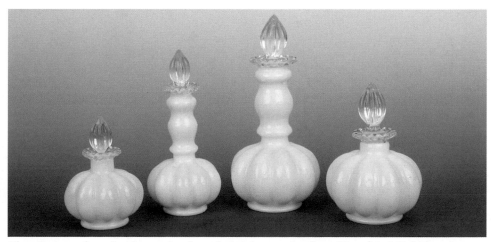

Silver Crest perfume bottles, melon form, in heights ranging from 5" to 9", **$40-$60** each.

Fenton by Era

Silver Crest perfume bottles, beaded melon form, 4-3/4" and 6-3/4" h, **$40-$60** each.

Silver Crest melon-form perfume bottle with Charleton decoration by Abels, Wasserberg of New York, mid-1940s, 7" h, **$85.**

Perfume set, two Silver Crest pieces, melon form, with Charleton decoration, 1950s, from left: powder box, 4-1/4" diameter; perfume bottle, 5" h, **$125+** set.

Silver Crest tall perfume bottles, melon form, with Charleton decoration, 1950s, each 9" h, **$150+** pair.

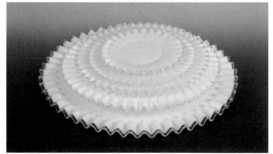

Silver Crest plates, from the bottom (expect to find width variations of up to 3/4"): 16" torte plate, **$72+**; 12" dinner plate, **$40+**; 10" dinner plate, **$35+**; 8-1/2" luncheon plate, **$15+**; 6" bread plate, **$20+**.

Silver Crest salt and pepper shakers, 4-1/2" and 5" h, **$125+** each pair.

Silver Crest cone or 8" vases, from left: standard crimp, smooth crimp (with quilted pattern), and pie-crust crimp; each about 8" h, **$75+** each.

Silver Crest toothpick holders (also called mini-vases), square crimp and fan (found in other configurations), each 2-1/4" h, **$250+** each.

Silver Crest baluster or urn vases, possibly made for Weller Pottery Co., 11" h, **$80+**; 7" h, **$50+**.

Silver Crest "bowling pin" salt and pepper shakers, 1940s, each 4" h, very rare, **$400+** pair.

Silver Crest sherbet, left, 3" h, **$18+**; center: Silver Crest mayonnaise set (which combines a 6" saucer and deep dessert) with ladle, **$40+** set; right: Silver Crest footed nut dish, 4" h, **$15+**.

Silver Crest pieces, 1940s: left, ribbed cone vase with wide turned-down crest, 8" h, **$200+**; right, bulbous jug with spout lip, 9" h, **$75+**.

fenton by Era

Silver Crest fan vase with transfer decoration, 1940s, decorated by Tyndale, 7" h, **$50.**

Silver Crest cornucopia vase, left, with smooth, tulip profile, **$65+**; right, a variation on a 13" Silver Crest fan vase, with large crimping, **$200+.**

Silver Crest 6" vases with smooth crimps, **$75+** each.

Silver Crest hat vases: 4-1/2" h, **$40+**; 7" h, **$150+**; 3" h, **$35+.**

Silver Crest 8" vases, from left: curled rim, fan, and flared; 7-1/2" h to 9" h, **$75+** each.

Silver Crest "8"" vases; left, melon form, and right, beaded melon, **$50+** each; center: new beaded melon vase showing irregular lobe sizes and larger beading, plus dense white glass, **$30+.**

Swirled Feather in Green, Blue, and French Satin, early 1950s (the lids on the powder boxes are new replacements; prices are for boxes with original lids); left and right, powder boxes, each 5-3/4" h; in Green, **$350+**; in French, **$225+**; center: hurricane lamp, 8" h, **$250+**.

Swirled Feather was part of the Satin Opalescent line introduced in 1953. All pieces, in all colors, are seldom seen.

Tiara Line beaded-melon vases, approximately 4" h, in Silver Crest, Gold Overlay, and Green Overlay, circa 1950, **$35+** each.

Tiara Line beaded-melon vases, approximately 4" h, in Emerald Crest, Yellow Overlay, and Peach Crest, circa 1950, **$50+** each.

The Tiara Line was introduced in 1949, and eventually collectors began referring to it as "beaded melon." The 4-inch vases seen have become a collecting area unto themselves.

Tiara Line beaded-melon vases, approximately 4" h, in Green Overlay and Blue Overlay, circa 1950, **$35+** each.

Fenton by Era

The pieces of Topaz Opalescent glass (Fenton's name for Vaseline glass) that were made in the late 1930s often featured the patterns of Rib and Spiral Optic, followed by Hobnail in 1939. Also see 1955 to 1980.

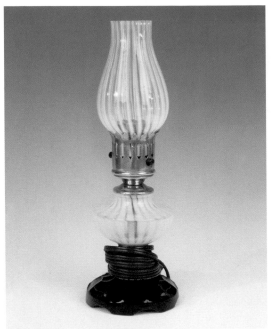

Topaz Opalescent electric lamp in Rib Optic, early 1930s, 11" h, **$150+**.

Topaz Opalescent basket in Coin Spot, 1930s, 12" h, **$300+**.

Topaz Opalescent fan vase in Hobnail, early 1940s, 8" h, **$175+**.

Three pieces of Topaz Opalescent in Hobnail: left, candleholder in style No. 3974, low Hobnail, **$40+**; candle bowl, **$95+**; miniature cornucopia candleholder, style No. 3971, 1940-57, 3-1/2" h, **$30+**.

Topaz Opalescent crimped vase in Hobnail, early 1940s, 8" h, **$225-$250**.

Topaz Opalescent creamer and sugar in Hobnail, early 1940s, each 2" h, **$50** pair.

To compare to Topaz Opalescent: Vaseline glass compote or nut dish with Grapevine pattern, made by U.S. Glass, circa 1910, 6-1/4" diameter, **$500+**.

Turquoise candleholders in Block and Star, one with finger ring, 1955, 4" diameter not including ring, **$30+** each.

Wild Rose cased-glass sample rose bowl with satin finish, unusual, hand painted, 1940s, 6-1/2" diameter, **$275+**.

To compare to Topaz Opalescent: Vaseline glass biscuit jar with cherries motif, maker unknown, 1950s (?), 8" h, **$100+**.

Wild Rose cased-glass covered jar, made for L.G. Wright, 1940s, 6-1/2" h, **$325+**.

Lawrence Gale Wright started his glass wholesale business in 1937 in New Martinsville, W.V., buying glass from several manufacturers, including Fenton. Wright commissioned new molds and also bought old molds, including some Northwood, Dugan and Diamond designs. The same molds were used to make L.G. Wright glass at several different glassworks at various times. By some estimates, 70 percent of the glass made for Wright was produced by Fenton. Since most pieces were unmarked, it's difficult to identify which glassworks made a particular piece of L.G. Wright glass, and the designs were not restricted to particular years, so most are difficult to date. The two Wild Rose pieces shown here are also called "Peach Blow" by some collectors. These values assume a Fenton attribution.

131

Fenton by Era

Wistaria was an acid-etched pattern from the late 1930s. The jug and tumbler shown here are particularly elusive.

Made for only one year, Yellow Overlay should not be confused with Goldenrod, which didn't arrive until 1956.

Wisteria footed flared bowl (Amethyst?) in Silvertone, mid-1930s, 6" diameter, **$25+**.

Yellow Overlay vase, beaded-melon form with tulip crimp, 1950, 8-3/4" h, **$80+**.

Yellow Overlay basket, beaded-melon form, 1950, 11" w, **$150+**.

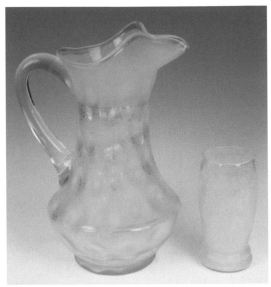

Wistaria jug and tumbler, part of a lemonade set that would have included six tumblers, late 1930s; jug with crimped ice lip, 11" h, **$225+**; tumbler, 5-1/4" h, **$55+**.

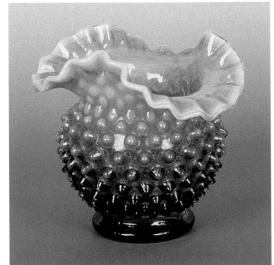

Wisteria Opalescent tri-crimp vase (Amethyst?) in Hobnail, 1944, 4-1/2" h, **$70+**.

Wisteria, Crystal and Amber footed candleholders in Silvertone, mid-1930s, 4-1/2" diameter; Crystal and Amber, **$15+** each; Wisteria, **$30+**.

In the third quarter of Fenton's history, the company returned to themes that had proved popular to preceding generations, and began adding special lines, like the Bicentennial series. Fenton also started marking its glass in the molds for the first time.

Opalescent patterns that were given new life included Cactus. Satin finishes also developed a strong following. But the star of this era was the yellow and blushing pink creation known as Burmese, which remains popular today. This was followed closely by a menagerie of animals, birds, and children.

There was the line of Colonial colors that debuted in 1963, including Amber, Blue, Green, Orange, and Ruby.

Based on a special order for an Ohio museum, Fenton in 1969 revisited its early success with "Original Formula Carnival Glass."

The '60s also wouldn't have been complete without Vasa Murrhina ("Vessel of Gems"), in Autumn Orange, Blue Mist, and "Aventurine."

In 1975, Robert Barber, an award-winning glass artist, was hired by Fenton to begin an artist-in-residence program with some of Fenton's most skilled craftsmen, producing a limited line of art-glass vases in a return to the off-hand, blown-glass creations of the mid-1920s.

Like other colors in the Crest line, Apple Blossom was made for only a short time, 1960-61.

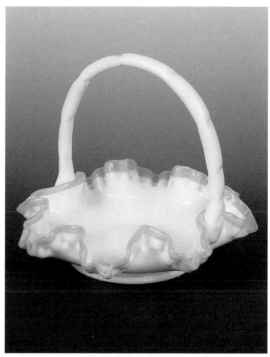

Apple Blossom Crest basket, 1960-61, 8" diameter, **$125+.**

Apple Blossom Crest three-horn epergne and candleholders, 1960-61; epergne, 10-1/2" h, **$400+;** candleholders, 3-1/2" h, **$150+ pair.**

Fenton by Era

Amberina finger bowl (?) in Hobnail, made for L.G. Wright Glass Co., 1970s, 3" h, **$15+**.

Swirl ashtrays in Amber and Blue, 1960s, 7-1/2" and 5" diameter, **$15** each.

Though Amber Overlay was first made in the late 1940s and early 1950s, this decorated example is later. Louise Piper worked at Fenton from 1968 to 1989. She died in 1995 at the age of 88.

Amber Overlay tri-crimp vase with hand-painted flowers by Louise Piper, 1970s, 7-1/2" h, **$150+**.

Aqua Opalescent comport in Cactus, 1979, 5-1/2" h, **$55+**.

All pieces of Aqua Opalescent in the Cactus pattern are hard to come by.

Aqua Crest, Apple Blossom Crest and Gold Crest candleholders, early 1960s, 3-1/2" and 5-1/2" h, Aqua, **$60+**; Apple Blossom, **$75+**; Gold, **$50+**.

Aurene Jefferson comport, one of only 75 made as a test color before the Bicentennial colors were established, circa 1973, 10-1/2" h, **$300+.**

Bicentennial eagle plate in Chocolate, 8-1/4" diameter (also found in Patriot Red, Independence Blue, and Valley Forge White), **$15+.**

The Bicentennial pieces were made in four colors beginning in 1974, and include the Jefferson comport, bell, eagle paperweight, stein, square planter, and two plates, showing the Bald Eagle and Lafayette.

Bicentennial planter and eagle paperweight in Chocolate, 4" h and 3-1/2" h (also found in Patriot Red, Independence Blue, and Valley Forge White), **$35+** each. The Patriot Red Planter was never produced for the regular line. There are reports that as many as 70 were made and sold through the Fenton Gift Shop as "seconds." This planter in Patriot Red is extremely rare and could sell for **$200.**

Bicentennial bells in Patriot Red and Chocolate, each 6-3/4" h (also found in Independence Blue and Valley Forge White), **$35+** each.

135

Fenton by Era

Bicentennial steins in Chocolate and Independence Blue, 7" h (also found in Patriot Red and Valley Forge White), **$45+** each.

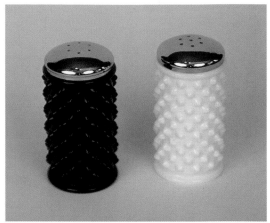

Black (Ebony) and Milk-glass kitchen shakers in Hobnail, sold in B&W (Fenton Gift Shop, 1968) and white pairs, late 1960s, 4-1/2" h; black, **$45+**; Milk-glass, **$20+**.

Blue Marble was made for four years from 1970 to 1973.

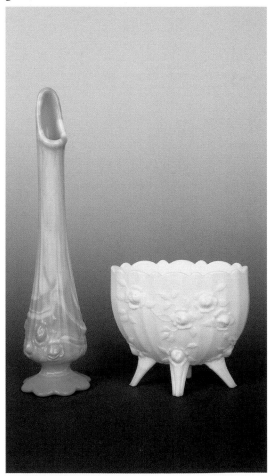

Blue Marble crimped comport in Hobnail, early 1970s, 6" h, **$30+**.

Blue Marble swung vase in Rose, early 1970s, 11" h; Milk-glass footed pillow vase in Rose, late 1960s, **$20** each.

Blue Opalescent hanging shade in Coin Dot, early 1960s, 13" h, **$250+.**

Blue Opalescent basket in Coin Dot, 1950s, 11" w, 13" h, **$500+.**

Blue Opalescent creamer and covered sugar in Cactus, 1979, 5" h and 6" h, **$100+** pair.

Blue Opalescent kerosene lamp in "Eye" Dot/Beaded Curtain, 1960s, 11" h including chimney, **$350+.**

Blue Opalescent glass has been produced throughout Fenton's history. Examples in Hobnail often date from about 1940 to 1954. It made a brief reappearance in 1960-61, and again in the early 1980s. Cactus was made in 1979. Blue Opalescent glass in a Spiral Optic pattern dates from about 1938-39. The pattern known as Coin Spot had wide production in the late 1930s and early 1940s. Pieces in Coin Dot were made primarily from 1947 to 1955. (In Coin Dot, the "coins" are clear; in Coin Spot, the coins are opaque.) Also see 1930 to 1955.

137

Fenton by Era

Blue Pastel, Blue Marble and Green Pastel candleholders in style No. 3974, low Hobnail, note size variations, 1950s-60s, 3" to 3-1/2" h, **$25+** each.

Blue Pastel, Milk-glass and black (Ebony) shakers in Block and Star, mid-1950s, 3-1/2" h, **$40+** each.

Blue Satin was one of several colors in a matte finish introduced in 1971 and made into the 1980s, including Crystal Velvet, Custard, Lime Sherbet, and White.

Blue Satin "Worker" elephant, 1960s, 3" h, **$400+**.

Blue Satin pitcher and basin in Water Lily, early 1970s; basin, 8-1/2" diameter; pitcher, 7-1/4" h, **$150+** pair.

Blue Satin pieces, 1970s; left: owl-form fairy light, 3-3/4" h, **$40**; right: hexagonal planter, 8" diameter, **$45**.

Two footed covered candy jars in Baroque, 6-1/2" h, from left: Blue Satin, 1970s, **$35**; Turquoise Iridized, 2003, **$45**.

Burmese vase with hand-painted landscape by Sue Foster, 1973, 5" h, **$130+**.

Burmese apothecary jar with hand-painted flowers, mid-1970s, made for L.G. Wright, 10" h, **$300+**.

Burmese crimped vase, 1970-71, with acid-washed satin finish (later pieces are sand-blasted), and slightly more intense color, 7" h, **$55+**; right, glossy Burmese ewer, mid-1990s, 9-1/2" h, **$65+**.

Leaves on Burmese fairy lamp, 1970s, 6" h, **$200+**.

Based on a popular 19th century glass, Fenton's Burmese was introduced in 1970 and remains popular today. It comes in glossy and matte finishes, decorated and in figures. Time-honored patterns include Daisy and Button, Peacock, and Hobnail. Blue Burmese followed in 1983. See more Burmese in 1980 to 2005.

Fenton by Era

The original Cameo Opalescent was put into wide production only for a short time in 1926-27. The revival of this glass in 1978 also included the opalescent colors of Blue, French, and Topaz.

Cameo Opalescent comport in Pineapple, made for the Fenton Art Glass Collectors of America, 1979, 6-1/2" diameter, **$60+.**

Cameo Opalescent covered margarine tub holder in Hobnail, 1979, 5" diameter, **$50+.**

Cameo Opalescent basket in Spiral Optic, 1979-80, 8" h, **$75+.**

Cameo Opalescent basket in Lily of the Valley, 1979, 7-1/2" h, **$45.**

Cameo Opalescent basket in Spiral Optic, 1979, 8" h, **$60+.**

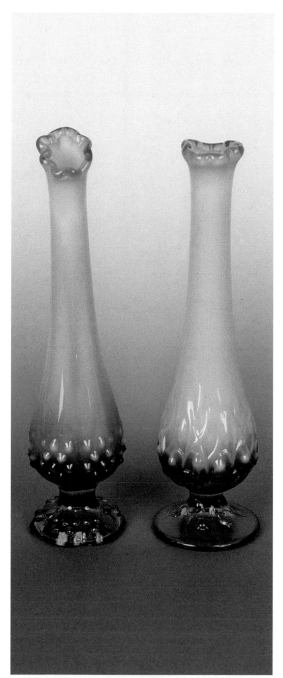

Cameo Opalescent swung bud vases in Lily of the Valley and Hobnail, 1979, each 10" h, **$25+** each.

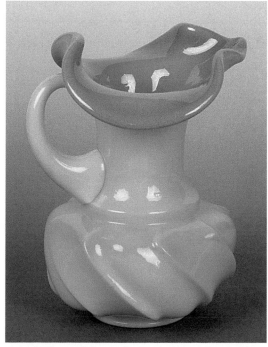

Cased Lilac and Turquoise jug in Wave Crest, 1955, 6-1/2" h, **$85+.**

Cased Lilac was a brief experiment in 1955.

Fenton by Era

The Colonial colors that debuted in 1963 included Amber, Blue, Green, Orange, and Ruby. They were made into the mid-1980s. As the prices here show, many collectors have yet to embrace these pieces.

Colonial Amber three-horn epergne in Thumb Print, early 1960s, 9" h, **$40+.**

Colonial Amber comport in Pineapple, late 1960s, 5-1/2" h, **$12+.**

Hobnail crimped vases, 4", in Colonial Amber and Colonial Blue, 1960s, **$12-$15** each.

Colonial Blue and Colonial Amber apothecary jars, 1960s, 11" h; Blue, **$85**; Amber, **$60.**

Colonial Amber, Blue and Green footed shakers in Thumb Print, and a Black (Ebony) example sold only through Fenton gift shop, 1960s-70s, 3-1/2" h; Colonial Blue, **$50+**; Amber and Green, **$25+** each; Black (Ebony), no established value.

Colonial Amber and Colonial Green shakers in Valencia, 1960s-70s, 5" h, **$35+** each.

Colonial Amber, Colonial Pink and Colonial Blue shakers in Thumb Print (flat bottom), 1960s to 1970s, 4" h; Pink and Blue, **$35+** each; Amber, **$15+.**

Colonial Blue, Milk-glass, Colonial Amber, Colonial Green and Colonial Orange shakers in Daisy and Button, 1970s, 3-1/2" h; Blue, **$20+**; Milk-glass, **$10+**; Amber, Green and Orange, **$15+** each.

Colonial Blue, Amber, Milk-glass (1960s-70s) and Blue Iridized (QVC, 1990s) shakers in Rose Pattern, 3-1/2" to 4-1/2" h; Colonial Blue, **$30+**; Amber, Milk-glass, **$20** each, and Blue Iridized, **$25+.**

Fenton by Era

Colonial Orange creamer and sugar in Daisy & Button, circa 1970, each 2-7/8" h, **$20+** pair.

Colonial Orange oval English basket, circa 1970, 6" l, **$10+.**

Colonial Green comport in Rose, late 1960s, 7-1/2" h, **$15.**

Colonial Orange crimped basket, circa 1970, 8" h, **$30+.**

Colonial Green pieces, mid-1960s: crimped basket in Thumb Print, 8-1/2" h, **$25+**; fairy light in Hobnail, 4-1/2" h, **$15+.**

Colonial Orange pieces, circa 1970, from left: covered candy dish in Hobnail, 8-1/2" h, **$12+**; cigarette box in Valencia, 7-1/2" h, **$15+**.

Colonial Orange pieces, circa 1970; left: comport in Rose, 6-1/2" h; right: swung handkerchief vase, 7" h, **$10+** each.

Left: Colonial Orange Empress vase, 1960s, 7-3/4" h, **$70**; right: Colonial Blue Fall-Spring Seasons vase, 1960s, ex-Fenton Museum, probably a sample piece, **$175**.

Coral baluster vase in Bubble Optic, 1961, 11" h, **$275+**.

Hobnail vases, in Colonial Orange and Ruby, circa 1970, 3", **$20+** each.

Fenton by Era

Cranberry—plain and Opalescent—is another color made by Fenton for decades in various patterns. Examples in Spiral Optic arrived in the late 1930s. The Hobnail alone was produced for almost four decades from 1940 until the late 1970s. Coin Dot was made for just under two decades, from the late 1940s to the mid-1960s. Also see 1930 to 1955.

Cranberry apothecary jar in Dot Optic, made for L.G. Wright, 1960s, 10" h, **$275+**.

Cranberry Opalescent basket in Coin Dot, 1950s, 11" w, 13" h, **$500+**.

Cranberry Opalescent deep basket in Hobnail, 1963, 10" h, 7" widest point, **$350**.

Cranberry Opalescent lampshade in Coin Dot, 1960s, 6-1/4" h, **$150+**.

Cranberry Opalescent pieces made for L.G. Wright, 1960s; left: barber bottle in Rib Optic, 9" h, **$100+**; right: syrup jug in Spiral Optic, 6-1/2" h, **$125+**.

Cranberry Satin apothecary jar in Daisy and Fern, made for L.G. Wright, 1950s and 1960s, 8" h, **$350+**.

Cranberry Polka Dot (1955) and Yellow Legacy Rib Optic shakers (1970s), 2-1/2" h; Cranberry, **$65+** each; Yellow (Candle Glow), **$23+** each.

Cranberry Polka Dot and Milk-glass covered butter with twig-form handle, 1955-6, 5-1/4" h and 8-1/4" diameter (base), **$400.**

Cranberry Opalescent pieces made for L.G. Wright, 1950s and 1960s; left and center: Daisy and Fern sugar shaker, 4-1/2" h, **$125+**; syrup, 6-1/2" h, **$250+**; right: Coin Spot sugar shaker, 4-1/2" h, **$125+**.

Fenton by Era

With few exceptions, Crystal pieces can often be dated by pattern. They are among the most affordable of all Fenton glass.

Crystal "epergne" in Sheffield, 1958, not sold with base because it was meant to fit in a candleholder, 6" diameter, **$25.**

Crystal covered cruet in Hobnail, 1968, 11-1/2" h, **$250+.**

Crystal Apollo II paperweight, 1969, 4" diameter, **$20-$25.**

Crystal Satin elephant figurine, 1972, 3" h (also made in White Satin and Blue Satin), **$175+.**

Crystal (1970s) and Original Formula Carnival Glass (1990s) shakers in Fine Cut and Block, and Milk-glass shaker in Old Virginia (1960s), 4" h; crystal and Milk-glass, **$15+** each; OFCG, **$35+.**

Crystal Velvet crimped vase in Basket Weave with Open Edge, 1970s, 3-1/2" h, **$20.**

Custard, Milk-glass and Topaz Opalescent shakers in Cactus, early 1960s to 1970s, 3-1/2" h; Custard, **$25+**; Milk, **$15+**; Topaz, **$45+.**

Crystal Velvet Cardinal hood ornament or car mascot, circa 1970, made for Crawford Auto Museum, Cleveland, Ohio, 6" h, **$200.**

Crystal Velvet was one of several colors in a matte finish introduced in 1971 and made into the 1980s, including Blue, Custard, Lime Sherbet, and White.

Crystal Velvet pieces, 1970s; left: water lily votive, 4" diameter, **$25+**; right: Butterfly covered candy, 5-1/4" h, **$35+.**

Fenton by Era

Custard Satin was one of several colors in a matte finish introduced in 1971 and made into the 1980s, including Blue, Crystal Velvet, Lime Sherbet, and White. The figures of animals, birds and children have proved to be among the most popular items in Fenton's history, and prices have risen along with demand.

Custard Satin animals, late 1970s: small bird, 2-3/4" h with hand-painted roses, **$45+**; donkey (also found with cart) with hand-painted daisies, 4-3/4" h, **$80+**; bunny with hand-painted daisies, 3-1/2" h, **$40+**.

Custard Satin animals, late 1970s: cat with hand-painted roses, 4" h, **$65+**; Happiness Bird with hand-painted roses, 5" h, **$40+**; frog with hand-painted pink blossoms, 3-1/2" l, **$140+**.

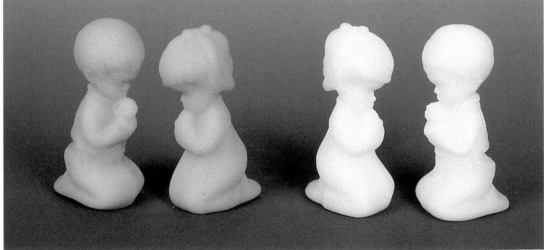

Praying Boys and Girls in Lime Sherbet and Custard Satin (found in other colors), late 1970s, each 4" h, **$25-$30** pair.

Custard Satin flared and crimped vase with hand-painted winter scene by Louise Piper, 1976, 6-1/4" h, **$125+.**

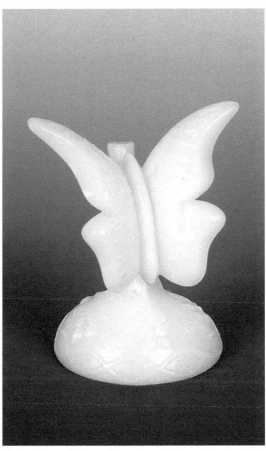

Shiny Custard Butterfly on Branch, late 1970s, 5" h, **$20+.**

Lavender Satin Bunny, 1977-78, 3-1/2" h, **$70+.**

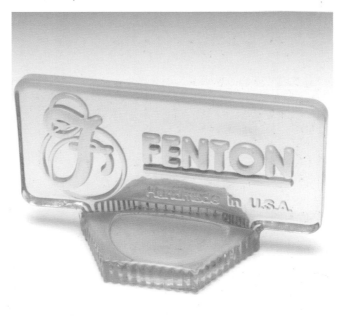

Dealer sign in Amethyst, 1950s (?), 5" w, **$150+.**

Fenton by Era

Ebony Crest was sold only at the Fenton gift shop in Williamstown, W.V., in 1968.

Ebony Crest basket, 6-1/2" h, **$110+**.

Ebony Crest candleholder, 3-1/2" h, **$50+**.

Plain-base Egg in Ebony glass (also found with leaf and footed bases), hand-painted, 3-1/2" h, **$40+**.

Plain-base Eggs, from left: hand-painted devil by Louise Piper, Violets in the Snow, Bluebells in the Snow, brown flowers on Shiny Cameo, **$60+** for devil; **$40+** each for the others.

Experimental shallow bowl, iridescent stretch glass, made 4/18/75, 7-1/2" diameter, **$50+**.

Experimental melon vase, multi-colored cased Milkglass tri-crimp, with Crystal Overlay and multi-colored "frit," sample made 10/13/64, 7-1/2" h, **$100+**. (Frit is composed of partly fused materials of which glass is made.)

Like Fenton figural items, the eggs have a legion of fans. Production began in the late 1970s.

Experimental pieces and oddities—sometimes called "lunch hour" or "end of the day"—have been finding their way into collectors' hands for decades. Valuations are not always easy, since these pieces may be one of a kind.

153

Fenton by Era

Experimental vase, cased Milk-glass tri-crimp, with mica flecks, possibly designed as lampshade, 1965, 7-1/2" h, **$100+**.

Experimental crimped melon vase resembling Vasa Murrhina in Blue Mist, purchased from the "special" room at the Fenton factory, 1960s, 6" h, **$100+**.

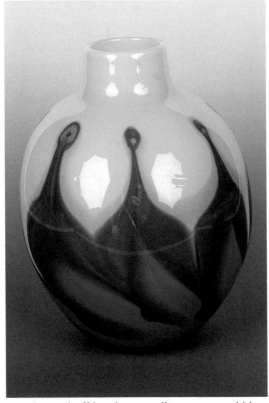

Experimental off-hand vase, yellow, green and blue, Robert Barber era, 1975-76, probably made by Dave Fetty or Delmar Stowasser, 8" h, **$700+**.

Amberina donut vase, Iridized plated, sample, Robert Barber era, 1975, probably made by Dave Fetty or Delmar Stowasser, 9" h, **$500+**.

Favrene vase, left, 4", mid-1970s, **$75+**; center: Jefferson comport in Favrene, mid-1970s, 10" h, **$450+**; right: Favrene off-hand vase, mid-1970s, 4-3/4" h, **$100+**.

Favrene pieces, mid-1970s, from left: Fat Bird, sample, 2-5/8" h, **$125+**; Quilted Grape nappy/bowl, 6" diameter, **$75+**.

Around 1974, Fenton was planning to put out a Bicentennial series. The original plan was to use Favrene, a new color, but due to production problems, Independence Blue was chosen. Favrene reappeared in the mid- to late 1980s, because there are some off-hand and some sample items found from that time frame. It first went into the line in the early '90s and has appeared almost annually, in limited quantities, ever since. It is very difficult to produce. Silver is incorporated in the glass, and it is brought to the surface using a reduced-oxygen atmosphere in the furnace. Also see 1980 to 2005.

Fenton by Era

Flame Crest was made for less than a year and is one of the more difficult Crest items to find.

Flame Crest crimped bonbon, 1963-64, 8" diameter, **$60+.**

Flame Crest crimped bonbon, 1963, 6" w, no established value.

Floral decorations from left: Silver Crest Violets in the Snow pitcher, 1968, 5-1/2" h, **$75+**; Milk-glass Roses in the Snow ashtray in Hobnail, 1974, 5" diameter, **$45+**; Milk-glass Bluebells in the Snow fairy light in Hobnail, 1971, 4-3/4" h, **$55.**

Heart-shaped candy dishes in Flame Crest (1963) and Ruby Snow Crest (early 1950s), each 6" l, **$35+** each.

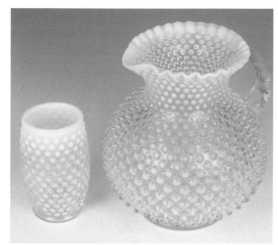

French Opalescent pitcher and tumbler in Hobnail, part of a water set that would have included six tumblers, 1970s; jug, 8" h, sometimes with crimped ice lip; tumbler, 4-3/4" h, **$250+** complete set.

Condiment set in Flower Panel, sold in Milk-glass and Jamestown Blue as shown, 1957-58, **$150+ set**; single Milk-glass shaker, **$25+**.

French Opalescent "Boxtle," combination powder box, perfume container and dauber, with original label, 1980 special order (this form introduced in 1953), 7" h, **$250**.

Flame lamp with blue satin shade, 1960s, 10-1/2" h, **$125+**.

"Glassblower" Craftsman plate in Original Formula Carnival Glass, 1970, the first in a series of eight; in raised letters on reverse, "The Fenton Art Glass Company commemorates with this handmade plate the earliest glass craftsmen of new America, Jamestown, 1608–(Fenton logo)–No. 1 in the annual series of collector's plates by Fenton 1970," 8-1/4" diameter, **$30+**.

Fenton by Era

Gold Crest made its debut in 1943, but only lasted until 1945. It was revived for two years in 1963-64. Since neither incarnation is marked, remember that old-formula Milk-glass from the 1940s is less opaque (called "skim milk" by collectors), while glass made after the late 1950s is usually a solid, shiny white. Also see 1930 to 1955.

The Goldenrod (1956-57) condiment set at top right is especially rare and may be an experimental piece. This color is not known to have been used in the Tear Drop pattern, which was made at the same time.

Gold Crest double-crimp melon vase, mid-1960s, 8" h, $45+.

Goldenrod condiment set (salt, pepper, mustard and stand) in Tear Drop, late 1950s, 7" h with handle, $350+.

Goldenrod candleholder, 1950s, 4-3/4" h, $75+.

Green Opalescent bud vase (also called Emerald Green) in Hobnail, 1959, 8" h, **$40.**

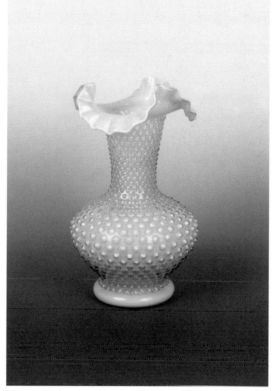

Honey Amber Overlay tri-crimp vase in Hobnail, mid-1960s, 11" h, **$110+.**

Honey Amber Overlay crimped vase in Bubble Optic with Gold Crest, early 1960s, 5" h, **$70+.**

Honey Amber Overlay and Milk-glass shakers in Wild Rose and Bowknot, 1960s, 3-1/2" h to 4-1/2" h; Honey Amber, **$35+**; Milk-glass, **$15+.**

Honey Amber Overlay, Milk-glass, Powder Blue Overlay and Apple Green Overlay shakers in Jacqueline, 1960s, 2-1/2" h; Milk-glass, **$20+**; Honey, Blue and Green, **$35+.**

Part of a group of Hobnail-pattern colors renewed in 1959, the Green items were only made until 1961.

Overlay colors on Hobnail that debuted in 1961 included Apple Green, Coral, Honey Amber, Powder Blue, and Wild Rose. Other colors were dropped, but Honey Amber lasted until about 1966.

159

Fenton by Era

Two styles of Jamestown Blue—cased and transparent—were made from 1957 to 1959. (Also see Silver Jamestown.)

Jamestown Blue Overlay ribbed pillar vase, late 1950s, 5" h, **$45.**

Jamestown Blue Transparent pieces, late 1950s, left: tri-crimp vase in Polka Dot, 6" h, **$65+**; right: rose bowl, 3 1/2" h, **$45+.**

Jamestown Blue Transparent pieces, late 1950s, from left: salt and pepper shakers, with swag and floral pattern, and beaded border, each 2-3/4" h, **$40+** pair; Wave Crest covered box, 4-1/2" h, **$125+**; creamer in Polka Dot, with clear handle, 4-1/4" h, **$45+.**

Jamestown Blue Overlay vases, late 1950s, from left: tri-crimp with ringed neck, 6-1/4" h, **$45+**; pinched and flared in Polka Dot, 8-1/4" h, **$90+**; swirl, **$55+.**

Jamestown Blue Transparent vases in Polka Dot, late 1950s, from left: tri-crimp urn, 7" h, **$65+**; ovoid with flared top, 10-1/4" h, **$95+**; pinched and flared, 7" h, **$45+**.

Lime Satin, Milk-glass and Custard Santa fairy lights, mid-1970s, two pieces, 5-1/2" h, **$30** each.

Midnight Blue, Amber and Blue Opalescent shakers in Hobnail, 1970s, 3-1/2" h, **$30+** each.

Malachite Green experimental chrysanthemum-motif planter, ex-Fenton Museum, late 1960s or early 1970s, 10" w, 4-1/2" h, 6-1/4" deep, **$375**.

Fenton by Era

What carnival glass was for the first quarter of Fenton's history, Milk-glass was for the second. Millions of pieces found their way into kitchen cupboards, sideboards, and china shelves. What began in the middle of the 19th century as a cheap alternative to porcelain was now a staple of American glass making. For more Milk-glass, see 1930 to 1955.

Though it isn't an infallible test, the density of the Milk-glass can help to date the pieces. Milk-glass made prior to the late 1950s frequently has greater opalescence (what Fenton collectors call "fire") than later examples. Also note differences in the opacity of the glass; less opaque Milk-glass is sometimes called "skim milk."

Three Milk-glass pieces in Hobnail, hand decorated with holly leaves and berries, 1974-75: bell, 5-1/2" h, **$35**; comport, 6" h, **$40**; fairy light, 4-1/2" h, **$45**.

Milk-glass cake plate in Tear Drop, late 1950s, 11" diameter, **$80+**.

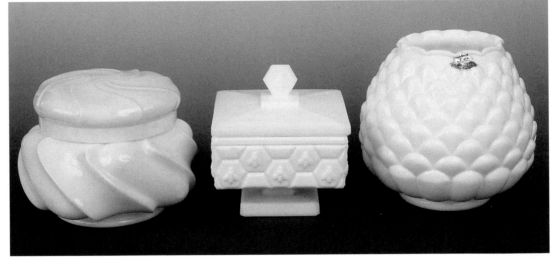

Milk-glass pieces from left: Wave Crest covered box, late 1960s, 5" h, **$35+**; Bee box, late 1960s, 5" h, **$30**; Jacqueline vase, early 1960s, 6" h, **$35+**.

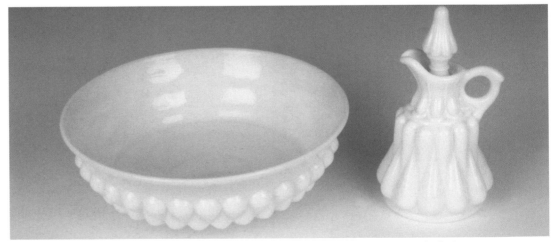

Milk-glass pieces in Tear Drop, late 1950s: bowl, 9" diameter, **$40+**; cruet, 6-3/4" h, **$70+**.

Milk-glass covered candy dishes (one footed, also note finial variation) in Tear Drop, mid-1950s, 9-1/4" and 4-1/2" h, **$55+** each.

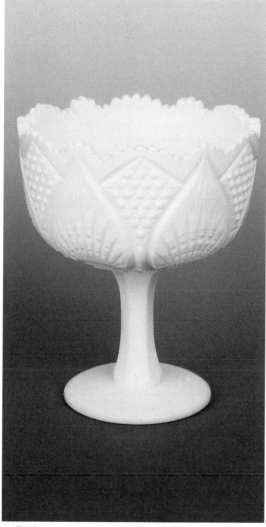

Milk-glass comport in Regency, late 1970s, 6-1/2" h, **$20+.**

Milk-glass covered candy jar in Daisy and Button, 1969, 6" h, **$35.**

Milk-glass candleholders in Tear Drop, late 1950s, each 6-1/4" h, **$90+** pair.

fenton by Era

Milk-glass condiment set (salt, pepper, mustard, and stand) in Tear Drop, late 1950s, 7" h with handle, **$95+.**

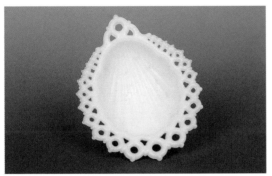

Milk-glass shell dish, late 1950s, 5" l, **$10+.**

Milk-glass one-horn epergne in Hobnail, mid-1970s, 7-1/2" h, **$100+.**

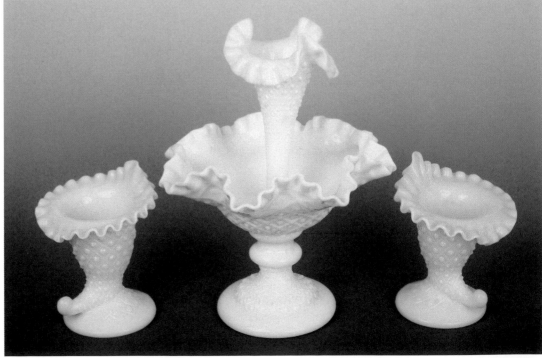

Milk-glass console set in Diamond Lace, late 1950s, including one-horn epergne (10-1/2" h) and cornucopia candleholders (each 5-1/2" h), **$90+** set.

Milk-glass and Topaz Opalescent shakers, 1970s, 4-1/2" h, Milk-glass, **$25+** each; Topaz (marked), **$45+**.

Left: Milk-glass toothpick or candleholder in Hobnail, 1971-76, 2-1/2" h, **$20+**; right: Milk-glass double candleholder in Daisy and Button, 1963, 4-1/2" h, **$25+**.

Milk-glass tidbit tray and covered sugar and creamer in Tear Drop, late 1950s; tray, 11" diameter, **$50+**; sugar, 5-1/4" h, and creamer, 3-1/2" h, **$60+** pair.

Milk-glass rectangular planter, 10" w, late 1960s, **$45.**

Fenton by Era

Milk-glass Laurel vase (using a 1930s Verlys mold), 1960s, 10-1/4" h, **$150.**

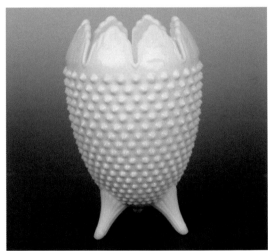

Milk-glass covered urn in Hobnail, late 1960s, 11" h, **$500+.**

Milk-glass three-footed cupped petal vase in Hobnail, late 1960s, though sometimes called the "12" vase," it's only 8-1/2" h, **$200+.**

Milk-glass pieces from left: 6-1/2" flared vase, (Cactus pattern?) circa 1960, **$25+**; Vessel of Gems vase, 1968, 7" h, **$45**; waffle vase, circa 1960, 4" h, **$30.**

Olde Virginia Glass three-piece, Milk-glass lavabo (wall-mounted fount, lid, and bowl) in Thumb Print, 1960, **$65+** set.

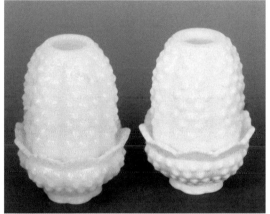

Opal fairy light in Hobnail, left, 1969, 4-3/4" h, **$35**; right, Milk-glass fairy light in Hobnail, 1970s, 4-3/4" h, **$25**.

Opaque Blue shoulder vase in Rib Optic, 1962, 10 3/4" h, **$90**.

Olde Virginia Glass was distributed by catalog through several resellers from 1960 to 1979. There is a wide range of colors in patterns that include Daisy and Button, Desert Tree (Cactus), and Thumb Print.

Left: Opaque Blue candleholder in Daisy and Button, 1970s, 4-1/2" h; right: Blue Satin candleholder in Orange Tree, 1970s, 5" h, **$25+** each.

167

Fenton by Era

It was 1969 when Rose Preznick placed an order for tobacco jars to sell at her Carnival Glass Museum in Lodi, Ohio. It marked the return of carnival glass (a term generally attributed to her and fellow collector Marion Hartung), and the debut of the Fenton logo, which eventually was added to virtually all Fenton glass over the next five years. Fenton used the term "Original Formula Carnival Glass."

Butterfly on a Branch in Original Formula Carnival Glass, left: 1981, 5" h, **$50+**; right: blown Rabbit in Original Formula Carnival Glass, 1971-72, 5-1/2" h, **$50+**.

Original Formula Carnival Glass swan candleholder, 1971, 6-1/2" h, **$50+**.

Original Formula Carnival Glass pieces, amethyst base, left: Persian Medallion chalice, 1972-73, 7" h, **$45+**; right: Grape and Cable tobacco jar, 1969, 7-1/4" h, marked, "Preznick's Carnival Glass Museum–Lodi, Ohio 1969," **$150+**.

Original Formula Carnival Glass pieces, amethyst base, 1971-73, from left: Quilted Grape nappy/bowl, 6" diameter, **$50+**; Strawberry toothpick holder, 3" h, **$30+**; cupped footed bowl in Leaf and Orange Tree, **$50+**.

Left: Plated Amberina courting lamp in Rib Optic; right: Opaque Blue Overlay courting lamp in Rib Optic, both circa 1962, 10-1/2" h, **$225** each.

Left: Plated Amberina shoulder vase in Rib Optic, 1962-63, 10-3/4" h, **$140**; right: Plated Amberina cracker jar in Rib Optic, 1962-63, 5-1/2" h, **$175.**

Plum Overlay "Gone With the Wind" lamp in Hobnail, melon form, 1970s, one of only two made, 23" h with chimney, **$800+.**

Plum Opalescent and Green Opalescent footed covered candy jars in Hobnail, late 1950s to early 1960s, 8-1/2" h; Plum, **$175**; Green, **$100.**

169

Fenton by Era

Left: Praying Children figurines in Blue Satin, made for Precious Moments, 1970s, 3-1/2" h to 4" h; right: Milk-glass Satin and Crystal Satin figurines, 1970s, 3-1/2" h to 4" h, all **$50-$60** pair.

Two sizes of Praying Children figurines in Iridized finish (current production) and Black (Ebony), 1980; current production girl, 4-1/8" h, and boy, 4" h; Iridized, 3-1/2" h to 4" h, **$50-$65** each pair.

Purple stretch-glass four-horn epergne, 1970s, made for Levay Co., 13" h, **$375+.**

Two sizes of Praying Children figurines in Lavender Satin, 1977-78, and hand painted (current production), Lavender 3-1/2" h to 4" h, current production girl, 4-1/8" h, and boy, 4" h; lavender, **$250+** pair; hand painted, **$90+** pair.

Robert Barber off-hand ashtray in orange swirl, dated 1976, 6-1/2" diameter, **$75+.**

In 1975, Robert Barber, an award-winning glass artist, was hired by Fenton to begin an artist-in-residence program with some of Fenton's most skilled craftsmen, producing a limited line of art-glass vases in a return to the off-hand, blown-glass creations of the mid-1920s.

Four pieces were offered initially in early 1975 and the remainder of the line was added toward the end of the year. Pieces that did not meet Barber's standards were either ground down if there was a structural problem with the top, or given a satin finish if the flaw was only in the pattern. Some of these seconds are lightly etched with the Fenton oval and "1975 S."

Two Fenton craftsmen are generally credited with making Barber pieces: David L. Fetty and Delmer Stowasser. (For more on Dave Fetty, see 1980 to 2005.)

Each Barber piece had to be individually blown, shaped, decorated and finished manually. Some originally sold for $200. The Barber experiment was a money-losing venture for Fenton, and lasted for less than a year.

Robert Barber off-hand eggs, 1975-76, 5" h and 4-1/2" h, **$200+** each.

Robert Barber off-hand vase in a glossy Blue Feather variation, 1975-76, 8-1/2" h, **$250+.**

Fenton by Era

Robert Barber off-hand vase in glossy Blue Feather, 1975-76, 8" h, **$300+**.

Robert Barber off-hand Cascade vase, 1975-76, 8" h, **$300+**.

Robert Barber-era off-hand Hanging Hearts basket in Turquoise, mid-1970s, 7-1/2" h, **$150+**.

Robert Barber off-hand Turquoise decanter in Hanging Hearts, with vine decoration on stopper, 1975-76, 8-1/2" h, **$325+**.

Robert Barber-era Turquoise mariner's lamp in Hanging Hearts, 1976, 20" h with chimney, **$1,600+.**

Robert Barber-era Lavender ewer, cased-glass, off-hand in Hanging Hearts, sample, mid-1970s, 6-3/4" h, **$350+.**

Robert Barber custard off-hand vase in Hanging Hearts, with ground top, 1975-76, 8" h, **$250+.**

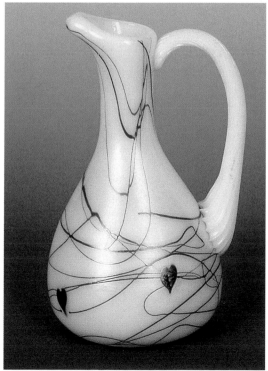

Robert Barber-era off-hand Hanging Hearts ewer in iridized Custard glass, circa 1976, 7" h, **$125+.**

173

Fenton by Era

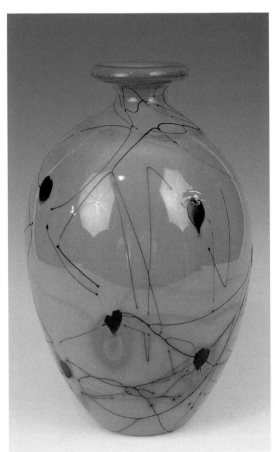

Robert Barber Turquoise Satin off-hand vase in Hanging Hearts, 1975-76, 11" h, **$250+.**

Robert Barber experimental off-hand vase in Hanging Hearts and Bittersweet glass, 1975-76, 10" h, **$550+.**

Robert Barber vases, 1975-76, each 6-1/2" h, with ground tops; left: Bittersweet with Hanging Hearts; right: zebra stripe, **$300+** each.

Robert Barber Satin Custard off-hand vase in Hanging Hearts, 1975-76, 9-1/2" h, **$275+**.

Robert Barber off-hand Hyacinth Feather vase with flared top (also found with tapered and ground top), 1975-76, 450 made, 13" h, **$450+**.

Robert Barber off-hand vase in cobalt and white swirls, 1975-76, 9" h, **$350+**.

Hand-blown vases with hang-hearts motif, from left: Imperial, 1920s, 6" h, **$450+**; bud vase, maker unknown, late 20th century, 9" h, **$300+**; flared vase, maker unknown, possibly Italian, late 20th century, 8" h, **$300+**.

By way of comparison to Robert Barber's work, here is some non-Fenton off-hand glass in the Hanging Hearts pattern.

Fenton by Era

Rosalene was originally made for three years, from 1976 to 1979. Though not wildly successful when introduced, it has become much more sought after in the last three decades. Also see 1980 to 2005.

Rosalene fan vase, late 1970s, 6-3/4" h, **$200+.**

Rosalene cracker jar in Cactus, circa 1980, 8" h, **$115.**

Rosalene low cake plate in a Holly pattern, mid-1970s (?), 10" diameter, **$95.**

Rosalene footed basket in Threaded Diamond Optic, 1976, 8-1/2" h, **$55+.**

Rosalene comport, flowered, 1976, 7" h, **$60+.**

Rose Overlay covered candy box in Corn (also called Maize), made for L.G. Wright, 1960s, 7-1/2" h, **$225+.**

Rose Overlay pieces in Corn (also called Maize), made for L.G. Wright, 1960s: jug, 9" h, **$300+;** sugar shaker, 5-1/2" h, **$150+.**

Rose Pastel swirl vase, mid-1950s, 6" h, **$30+.**

Rose Overlay crimped vase in Wild Rose and Bowknot, early 1960s, 7-1/2" h, **$50+.**

Rose Satin melon vase, mid-1970s, 6" h, **$50+.**

Fenton by Era

Ruby made its debut in 1921, and pieces may also be found with dolphin handles and in the Diamond Optic pattern. Some forms may have a gold tinge around rims and bases.

Ruby handled bonbon in Hobnail, mid-1970s, 8" diameter, $35+.

Ruby bonbon in Hobnail, mid-1970s, 7-1/2" diameter, $45+.

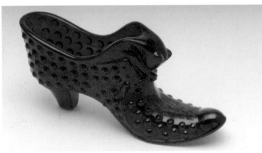

Ruby shoe ashtray in Hobnail, pre-1970, 5-1/2" l, $25+.

Ruby basket in Hobnail, early 1970s, 7-3/4" h, $35+.

Iridized Ruby pieces, from left: Butterfly candy box, 1978, 6-3/4" l, $75+; Pineapple cupped comport, 1979, made for the Fenton Art Glass Collectors of America, 3-1/2" h, $50+.

Ruby comport in Hobnail, early 1970s, 6" h, **$35+.**

Ruby and Colonial Green Santa fairy lights, mid- to late 1970s, two pieces, 5-1/2" h, **$40** each.

Ruby candleholders in Thumbprint, 1950s, each 9" h, **$125+.**

Ruby fairy light in Hobnail, two pieces, 4-1/2" h, pre-1970, **$25+.**

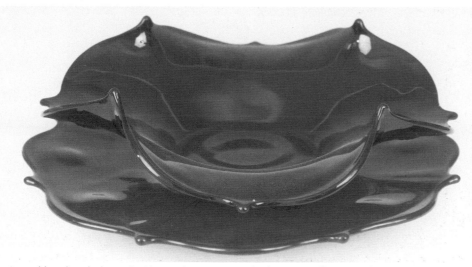

Ruby crimped bowl and platter in Pineapple, 1970s, each about 14" diameter, **$250+** pair.

fenton by Era

Ruby plate in Thumb Print, 1960s, 8-1/2" diameter, $35+.

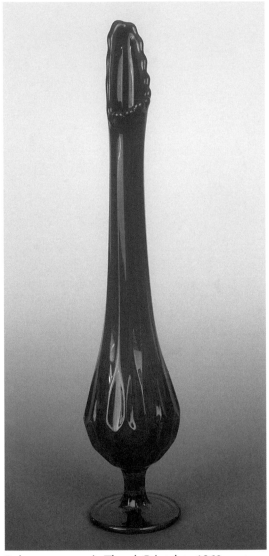

Ruby platter in Priscilla, 1970s, 12" diameter, $40+.

Ruby swung vase in Thumb Print, late 1960s, 17" h, $25+.

Ruby, Milk-glass and Colonial Green shakers in Thumb Print (flat bottom), 1960s to 1970s, 4" h; Ruby, $50+; Milk and Green, $15+.

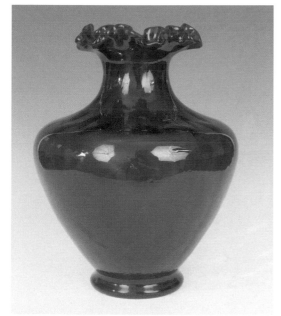

Ruby baluster vase with crimped top in Diamond Optic, 1970s, 11" h, **$80+**.

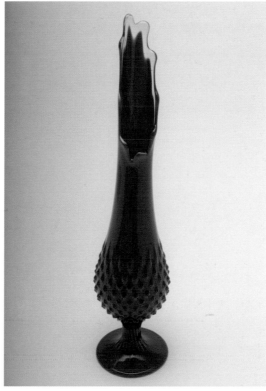

Ruby swung footed vase in Hobnail, pre-1970, 16-1/2" h, **$50+**.

Ruby Satin Cardinal hood ornament or car mascot, circa 1970, made for Crawford Auto Museum, Cleveland, Ohio, 6" h, **$200**.

Ruby Overlay shaker in Dot Optic and Jamestown shaker in Polka Dot, 1955, 2-1/2" h, **$45+** each.

Ruby, Rose Pastel and Plum Opalescent candleholders in style No. 3974, low Hobnail, 1950s-60s, 3" h to 3-1/2" h; Ruby, **$50+**; Rose, **$25+**; Plum, **$90+**.

Fenton by Era

Silver Crest comport, Violets in the Snow, Spanish Lace, 1975, 7" h, **$50+**. (Also see Silver Crest, 1930 to 1955.)

Elaborate Silver Crest tall comport with unusual pink streaked interior similar to Vasa Murrhina Rose Mist, possibly an experimental or lunch-hour piece, age unknown but probably 1960s, 9" h, 11" diameter, **$1,000+**.

Silver Crest bell in Spanish Lace, mid-1970s, 6-1/2" h, **$40+**.

Silver Crest Spanish Lace bell, Violets in the Snow, late 1970s, 6-1/2" h, **$45+**.

Left: Silver Crest candleholder, style No. 7272, 1950s, 4-1/2" h, **$25+**; center: Silver Turquoise candleholder, style No. 7271, 1956, 3-1/2" h, **$45+**; right: Silver Turquoise candleholder, style No. 7272, 1956, 4-1/2" h, **$35+**.

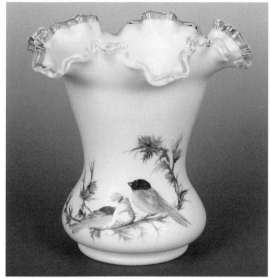

Silver Crest crimped vase, painted by Louise Piper, 1976, signed and dated, 6-1/2" h, **$150+.**

Silver Jamestown basket, late 1950s, 7-1/2" h, **$60+.** (Also see Jamestown, P. 160-161.)

Silver Jamestown crimped vase, left: late 1950s, 5-1/4" h, **$55+;** right: Jamestown Blue ribbed vase with piecrust rim, late 1950s, 4-7/8" h, **$50+.**

Silver Jamestown vase in Wave Crest, left: white exterior, late 1950s, 6" h, **$45+;** right: Jamestown Blue Overlay flared and crimped bowl, late 1950s, 8" diameter, **$70+.**

Silver Jamestown flared, footed vase with irregular crimp, late 1950s, 13" h, **$145+.**

Fenton by Era

Silver Rose and Silver Turquoise both arrived in 1956, but the Rose lasted little more than a year, while the Turquoise remained in production until 1959.

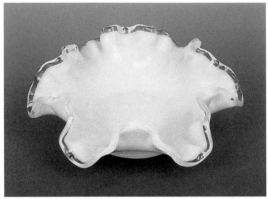

Silver Rose bonbon, mid-1950s, 6" diameter, **$25+.**

Silver Turquoise crimped comport, mid-1950s, 7" diameter, **$25+.**

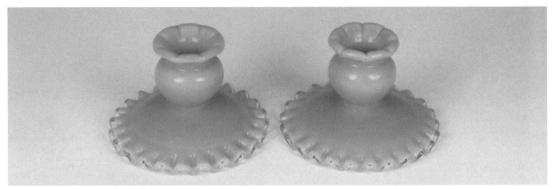

Silver Turquoise candleholders, 1950s, each 3-1/4" h, **$75+ pair.**

Topaz Opalescent returned in 1959 in Hobnail, and was featured in Cactus shortly thereafter. Also see 1930 to 1955.

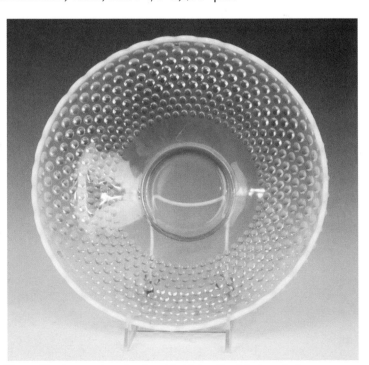

Topaz Opalescent hanging bowl in Hobnail, with three holes to accept chain hooks, late 1950s, 11" diameter, **$350+.**

Topaz Opalescent crimped bowl in Hobnail, 1959-60, 8" diameter, **$75.**

Topaz Opalescent "chip and dip" set in Thumb Print, with lipped platter and footed bowl, 1960s; platter, 12" diameter; bowl, 4-3/4" h, **$125+** set.

Topaz Opalescent comport in Cactus, circa 1960, 7" h, **$300+.**

Topaz Opalescent comport in Hobnail with ruffled edge, 1970s, 11" diameter, 8" h, **$150+.**

Fenton by Era

Topaz Opalescent one-horn epergne in Cactus, circa 1960, 8" h, **$500+**.

Topaz Opalescent three-horn epergne, "apartment size" in Diamond Lace, 1970, 9-1/2" h, **$225+**.

Topaz Opalescent bud vase, late 1950s, 7-1/2" h, $45.

Topaz Opalescent pitcher and goblet in Cactus, part of a lemonade set that would have included six tumblers, circa 1960; pitcher, 11" h; goblet, 6" h, **$550+** for complete set.

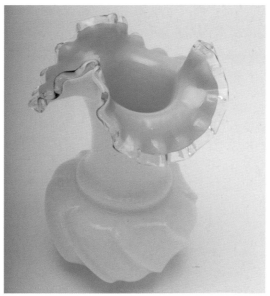

Topaz Opalescent footed fan vase in Cactus, circa 1960, 6" h, **$150+**.

Turquoise Overlay vase in Wave Crest, 1957-59, 7" h, no established value.

Turquoise Pastel "star-crimp" creamer and sugar in Hobnail, 1955-56, **$50+** pair.

Turquoise condiment set (salt, pepper, mustard, and stand), left, in Tear Drop, mid-1950s, 7" h with handle, **$200+**; turquoise covered candy dish in Tear Drop, mid-1950s, 4-3/4" h, **$70+**.

fenton by Era

Dating from 1964-68, Vasa Murrhina ("Vessel of Gems") came in Autumn Orange, Blue Mist, and "Aventurine" (which simply means glass containing opaque sparkling particles of foreign material, usually copper or chromic oxide) in predominantly Green/Blue and Rose. There are also confetti variations, and rare pieces cased in glass other than clear.

Vasa Murrhina basket in Aventurine Green with Blue, mid-1960s, 11" h, **$85+**.

Vasa Murrhina ribbed vase in Blue Mist, mid-1960s, 14" h, **$200**.

Vasa Murrhina baskets in Rose with Aventurine Green, two from mid- to late 1960s, from left: satin finish, 8" h, **$80+**; 11" h, **$150+**; made in 2000 for QVC, 9" h, **$75+**.

Vasa Murrhina vase in Aventurine Green with Blue, mid-1960s, 14-3/4" h, **$180+.**

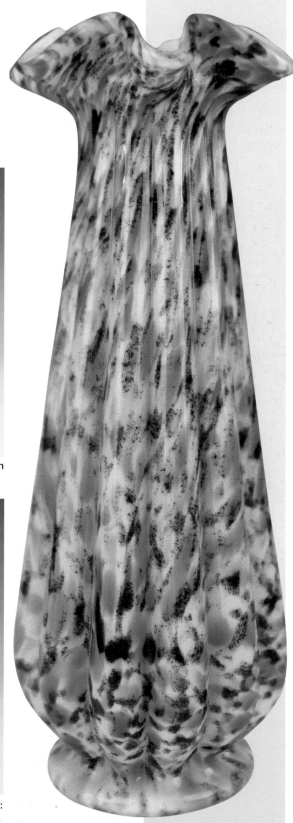

Vasa Murrhina fan vases, mid-1960s, 7" h, left: Rose Mist, **$85+**; right: Autumn Orange, **$75+.**

Vasa Murrhina fan vases, mid-1960s, 7" h, left: confetti, experimental, **$150+**; right: Aventurine Green with Blue, **$75+.**

Fenton by Era

Vasa Murrhina vases, mid- to late 1960s, 11-1/2" h, from left: Aventurine Green with Blue, **$125+**; Cranberry Mist Crest, sold at Sears in 1967 as part of the Vincent Price National Treasures Collection, **$175+**.

Vasa Murrhina experimental vases, mid-1960s, 5-1/4" h; left: confetti with clear overlay, **$100+**; right: confetti with Colonial Green overlay, **$125+**.

Vasa Murrhina crimped melon vase in Autumn Orange, mid-1960s, 8" h, **$45+**.

Vasa Murrhina melon vase in Aventurine Green, mid-1960s, 11-1/2" h, **$95+**.

White Satin was one of several colors in a matte finish introduced in 1971 and made into the 1980s, including Blue, Crystal Velvet, Custard, and Lime Sherbet.

Left: Violets in the Snow candlestick, 6" h; right: Yellow Rose candleholder, 3-1/2" h, both 1960s to '70s, $45+ each.

White Satin bookend, Girl and Fawn, late 1960s, 6-1/2" h, $100+ pair.

Violets in the Snow on White Satin mariner's lamp, late 1960s, 20" h, $400+.

Violets in the Snow on Silver Crest mariner's lamp, late 1960s, 20" h, $400+.

Fenton by Era

Wild Rose and Bowknot was a short-lived experiment from 1961-62.

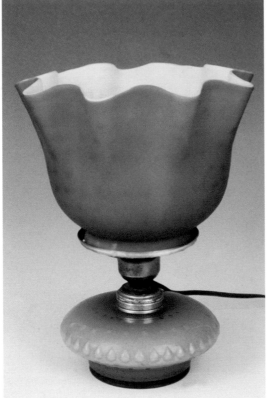

Wild Rose cased-glass electric lamp with flared shade, 1960s, made for L.G. Wright, 11" h, **$350+.**

Wild Rose cased-glass electric lamp in Blown Out Roses, 1960s, made for L.G. Wright, 18-1/2" h with chimney, **$400+.**

Wild Rose cased-glass kerosene lamp in Beaded Curtain, 1960s, made for L.G. Wright, 10-1/2" h with chimney, **$450+.**

Wild Rose and Bowknot overlay vase, 1961, 5" h, $50.

The Jacqueline vase was named for Jackie Kennedy in 1960, and is found in a variety of colors.

Unusual Wild Rose cased glass vase in Jacqueline, early 1960s, with collared base remaining (normally this was cut off), 6-3/4" h, **$80+.**

Yellow Opaline vase in Jacqueline, early 1960s, 4-3/4" h, **$55+.**

Yellow shaker in Rib Optic, made for Foreman, 1970s, 4" h (would have been paired with a taller example), **$45+ each.**

Wisteria bell in Threaded Diamond Optic, 1977, 5-1/2" h, **$50.**

Fenton by Era

The last chapter of the Fenton story was as much about technology as changing public taste.

Shopping at home via television was a recent phenomenon in the late 1980s when the Birthstone Bears became the first Fenton product to appear on QVC (established in 1986 by Joseph Segel, founder of The Franklin Mint). Since that first bear, more than 1,400 different Fenton pieces have been sold on QVC.

The Fenton Web site—www.fentonartglass.com—was created as a user-friendly online experience where collectors could learn about catalog and gift shop sales, upcoming events, and the history of the company.

Black (Ebony) miniature basket novelty with pink crest, 1980s, 4-1/4" h, **$90+.**

Like the Fenton eggs, animal figurines have become a significant collecting area, with some collectors focusing on specific creatures, like the bears seen here (note the height variation).

Bear figurines, four in smaller size (2-1/2" h,) not put into wide production; Burmese example at right is common production size, 2-3/4" h, 2000; smaller size, **$45+** each; larger, **$30+.**

The sand-carved iris vases seen here and on P. 195 were made for only a short time, 1982-83. A cobalt vase made at the same time as a sand-carved morning glory.

Sand-carved iris on Amethyst, 1982, from left: vase, 6-1/2" h, **$55+**; basket, 7" h, **$50+**; bell, 6" h, **$35+**; temple jar, 5-3/4" h, **$35+.**

Sand-carved iris on Amethyst vase, 1982, 11" h, **$90+**.

Amethyst shoe, hand-painted by Martha Reynolds, 1998, not a production piece, 4-1/2" l, no established value.

Blue Burmese hurricane lamps with hand-painted blossoms and butterflies by C. Sue Jackson, made for the 1999 Fenton Art Glass Collectors Association Convention, each about 10" h, including bases, **$400+** pair.

Originally called Rose Quartz, Blue Burmese had wide production from 1983-85, though other pieces were made as specialty items, like convention souvenirs.

Blue Burmese fairy light made for members of the National Fenton Glass Society, hand painted by Linda Everson, two pieces, 2005, 5-1/2" h, **$150+**.

Blue Burmese pieces, 1984, from left: cruet with satin finish, 7-3/4" h, **$55+**; two-handle glossy vase, melon form, with irregular swirled decoration called Pelaton Treatment, 5-1/4" h, **$70+**.

Fenton by Era

Blue Burmese guest set (cup fits inside pitcher), hand painted by T. Kelly, No. 571 out of an edition of 1,950, 1999, 7-1/4" h and 3-1/2" h, **$165** set.

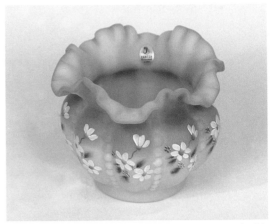

Blue Burmese beaded-melon vase, hand painted with daisies and forget-me-nots, made for QVC in 2003, 5" h, **$90.**

Blue Burmese night set or "tumble up," with hand-painted flowers, 2003, *Glass Messenger* exclusive, 6-1/2" and 3-1/4" h, **$175+**. *Glass Messenger* is Fenton's quarterly publication for collectors.

Blue Burmese basket whimsy, with "frit" mixed into body, early 1980s, 8" h, **$150+.**

Blue Burmese Iridized fish whimsy, probably 1990s, 8" l and 6" h, **$100.**

Blue Burmese (shiny) ribbed hexagonal vase, 1984, 5" h, **$70.**

Blue-gray transparent vase (Salem Blue?) with thistle pattern, 1985, 9" h, purchased from the Fenton gift shop in Williamstown, W.Va., **$60+**.

Blue, Ruby and Black (Ebony, with Autumn Leaf decoration) candlesticks, 1990s, 8-1/2" h; Blue and Ruby, **$30+** each; decorated Black, **$40+**.

From left: Blue Satin covered candy jar in Wild Strawberry, 1980s, 9" h, **$30**; Blue Opalescent covered candy jar in Paneled Daisy, 1970s, 9" h, **$45**.

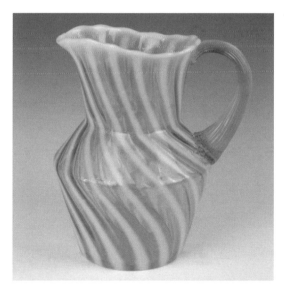

Blue Opalescent 44-ounce pitcher in Spiral Optic, circa 1980, 8" h, **$100+**.

Blue, Green and Black (Ebony) shakers in a swirl pattern, hand painted, 1990s, 2-1/2" h, **$25+** each.

Two "tumble-ups" (carafe and cup), in glossy Burmese and Lotus Mist Burmese in Diamond Optic, with Circle of Love decoration made for Joyce Colella, 2001, 6" h and 3" h, **$200** each set.

The Connoisseur Collection was a wide-ranging group of limited-edition pieces begun in 1983.

Brown Crest basket in opalescent Hobnail, 1998 and signed by Don Fenton, made in limited numbers, 9-1/2" h, and 10" w, **$150+.**

Blue Ridge 80th Anniversary dresser set, part of the Connoisseur Collection, limited to 1,000 sets including two perfumes, powder box and tray, 1985-86; perfumes, 5-3/4" h; powder box, 4" h; tray, 7" diameter, **$325+ set.**

Blue Overlay "Gabrielle" sand-carved oval vase, Connoisseur Collection, 1985, 12" h, **$175+.**

Based on a popular 19th century glass, Fenton's Burmese was introduced in 1970 and remained popular until the end. It came in glossy and matte finishes, decorated and in figures. Time-honored patterns include Daisy and Button, Peacock and Hobnail. Blue Burmese followed in 1983. See more Burmese in 1955 to 1980.

Burmese ginger jar, three pieces with base, decorated with butterflies, 2000, designed by J.K. (Robin) Spindler, with facsimiles of Fenton family signatures, 8-1/2" h, **$275.**

Burmese covered candy jar showing Little Brown Church in Nashua, Iowa, 1980s, 8-1/4" h, **$85+.**

Three hand-painted shakers in Tear Drop, 1990s, 2-1/2" h, **$20+** each.

Three Burmese shakers, two in Tear Drop (one hand painted), one in Rose, 1990s, 2-1/2" h and 3-1/2" h, Rose and plain Tear Drop, **$50+** each; hand painted Tear Drop, **$75+.**

Burmese spherical lamp shade with hand-painted railroad motif, 1999, 13" h, no established value.

Burmese vase with hand-painted floral motif by Martha Reynolds, 1997, 11" h, **$450+.**

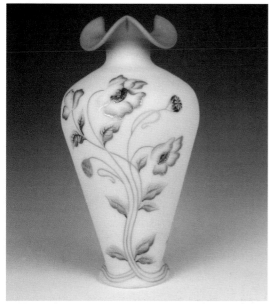

Burmese vase with hand-painted flowers by Martha Reynolds, 1990s, 13" h, **$350+.**

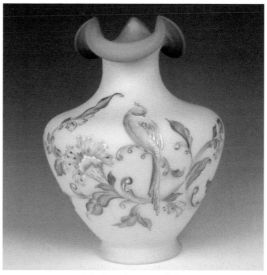

Burmese vase with hand-painted flowers and birds by Martha Reynolds, 1990s, 12" h, **$350+.**

Fenton by Era

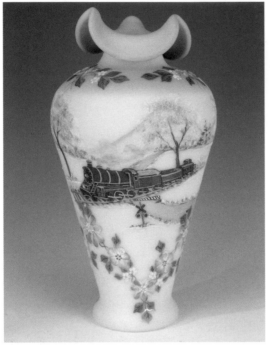

Burmese vase with hand-painted scenes, including steam-powered train and rural delivery wagon, 2000, 12-1/4" h, **$300+**.

Two limited-edition Burmese feather vases, each with three hand-painted panels honoring Mary Walrath-Jachim, who died in 2004, made in 2005, 9-1/2" h, **$300 to $325** each.

Two Burmese flared vases, Regal Peacock with applied jewels, Connoisseur Collection, designed by J.K. (Robin) Spindler, 2004; rose decoration designed and painted by Linda Everson, 2005, Fenton Gift Shop exclusive, 10" h, **$250** each.

Left: Burmese Trout vase, 1996, designed by J.K. Spindler and painted by Diane Gessel, 8" h, **$150**; right: Burmese Sea Dreams vase, 1995, designed by Frances Burton and painted by Tammy Watson, 9-1/2" h, **$350**.

Three Canaan Valley pieces, 2004-06, from left: hat vase, 3-1/4" h, **$80**; basket with clear spiral-twist handle, 10-1/2" h, **$85**; covered candy jar with opalescent snowflake pattern on lid and applied frit snowflakes, 4-1/2" h, **$75**.

Four pieces of decorated Burmese in Love Bouquet, designed by Mary Walrath, painted by Diane Gessel and Pam Miller, early to mid-1980s, from left: basket, 6-1/2" h, **$90**; tulip-crimp vase, 10-1/2" h, **$125**; bud vase, **$80**; toothpick holder, 2-1/2" h, **$55**.

Burmese whimsy basket with hand-painted decoration by Diana Barber, post-2000, not a production piece, 9" h, **$200+**.

Overlay vases, Candleglow Yellow and Heritage Green, in Flute and Dot, mid-1980s, 5-1/2" h, **$35+** each.

Champagne Satin, Ruby and Amber Iridized shakers in Daisy and Button, late 1990s to 2000, 3-1/2" h, **$20+** each.

Three pieces of Chardonnay on Mulberry, 1999, from left: baluster vase in Spiral Optic with ruffled edge, 8-1/2" h, **$120**; basket in Rib Optic, 11-1/2" h, **$135**; tri-crimp vase in Spiral Optic, 7" h, **$120**.

201

Fenton by Era

Chiffon Pink Iridized Mermaid vase, 2000, 6-1/2" h, **$90+**.

Candleglow decanter, 1980s, 11-1/2" h, **$80+**.

Charleston Collection beaded melon jug, exclusive from QVC, 2002, signed by Don and Randy Fenton, marking the company's 95th anniversary, 5-1/2" h, **$130+**.

Two Christmas Compotes (using an old Dugan mold with holly pattern), 1997, in Green Radium (also called Sea Green Opalescent Iridized) and Plum Opalescent Satin, 9-1/2" diameter, **$150-$200** each.

Left: Cobalt shoe with snowflake decoration, 2004-05, 4-1/4" l, **$30**; center: White Satin shoe with airbrush decoration and hand-painted holly leaves and berries, 2004-05, 4-1/4" l, **$30**; right: Periwinkle Blue Bear Cub with hand-painted holly leaves and berries, 2004-05, 3-3/4" h, **$45**.

Cobalt and Amber cornucopia candleholders, style No. 950, late 1990s, 6" h: Cobalt, **$45+**; Amber, **$25+**.

Cobalt and Ruby candlesticks in Spiral, 1990s, 7-1/2" h, **$35+ each**.

New World shakers in Cobalt Opalescent Rib Optic, 2000, made for QVC, 5" h, **$125+** pair.

Cranberry basket with hand-painted roses, 2003, 10-1/2" h, **$300+**.

Cranberry cameo glass platter with sand-carved floral decoration by Martha Reynolds, 1994, one of 500, 14-1/2" diameter, **$275+**.

Country Cranberry vase, 1995, signed by Don Fenton, sold to dealers attending the UMAGA trade show, 4-1/2" h, **$65+**.

Cobalt Snowflake ornaments, various winter scenes, 2000-2005, 3-1/4" diameter, **$35** each.

Two Cranberry Christmas trees, blown into molds, circa 2000, 6-1/4" h and 7" h, no other examples known, **$150** each.

Left: Cranberry rose bowl with Mary Gregory decoration, 2004, 3-1/4" h, **$85**; right: Rosalene covered powder jar, decorated with poinsettias, 2004, 3-1/4" h, **$75**.

Fenton by Era

Cranberry Opalescent fairy light in Hobnail, three pieces, 1995, 7" h, **$175+.**

Cranberry Opalescent Grasshopper vase made for QVC, 2004, 7" h, **$65.**

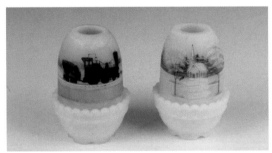

Custard Satin fairy lamps with hand-painted decoration, early 1980s, from left: locomotive and coal car; winter scene, each 4-1/2" h, **$65+** each.

Crystal and Milk-glass cornucopia candleholders, style No. 950, late 1990s, **$25+** each.

Custard Satin ginger jar with hand-painted log cabin, early 1980s, 7-3/4" h, **$100+.**

Four shakers, from left: Crystal in Regency, Light Blue and Crystal in Flower Band, and Crystal in Strawberry, 1980s, each approximately 3-1/2" h, **$15-$20** each.

Dave Fetty off-hand animals, 1980s, from left: whale, 5" l; penguin, 5-3/4" h, **$125+** each.

Dave Fetty off-hand fish in Rosalene, circa 2000, 4-1/4" h, **$350+**.

Dave Fetty off-hand mushrooms, 2000, 4-1/2" h and 5" h, **$100+** each.

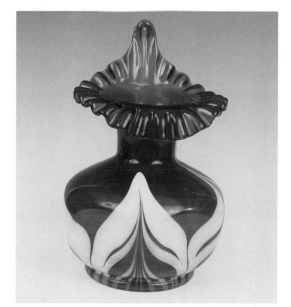

Dave Fetty off-hand pulled-feather vase in cobalt and white with tulip crimp, 2000, **$300+**.

Dave Fetty off-hand vase in a pulled-feather design, decorated by Martha Reynolds, with applied glass butterfly, 1998, 8-3/4" h, **$350+**.

Dave Fetty started working for Fenton in 1964 after learning his trade at the Blenko Glass Co. in Milton, W.Va.

In the mid-1970s, Fetty worked with glass artisan Robert Barber, helping to design and create some of Fenton's first limited-edition pieces.

Even after his "official" retirement in 1999, Fetty has continued to contribute to Fenton. During 2000, he worked with the glassworkers who produced a "Hanging Hearts" vase for the Connoisseur Collection. His contribution to the Collection in 2002 was his "Favrene Feathers Vase." Fetty also handcrafts pieces for the Collectors Room at the convention of the Fenton Art Glass Collectors Association held each year.

Fenton by Era

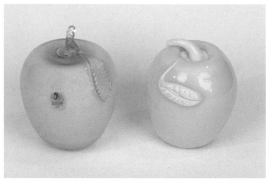

Two Dave Fetty handmade apples in overlay colors, post-2000, 4" h to 5" h, **$95** each.

Two Dave Fetty handmade pieces from left: Hanging Hearts vase with Black (Ebony) trim and red interior, 2005, 6-1/4" h, **$275**; Hanging Hearts egg, post-2000, 5-1/4" h, **$125**.

Two Dave Fetty handmade ornaments, after 2000, in a pulled-feather design, 6" iridized and 4" Milk-glass on Ruby, sold with stands, **$100-$150** each.

Dave Fetty handmade vase in chocolate and cobalt, 2005, 7" h, **$300**.

Dave Fetty handmade pitcher in Willow Green Opalescent Hanging Hearts, with iridized cobalt trim and handle, Connoisseur Collection, 2003, 8-1/2" h, **$425**.

Dave Fetty off-hand "controlled bubble" vase, teal and clear, circa 1980, 5-1/4" h, not a production piece, **$100+**.

Dealer signs in Lilac and Lavender Cobalt, late 1990s, each 5" l, **$35+** each.

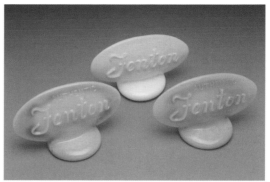

Dealer signs made for the Fenton Art Glass Collectors of America, 1990s, 5" w, each **$100-$150+.**

Ebony fan vase with hand-painted sunflowers, designed by Beverly Cumberledge and custom-made in 2002 for Randy's Antiques & Gifts of St. Paul, Minn., 8-1/4" h, **$75+.**

Dealer signs with collars still attached, made for the Fenton Art Glass Collectors of America, in iridescent, purple and ruby iridized glass, 1990s, 5" w; ruby iridized, **$300**; purple, **$100+**; iridescent, **$75-$125.**

Fenton pieces designed by Beverly Cumberledge and custom-made in 2002 for Randy's Antiques & Gifts of St. Paul, Minn., from left: Burmese duck with hand-painted pine cones, 5" l, **$70+**; Rosalene ribbed pitcher with hand-painted tulips, 7-1/4" h, **$100+**; Blue Burmese butterfly with hand-painted morning glories, 3" h, **$65+.**

Custom-made and decorated pieces of Fenton also began appearing with greater frequency, and prices have risen dramatically. Collectors could even commission Fenton artists to create special designs.

Fenton by Era

Lamp with scenic motif ("Log Cabin") hand-painted on Custard glass and signed by Louise Piper, circa 1980, 21" h, **$850+**.

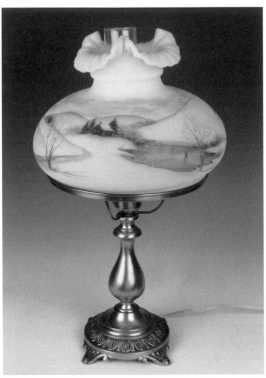

Lamp with hand-painted winter scene by Beverly Cumberledge, 2002, one of only six made this style, 22" h, **$850+**.

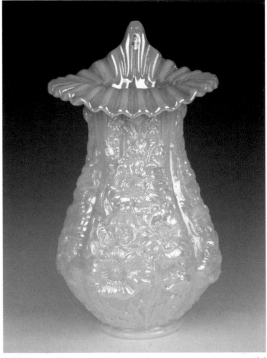

Iridescent Burmese Poppy Show Vase using an old Imperial mold, 2003, custom-made for Singleton Bailey, 13-3/4" h, **$185+**.

Sea Mist Green vase with hand-painted swallowtail butterflies by Martha Reynolds, made for the 2000 Fenton Convention auction in Williamstown, W.Va., sample only, not in the regular Fenton line, 10" h, **$300+**.

Silver Crest shallow bowl with hand-painted pansies by Louise Piper, 1981, 8" diameter, **$100+**.

Willow Green Opalescent "flip vase" with Purple Crest in Diamond Optic, with hand-painted irises and signed by Martha Reynolds, and Purple base, 2001 QVC exclusive, 7" h including base, **$200+**.

Favrene "Seasons" vase, part of the Connoisseur Collection, limited to 1,350 pieces, 1998, 8-1/2" h, **$300+**.

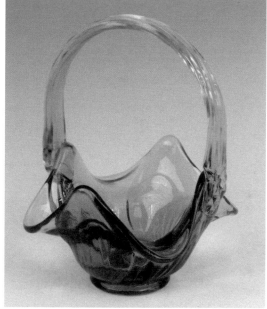

Dusty Rose basket, 1980s, 6" h, **$25+**.

Favrene ginger jar with iridescent Hanging Hearts, sand-carved, with stand, 1990s, 8-1/2" h, one of a kind, no established value.

Fairy lamps, late 1990s, each 6" h; left: Topaz Opalescent with black crest, possibly one of a kind; sample sold at FAGCA auction in 2000, **$200+**; right: Blue Burmese, FAGCA exclusive, **$250+**.

Dusty Rose was part of an overlay series from 1983 to 1985 that included Candleglow Yellow, Heritage Green, and Federal and Periwinkle Blue. A few colors were made until the late 1980s.

In 1974, when Fenton was planning its Bicentennial series, the iridescent silver and blue color known as Favrene was going to be used, but production problems prompted them to go with Independence Blue. Favrene was tried again in the mid- to late 1980s, and some off-hand and some sample items were made at that time. It eventually went into the line in the early '90s and has appeared almost annually, in limited quantities, ever since. Also see 1955 to 1980.

Fenton by Era

Favrene temple jar with base hand-painted and signed by Martha Reynolds, 1995, 9-1/2" h with base, **$450+.**

Two Fenton 100th anniversary (2005) pieces, part of the four-piece President's Collection to commemorate the company's four presidents (for QVC), from left: Lotus Mist Burmese square vase with hand-painted landscape, 8-3/4" h; Burmese basket with hand-painted poppies, 9" h, **$90** each.

Two Fenton 100th anniversary (2005) pieces, part of the four-piece President's Collection to commemorate the company's four presidents (for QVC), from left: Turquoise cannonball pitcher, hand painted in flowering quince, 7" h; Red Carnival covered candy jar with gold leaf decoration in a grape pattern, 6-1/2" h, **$90** each; plus a Fenton logo in Original Formula Carnival Glass, 3-1/4" h, **$30.**

Favrene ovoid vase with specially commissioned sand-carved southwestern motif by Martha Reynolds, 2001, signed and dated by Reynolds, numbered "141," 12" h, no established value.

Favrene pillow vase with specially commissioned sand-carved equine motif by Martha Reynolds, 2001, 9-1/2" h, no established value.

Favrene covered urn in Dancing Ladies, available with purchase of company-published book commemorating 100th anniversary, 2005, with facsimile signatures of 10 members of the Fenton family, 10" h, **$150+.**

Along with Teal Marigold and Teal Royale, French Cranberry, and French Royale were richly colored pieces from the late 1980s and early 1990s.

French Cranberry experimental vase in Spiral Optic, late 1980s, 13" h, **$350+**. (Also found with satin finish and clear handles, same value.)

French Royale experimental vase in Spiral Optic with cobalt handles, late 1980s, 14-1/4" h, **$450+**. (Also found in 13" size without handles, same value.)

Green, Iridized Opalescent and Purple shakers in Daisy and Button, late 1990s to 2000, 3-1/2" h, **$20+** each.

Green iridized vase with hand-painted flowers, 2000 QVC Designer Showcase Series, signed by Bill Fenton, 8-1/2" h, **$100+**.

Fenton by Era

Heritage Green was part of an overlay series from 1983 to 1985 that included Candleglow Yellow, Dusty Rose, and Federal and Periwinkle Blue. A few colors were made until the late 1980s.

Heritage Green, Ruby and Green Opalescent Santa votives, 4-1/2" h, 1983-85; Heritage Green and Green Opalescent, **$40** each; Ruby, **$30**.

Three Holly on Ruby pieces, 1980-81, from left: covered candy jar with oval panels, 8" h, **$55**; hurricane lamp, two pieces, 9-1/2" h, **$85**; Happiness Bird, 5" h, **$35**.

Ivory on Cameo Satin Empress vase, 1980s, 7-1/2" h, **$100+**.

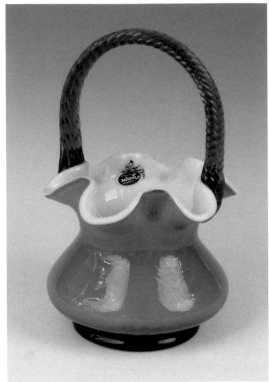

Heritage Green Overlay basket, mid-1980s, 8" h, **$65+**.

Lamp with interior and exterior hand-painted autumn-scene shade by Michael Dickinson, 1992, 21" h, **$500**.

Lamp with interior and exterior hand-painted birches and evergreen shade by Michael Dickinson, 1992, marked "Sample," 22" h, **$500.**

Lotus Mist Burmese vase with smooth tri-crimp, designed and hand painted with the boat Leviathan II by Beverly Cumberledge, one of a kind and custom made for Chuck Bingham, 2002, 11-1/2" h, **$400.**

Lotus Mist Burmese Apple Tree pitcher, hand painted, made for QVC in 2003, 10" h, **$150.**

Lotus Mist Burmese pillar vase, hand painted with a lighthouse by M. Kibbee, 2004, FAGCA convention souvenir, 9-1/4" h, **$110.**

Lotus Mist Burmese vase with hand-painted hummingbird by Susan Bryan, Fenton Gift Shop exclusive, No. 42 out of 100, 2004, 10-3/4" h, **$165.**

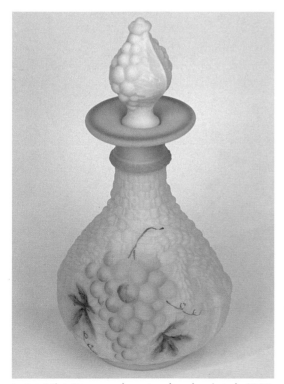

Lotus Mist Burmese decanter, hand painted, 2004, 11-1/2" h, **$120.**

Mary Gregory pitcher and two cups, 2004, 7" h and 3" h, **$300+** set.

Fenton by Era

Mary Gregory vase, 2000, 7" h, **$110+**.

Milady Vase in Ivy Overlay, sold through QVC from the Columbus, Ga., Museum of Fenton Art Glass, 11" h, **$100+**.

Mulberry Crest bell with ruffled edge, hand-painted, Designer Series, 2003, 7" h, **$90+**.

Three Mulberry vases, 1989, from left: Caprice, 6-1/2" h, **$85**; Daffodils, 8" h, **$95**; Jacqueline, 4-1/2" h, **$80**.

Three pieces of Mulberry showing color variations, 1999-2000, from left: covered box with pierced brass cover and Evening Blossoms decoration, 5-3/4" h, **$150**; hexagonal basket, 10-1/2" h, **$90**; jug or pitcher in Drapery Optic, 6-1/2" h, **$80**.

Original Formula Carnival Glass candle lamps made for the HOACGA (Heart of America Carnival Glass Association in Kansas City) in red, white, and cobalt, in Grape and Cable with horseshoe and "Good Luck," dated 1981, each 10-1/2" h, **$175-$250** each.

Original Formula Carnival Glass Red wine decanter and wine goblet in Hobnail, purchased from the "special" room at the Fenton factory, early 1980s, 12" h and 4-1/2" h, **$300+** pair.

Off-hand elephant, experimental, 1980, 3-3/4" h, **$150+**.

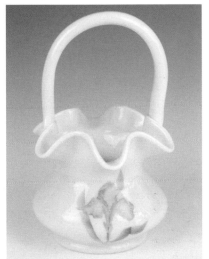

Milk-glass basket with hand-painted iris, 1980, 7-1/2" h, **$60+**.

Peking Blue Mandarin vase, 1980, 7-1/2" h, **$125+**.

It was 1969 when Rose Preznick placed an order for tobacco jars to sell at her Carnival Glass Museum in Lodi, Ohio. It marked the return of carnival glass (a term generally attributed to her and fellow collector Marion Hartung), and the debut of the Fenton logo, which eventually was added to virtually all Fenton glass over the next five years. Fenton used the term "Original Formula Carnival Glass."

Sometimes called Pekin Blue after the glass made the early 1930s, this color was joined by a renewed Jade Green for one year.

fenton by Era

Periwinkle Blue vase with thistle pattern, 2004, 9" h, **$130+**.

Pink Iridized trinket box made for Cracker Barrel, 2000, 4-1/2" l, **$50+**.

Plated Amberina (1984) top hat, 9" w and 6" h, and cane, 18" l; hat, **$150**; cane, **$100**.

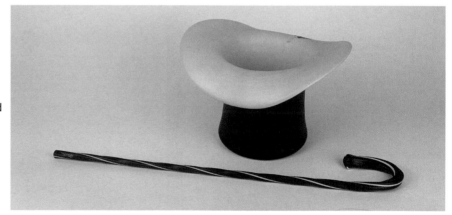

Two Plated Amberina baskets in Spiral Optic, one glossy, one satin, 1984, each 10-1/2" h, **$150** each.

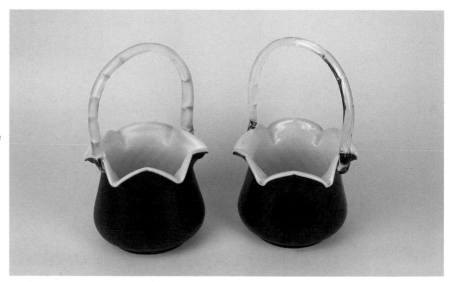

Plum Opalescent tri-crimp bowl in Sheffield, 1999-2000, 10" diameter, **$200+.**

Plum Opalescent cupped vase in Sheffield, 1999-2000, 5" h, **$200+.**

Though Sheffield was a Fenton pattern popular in the late 1930s, these examples are contemporary forms. The following six pieces are all from the same mold, with different crimping and treatments.

Plum Opalescent banana boat in Sheffield, 1999-2000, 12" w, **$200+.**

Plum Opalescent shallow bowl with ruffled edge in Sheffield, 1999-2000, 11-1/4" diameter, **$200+.**

Plum Opalescent center bowl with rolled rim in Sheffield, with Ebony base, 1999-2000, 10" diameter, **$100+.**

Plum Opalescent center bowl with rolled rim in Sheffield, with Ebony base and hand-painted flowers, 2000, 9-1/2" diameter, **$150+.**

Fenton by Era

Poppy Show Vase whimsy, made as a pitcher in Turquoise Iridized for Singleton Bailey, 2005, 12" h, **$275.**

Poppy Show Vase in Blue Burmese Iridized, made for Singleton Bailey, 2000, 12-1/2" h, **$150.**

Plum Opalescent jug and tumbler in Hobnail, part of a lemonade set that would have included six tumblers, 1980s; jug, 10" h, with crimped ice lip; tumbler, 4" h, **$500+** for complete set.

Poppy Show Vase in Red Carnival with tulip crimp, made for Singleton Bailey, 2002, 14-1/2" h, **$110.**

Poppy Show Vase in Cobalt Iridized with tulip crimp, made for Singleton Bailey, 2001, 14" h, **$110.**

Plum Opalescent donkey, 1995, 5" h, **$125+.**

Two pairs of New World shakers in Plum Opalescent and Topaz Opalescent in Rib Optic, made for the National Fenton Glass Society, early 2000s, 4" h and 5" h; Plum, **$125+** pair; Topaz, **$150+** pair.

Two Poppy Show Vases in Cranberry Opalescent (2001) and Cranberry Opalescent Iridized (2003), made for Singleton Bailey, 12-1/4" h and 14-1/2" h, **$150** each.

Poppy Show Vase in Emerald Green Overlay Carnival, made for Singleton Bailey, 2002, 12-1/2" h, **$125.**

Poppy Show Vase in Violet Opalescent Iridized, made for Singleton Bailey, 2003, 12-1/4" h, **$110.**

Poppy Show Vase in Violet, made for Singleton Bailey, late 1990s, 12-1/2" h, **$110.**

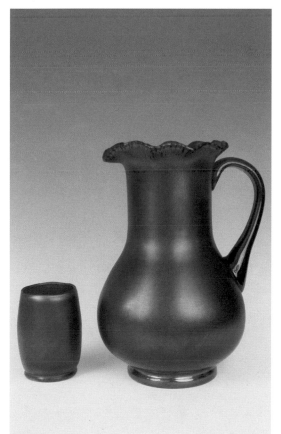

Purple stretch-glass tankard and tumbler, part of a water set that would have included six tumblers, 1980s; tankard, 10-1/2" h; tumbler, 4" h, **$500+** for complete set.

Red Iridized three-horn epergne, "apartment size," 1990s, 7" h, 9" w, **$200+.**

Fenton by Era

Rosalene was originally made for three years, from 1976 to 1979. Though not wildly successful when introduced, it has become much more sought after in the last three decades. It still can be found in later specialty items. Also see 1955 to 1980.

Rosalene three-piece fairy light, satin finish, with clear candleholder, 1990, 7-1/4" h, **$85.**

Rosalene three-piece fairy light in Spiral Optic, with clear candleholder, 1999 for QVC, 7-1/4" h, **$100.**

Rosalene lightning rod ball, made for Harker, 1980s, 5-1/2" h, **$150+.**

Rosalene sand-carved egg sample, late 1990s, 5" h, **$150+.**

Rosalene Iridized shell bowl, 1980s (?), 10-1/2" w, **$100.**

Rosalene covered candy jar showing the Chessie Cat, 1980s, 8-1/4" h, **$300+.**

Rosalene Water Lily pitcher, signed by Bill Fenton, 1987, Museum Collection, 7-3/4" h, **$85.**

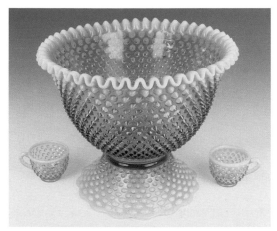

Rose Opalescent bowl in Sheffield, 1980s, 6" w, **$25+.**

Rose Magnolia two-piece punch bowl and cups in Hobnail (complete set includes 12 cups), 1994, 11" h, overall and 2-1/2" h, **$400+** for complete set.

Rose Quartz sand-carved bud vase in a dogwood motif, 1983, Connoisseur Collection, 5" h, **$75.**

Rose Quartz sand-carved Lady Vase, 1983, Connoisseur Collection, No. 815 from an edition of 850, 8-1/2" h, **$250.**

Rose Quartz sand-carved Girl Blowing Dandelions Vase, 1983, Connoisseur Collection, 7" h, **$110.**

Roselle on Cranberry basket, 1990s, 11-1/2" h, **$160+.**

Rose Magnolia from 1993-94 was part of Fenton's Historic Collection.

Fenton by Era

Royal Purple basket in Swirled Berry decoration by Frances Burton, Fenton Connoisseur Collection 2002, edition of 1,750, 10" h, **$225+.**

Left: Ruby bonbon in Hobnail, 1980s, 6" diameter, **$50+**; right: Mandarin Red bonbon in Hobnail, date unknown, 6" diameter, possibly a whimsy, no established value.

Ruby basket in Hobnail, 6-1/2" h, 2000, **$40+.**

Ruby candlesticks in a spiral pattern, 2003, 7" h, **$65+** pair.

Ruby bell with hand-painted roses, indistinctly signed, 1990s, 6-1/2" h, **$50+.**

Ruby bud vase, 1980s, 7-1/2" h, **$25+.**

Ruby water goblet in Empress, 1980s, 6-1/2" h, **$25+.**

Ruby Carnival footed plate in a Holly pattern, made to commemorate Frank M. Fenton's 85th birthday in 2000, 10" diameter, **$125+.**

Ruby Overlay shaker in Leaf, 1990s, 3-1/2" h, **$50+.**

Two hand-painted Santa Head fairy lights, 2003-04, two pieces, 4-1/2" h, from left: Burmese decorated with roses, **$85;** Opal Satin Iridized, **$50.**

Two Ruby Silvercrest three-horn epergnes in Diamond Optic, one with satin finish, 2005 special order, 10" h, **$300** each.

Three hand-painted Santa figurines, from left: Tyrolean with cat, 2000, 8-1/2" h, **$90;** with sack and flocked coat, from QVC, 2006, 6-1/2" h, **$90;** with list, from QVC, 2006, 8" h, **$90.**

Ruby Iridized paneled pitcher, 2002, 4-1/2" h, **$55+.**

Fenton by Era

Like the Dancing Ladies from the 1930s, the Sophisticated Ladies vases are one of the few Fenton lines to feature the human form. The stylized women (and men) in 1930s dress are a tribute to Duke Ellington.

Sophisticated Ladies Cobalt vase with sand-carved decoration, early 1980s, 10-1/4" h, **$75+.**

Sophisticated Ladies tapered vase, Ebony (Black) with sand-carved decoration, early 1980s, 10-1/4" h, **$110+.**

Sophisticated Ladies spherical vase, Ebony (Black) with sand-carved decoration and original label, early 1980s, 8-1/4" h, **$200+.**

Sophisticated Ladies vase, Ebony (Black) with sand-carved decoration and original label, early 1980s, 10-3/4" h, **$200+.**

Left: Spruce Green Fawn, hand painted, 1999, 3-3/4" h, **$35**; right: Emerald Green candy jar in a Mary Gregory pattern, 2005, 10" h, **$60.**

Three pieces of Star Bright on Ruby, 2004-06, from left: paneled covered candy jar, 6" h, **$75**; vase, 11" h, **$110**; Bridesmaid Doll, 7" h, **$65.**

Three "Stars & Stripes" pieces made in 2002 to commemorate the 9/11 terrorist attacks, from left: baluster vase, 5-3/4" h, **$70**; hat vase, 4" h, **$65**; fairy light (two pieces), 5-1/2" h, **$70.**

"Stars & Stripes" Cranberry Opalescent hat basket with cobalt crest and star pattern, to commemorate 9/11 terrorist attacks, 2001, 7-1/2" h, **$150+.**

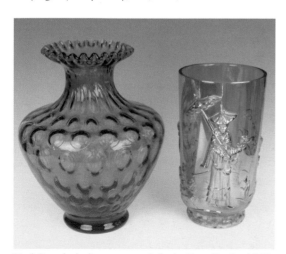

Teal Royale baluster vase, left, in Dot Optic, 1989-90, 11" h, **$90+**; right: Teal Marigold Mandarin vase, 1989-90, 9-1/2" h, **$80+.**

Topaz Blue Overlay Grasshopper vase made for QVC, 2004, hand painted, 6-3/4" h, **$50.**

Fenton by Era

Topaz Opalescent footed vase, left, with cattails and swan handles, Fenton special commission, late 1980s, 6-1/2" h, **$50+**; right: vaseline glass footed bowl with floral pattern, made by Davidson of England, circa 1890, with raised registration number inside bowl, 5" h, **$200+**.

From left: True Blue Friends Fawn, 1986, 3-3/4" h, **$35**; Opal Iridized Christmas Cactus bell, 1992, 4-1/4" h, **$30**; Spruce Green bell in Magnolia and Berry decoration, 1996, 6-1/2" h, **$35**; White Satin mini boot with Poinsettia Glow decoration, 1996, 2-1/2" h, **$25**.

The original Velva Rose was in production from 1926 to 1928.

Velva Rose pieces, 1980s, made to commemorate the company's 75th anniversary, from left: bud vase, 8" h, **$30**; deep comport, 6" h, **$50**.

Two Gems vases (using an old Verlys mold) in Red Carnival (1994) and Colonial Orange (1968), 6-3/4" h, **$75-$85** each.

Velva Rose pieces, early 1980s, from left: dolphin-handled fan vase, 6" h, **$50+**; sherbet, 4" h, **$30+**.

Velva Rose crimped basket, early 1980s, 8-1/2" h, **$70+**.

Violet Satin "Lance" vase (using an old Verlys mold from the 1930s), 1999, 8" h, **$85.**

White Satin and Milk-glass Santa votives, one hand painted, 4-1/2" h, 1983-85; White Satin, **$35**; Milk-glass, **$30.**

Violet Crest footed vase in Spanish Lace, with "frit" mixed into body, 4" h, circa 1985, **$50+.**

Willow Green trumpet basket, Glass Legacy Collection, hand painted, 2000, 10" h, **$125+.**

Three decorated Winter on Opal Satin pieces, 1985: votive on stand, 4-1/2" h, **$25**; smooth-crimp comport, 6" h, **$35**; music box bell, plays "White Christmas," 4-1/4" h, **$25.**

Yankee Doodle Puppy, hand painted, one of 500, the first piece that Fenton marketed on eBay, 2004, 4-1/2" h, **$35+.**

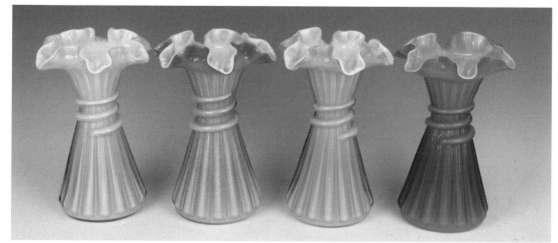

Wheat vases, early 1980s, each 7-1/2" h, in overlay colors of Honey Amber, Wild Rose, Apple Green, and Glacial Blue, **$55+.**

Christmas bells: "Going Home" and "Sleigh Ride" in Custard Satin, early 1980s, each 6" h, **45+** each.

Rosalene bell in Paisley, 1990s, 6-1/2" h, **45+**.

BELLS

		Original price	Current price
BIRDS OF WINTER SERIES			
BELL 7667BL, DOWNY WOODPECKER - CHISELED SONG, OPAL SATIN	1989	$30	$50
BELL 7667NB, A BLUEBIRD IN SNOWFALL, OPAL SATIN	1990	30	50
BELL 7668BC, CARDINAL IN THE CHURCHYARD, OPAL SATIN	1987	30	51
BELL 7668BD, CHICKADEE BALLET ON OPAL SATIN	1988	30	51
CHRISTMAS BELLS			
ANGEL BELL 5143P7, BOY, POINSETTIA GLOW, 6"	1997	35	55
ANGEL BELL 5144BM, GIRL, 6"	1997	45	55
ANGEL BELL 5144P7, GIRL, POINSETTIA GLOW, 6"	1997	35	55
BELL 1127P7, POINSETTIA GLOW ON IVORY SATIN, 6-1/2"	1997	38	55
BELL 2967AC, GOLDEN WINGED ANGEL	1996	40	56
BELL 2967TH, BOW & HOLLY ON IVORY, 6-1/2"	1995	40	49
BELL 5144AV, ANGEL, 6"	1996	40	48
BELL 5145FU, HOLLY BERRIES ON OPALESCENT, 6-1/2"	1997	38	48
BELL 6662CH, HOLLY BERRIES ON GOLD IRIDESCENT, 6-1/2"	1996	40	55
BELL 6662RX, THE WAY HOME ON RUBY SATIN, 6-1/2"	1997	65	76
BELL 7300BS, TULIP DELIGHT ON ROSEMILK OPALESCENT, 5-1/2"	2004	35	38
BELL 7463SD, MANGER SCENE ON RUBY, 6-1/2"	1993	40	49
BELL 7463SN, STAR OF WONDER ON GOLD SATIN, 6-1/2"	1996	48	65
BELL 7463TP, CHICKADEE ON GOLD, 6-1/2"	1995	40	49
BELL 7463TV, REINDEER ON BLUE, 6-1/2"	1993	30	38
BELL 7463VG, MAGNOLIA ON GOLD, 6-1/2"	1994	35	45
BELL 7463VP, ANGEL ON IVORY, 6-1/2"	1994	39	55
BELL 7463VS, SILENT NIGHT ON BLUE SATIN, 6-1/2"	1992	45	55
BELL 7463ZW, WINTER ON TWILIGHT BLUE, 6-1/2"	1992	30	45
BELL 7466AC, ALL IS CALM, 6-1/2"	1981	35	45
BELL 7466CV, CHRISTMAS MORN, 6-1/2"	1978	25	49
BELL 7466GH, GOING HOME, 6-1/2"	1980	32	55
BELL 7466NC, NATURE'S CHRISTMAS, 6-1/2"	1979	30	45
BELL 7466OC, COUNTRY CHRISTMAS, 6-1/2"	1982	35	49
BELL 7667AI, ANTICIPATION, 6-1/2"	1983	35	46
BELL 7667GE, EXPECTATION, 6-1/2"	1984	38	49
BELL 7667TQ, ICED POINSETTIA ON RUBY, 5-1/2"	1995	45	55
BELL 7667WP, HEART'S DESIRE, 6-1/2"	1985	38	71
BELL 7667XS, CHRISTMAS FAITH, CUSTARD SATIN, 6"	1986	35	70
BELL 7668HD, SLEIGH RIDE, 6-1/2"	1990	39	71
BELL 7668HJ, CHRISTMAS EVE, 6-1/2"	1991	35	67
BELL 7668HQ, FAMILY TRADITIONS, 6-1/2"	1992	39	56
BELL 7668HT, FAMILY HOLIDAY, 6-1/2"	1993	40	49
BELL 7668QP, PATRIDGE ON SPRUCE, 6-1/2"	1996	35	49
BELL 7668VT, OUR HOME IS BLESSED, GREEN SATIN , 6-1/2"	1995	45	55
BELL 7768QV, MOONLIT ON RUBY, 6-1/2"	1996	45	55
BELL, MUSIC BOX 7465GQ, FLORAL ON GREEN	1993	40	49
BELL, MUSIC BOX 7465VK, PATRIDGE ON RUBY, 6-1/2"	1994	48	61
CONNOISSEUR COLLECTION			
BELL 6761UZ, PAISLEY, ROSALENE, 7"	1991	50	93
BELL 7562UF, HAND-PAINTED BURMESE SATIN	1983	50	103
BELL 7666EB, BUTTERFLY AND FLOWERING BRANCH ON BURMESE, 6-1/2"	1985	55	135
BELL 7666SB, SHELLS ON BURMESE, 6-1/2"	1986	60	135
BELL 7666ZW, FLORAL ON WISTERIA, 7"	1988	45	85
BELL 9163UR, FAMOUS WOMEN BELL, RUBY SATIN IRIDESCENT	1984	25	67
BELL 9660WI, CRAFTSMAN BELL IN WHITE SATIN CARNIVAL	1983	25	66
BELL 9667KT, BLUEBIRD ON ROSALENE SATIN	1989	50	82
DESIGNER BELLS			
BELL 1145GF, BUTTERFLIES, 6" (DESIGNER: REYNOLDS)	1997	59	92
BELL 2962YD, TOPAZ SWIRL, 7" (DESIGNER: REYNOLDS)	1998	59	104
BELL 3279GN, HIBISCUS, 6-1/2" (DESIGNER: BURTON)	1998	59	92
BELL 4564IN, FLORAL MEDALLION , 6" (DESIGNER: REYNOLDS)	1996	59	92
BELL 4568EB, GILDED BERRY, 6-1/2" (DESIGNER: BURTON)	1996	59	92
BELL 4629AF, ROSES ON RIBBONS, 6-1/2" (DESIGNER: PLAUCHE)	1997	59	92
BELL 6662NI, GILDED DAISY, 6" (DESIGNER: SPINDLER)	1999	65	92
BELL 6864UL, VICTORIAN STRIPES, 6" (DESIGNER: REYNOLDS)	2000	65	83
BELL 7455FV, DOWN HOME (FARM VIEW) ON CUSTARD SATIN (DESIGNER: FINN)	1983	65	88
BELL 7466LT, LIGHTHOUSE POINT ON CUSTARD SATIN (DESIGNER: DICKINSON)	1983	65	93
BELL 7562AG, DECO FUSHIA, 7" (DESIGNER: PLAUCHE)	1999	65	83
BELL 7562IL, MIDNIGHT SAFARI, 7" (DESIGNER: REYNOLDS)	2001	65	82
BELL 7562PP, GARDENIA, 7" (DESIGNER: SPINDLER)	1996	55	83
BELL 7566HT, IRIDESCENCE, OVAL, WHITE FLORAL ON BLUE (DESIGNER: REYNOLDS)	1999	65	83
BELL 7568IQ, ROSE COURT, 6-1/2" (DESIGNER: BURTON)	2001	65	82
BELL 7568YB, WATER LILIES, 6" (DESIGNER: SPINDLER)	2000	65	82
BELL 7667HW, WILD ROSE, 5-1/2"	1996	50	82
BELL 7667TW, DOLPHIN FROLIC, 5-1/2" (DESIGNER: PLAUCHE)	2000	65	82

		Original price	Current price
BELL 9474IV, COTTON BERRY, 7" (DESIGNER: PLAUCHE)	2001	$65	$82
BELL 9667UJ, BLEEDING HEART, 7" (DESIGNER: SPINDLER)	1998	59	84
BELL 9862BF, WHITTON, FEATHERS, 6-3/4" (DESIGNER: SPINDLER)	1997	59	93

GENERAL ISSUE

BELL 1127SE, MAGNOLIA AND BERRY ON SPRUCE, 6-1/2"	1997	33	45
BELL 1145DX, TRELLIS ON FRENCH OPALESCENT, 6-1/2"	1999	40	49
BELL 3271CC, BLOWN, COUNTRY CRANBERRY WITH LOOPED CRYSTAL HANDLE	1999	75	82
BELL 3368GY, WILLOW GREEN HOBNAIL, 5"	2002	23	26
BELL 3645RN, RED CARNIVAL, 5-1/2"	1993	25	34
BELL 3645RV, ROSE MAGNOLIA HOBNAIL, 5-1/2"	1993	18	28
BELL 3645XC, PERSIAN BLUE OPALESCENT	1989	18	28
BELL 4629PD, MEADOW BEAUTY, 6"	1997	39	48
BELL 4694S3, INSPIRATIONS, STAR LIGHT ON COBALT: "ALL ARE PRECIOUS IN HIS SIGHT"	2004	40	48
BELL 4764UN, THREADED, GOLDEN DAISY ON AMETHYST CARNIVAL, 5-1/2"	2004	48	53
BELL 5762HT, HYDRANGEAS ON ROSEMILK OPALESCENT, 5-1/2"	2003	30	38
BELL 5966JP, PRISCILLA, APPLE GREEN STRETCH, 4-1/2"	2004	25	28
BELL 5966SY, PRISCILLA, BLUE TOPAZ, 4-1/2"	2002	20	23
BELL 6536KA, CELESTE BLUE STRETCH DRAPERY BELL	2004	29	34
BELL 6761RU, PAISLEY, RUBY, 7"	1997	23	39
BELL 6863FT, MELON, COTTAGE ROSES ON FRENCH OPALESCENT, 6"	2002	40	45
BELL 7463/6T, INSPIRATIONS ON VIOLET: "GOD'S LIGHT IS EVERYWHERE"	2003	38	49
BELL 7463BY, TIGER LILY ON BLACK, 6"	2002	45	49
BELL 7768FJ, ROYAL LENTEN ROSE, 6"	2002	40	44
BELL 7768GG, FLORAL INTERLUDE ON SEA GREEN SATIN, 6-1/2"	1998	45	54
BELL 8265BX, LILY OF THE VALLEY IN SAPPHIRE BLUE OPALESCENT, 6"	1990	16	27
BELL 8265PQ, LILY OF THE VALLEY IN CHAMPAGNE SATIN	1997	20	27
BELL 9065DT, LIGHT AMETHYST CARNIVAL, 5-1/2"	1991	25	38
BELL 9474Q4, INSPIRATIONS ON FRENCH OPALESCENT. "THOSE WHO LOVE THE LORD SHINE AS THE SUN"	2003	40	48
BELL 9560BO, TEMPLE BELLS IN STIEGEL BLUE OPALESCENT, 6-3/4"	1991	18	28
BELL 9560P2, TEMPLE BELLS IN PERIWINKLE BLUE SLAG, 6-1/2"	2004	30	34
BELL 9665TS, TOPAZ OPALESCENT, 6-1/2"	1997	25	34
BELL 9667GF, AURORA, STARFLOWER ON GOLD PEARL, 7"	1992	29	45
BELL 9667JE, CORALENE FLORAL ON CELESTE BLUE STRETCH, 7" (90TH ANNIVERSARY)	1995	35	49
BELL 9667SS, AURORA, STIEGEL GREEN STRETCH, 7"	1994	25	38

MADE FOR OTHER COMPANIES

BELL 3645AO, AQUA OPALESCENT HOBNAIL, RUFFLED	1982	—	39
BELL 3645PO, DEEP PLUM OPALESCENT HOBNAIL (LEVAY)	1984	—	109
BELL 7563VY, STAR-CRIMPED PURPLE STRETCH (LEVAY)	1981	—	782
BELL 7662WQ, PETITE, LOVE BOUQUET ON BURMESE, 4-1/2" (MARY WALRATH)	1986	—	55
BELL 7668XA, CLYDESDALES ON WHITE SATIN (BUDWEISER)	1984	—	221
BELL 9462DR, BASKETWEAVE, CHOCOLATE ROSES ON CUSTARD	1981	—	49

MADE FOR QVC

BELL C1773UQ, LAMB IN OPAL SATIN (MOTHER'S DAY)	1989	—	49
BELL C2052, SPANISH LACE IN TEAL MARIGOLD CARNIVAL WITH SNOW CREST	1988	—	55
BELL C40995, BUTTERFLY HANDLE, VIOLETS ON TOPAZ OPALESCENT IRIDESCENT	1997	—	54
BELL C62419, SHEFFIELD, VIOLET IRIDESCENT	1999	—	48
BELL C6719, CHRISTMAS CHURCH SCENE ON WHITE OPAL IRIDESCENT, BLUE SKIRT	1990	—	44
BELL C7562JQ, POINSETTIA ON MILK-GLASS WITH RUBY CREST	1988	—	55
BELL C7662EQ, PETITE, BLUE FLOWERS ON SHELL PINK, 4-1/2"	1988	—	39
BELL C7666KP, COPPER ROSES ON EBONY	1990	—	56
BELL C7667EQ, CLUE FLOWERS ON SHELL PINK, 6-1/2"	1988	—	56
BELL C7668UW, THANKSGIVING, 6-1/2"	1990	—	48
BELL C7668VD, VALENTINE'S DAY, PORCELAIN ROSE ON IRIDIZED OPAL, 6-1/2"	1990	—	49
BELL C7668XA, CHRISTMAS ROSES AND PINE ON OPAL SATIN, 6-1/2" (CHRISTMAS)	1990	—	49
BELL C7668XA, CHURCH ON OPAL SATIN, GREEN BORDER (CHRISTMAS)	1990	—	49
BELL C9268ET, FLORAL ON PEACH VELVET (EASTER)	1990	—	48
BELL, MUSIC BOX C7668QC, CHURCH AND LORD'S PRAYER ON OPAL SATIN (CHRISTMAS)	1988	—	56

MARY GREGORY

BELL 7463RG, BUTTERFLY DELIGHT ON RUBY, 6-1/2"	1995	49	72
BELL 7463RY, HE LOVES ME, HE LOVES ME NOT, RUBY, 6"	1994	49	72

FIGURINES

Assorted other items

BOTTLE K7761KN, SMALL WITH HICKORY BAND, 4" (KATJA)	1983	23	48
BOTTLE K7761KO, SMALL WITH FLAME BAND, 4" (KATJA)	1983	23	48
BOTTLE K7763KN, LARGE WITH HICKORY BAND, 8" (KATJA)	1983	50	93
BOTTLE K7763KO, LARGE WITH FLAME BAND, 8" (KATJA)	1983	50	93
CAKE PLATE 4671BO, RING AND PETAL IN STIEGEL BLUE OPALESCENT, OPEN-EDGE, 11-1/4"	1991	40	52
CANE 5090PV, PLATED AMBERINA VELVET (CONNOISSEUR)	1984	35	135
CENTERPIECE WITH NYMPH 2990KA, 4-PIECE, CELESTE BLUE STRETCH (90TH ANNIVERSARY)	1995	95	147
COVERED HEN EGG PLATE 5188TJ, FLORAL ON IRIDIZED OPAL, 12"	1997	115	157

Dolphin Frolic bell in window green, 2000, 5-1/2" h, **65+.**

Price Guide

		Original price	Current price
CRAFTSMAN STEIN 9640WI, WHITE SATIN CARNIVAL (CONNOISSEUR)	1983	$35	$54
CUSPIDOR 4634DT, 3-TOED, INNOVATION, LIGHT AMETHYST CARNIVAL	1991	23	43
FENTON LOGO 9499GE, OVAL, SEA GREEN SATIN, 5"	1998	28	32
FENTON LOGO 9499KA, OVAL, CELESTE BLUE STRETCH, 5" (90TH ANNIVERSARY)	1995	25	43
FENTON LOGO 9499TG, OVAL, OPALINE	1996	25	28
FENTON LOGO 9499TS, OVAL, TOPAZ OPALESCENT	1997	28	34
FENTON LOGO 9799BX, RECTANGULAR, SAPPHIRE BLUE OPALESCENT	1990	15	28
FENTON LOGO 9799DT, RECTANGULAR, LIGHT AMETHYST CARNIVAL	1991	20	28
FENTON LOGO 9799FO, RECTANGULAR, FRENCH OPALESCENT	1986	—	29
FENTON LOGO 9799RV, RECTANGULAR, ROSE MAGNOLIA	1991	20	28
FENTON LOGO 9799SS, RECTANGULAR, STIEGEL GREEN STRETCH	1994	25	28
FENTON LOGO 9799XV, RECTANGULAR, PERSIAN PEARL	1992	20	28
GOBLET 5561SS, STIEGEL GREEN STRETCH, 6-1/2"	1994	23	34
GUEST SET 1500DI, CRANBERRY (MARY GREGORY)	1997	115	163
NAPPY 8442TO, 3-TOED, TOPAZ OPALESCENT	1988	18	49
TUMBLER 1876XV, FERN IN PERSIAN PEARL	1992	25	38
TUMBLER 3949RV, ROSE MAGNOLIA HOBNAIL, 9 OZ	1993	12	22
VANITY SET 3104BI, 4-PIECE, BLUE RIDGE (CONNOISSEUR)	1986	125	435
VANITY SET 7199WB, 3-PIECE ON CRYSTAL TRAY, HAND-PAINTED MILK-GLASS	1996	250	328

BASKETS

		Original price	Current price
BASKET 1131DX, TRELLIS 8-1/2" (FAMILY SIGNATURE, LYNN FENTON)	1995	85	93
BASKET 1135JE, CORALENE FLORAL IN CELESTE BLUE STRETCH (90TH ANNIVERSARY)	1995	75	93
BASKET 1142JE, CORALENE FLORAL ON CELESTE BLUE STRETCH, FOOTED 7" (90TH ANNIVERSARY)	1995	38	49
BASKET 1158TS, TOPAZ OPALESCENT HOBNAIL, 8-1/2"	1997	45	78
BASKET 1217AO AUTUMN GOLD OPALESCENT 11" (FAMILY SIGNATURE, FRANK FENTON)	1994	70	93
BASKET 1330TE 7" BUBBLE OPTIC (CONNOISSEUR COLLECTION)	1989	85	119
BASKET 1435XC, PERSIAN BLUE OPALESCENT, 5"	1989	37	81
BASKET 1531MS, HUMMINGBIRD AND WILD ROSE, 8"	1996	95	104
BASKET 1533DI, BREEZY DAY ON CRANBERRY (MARY GREGORY)	1998	150	190
BASKET 1533JN, ROSELLE ON CRANBERRY, 11" (GLASS MESSENGER EXCLUSIVE)	1996	89	325
BASKET 1533OS, HEXAGONAL, LAVENDER LADY ON VIOLET OVERLAY, 11" (FAMILY SIGNATURE SERIES, TOM FENTON & SCOTT FENTON)	2000	109	136
BASKET 1539DQ, GIRL SWINGING (MARY GREGORY)	1997	115	157
BASKET 1617N4, COLONIAL SCROLL ON ROYAL PURPLE	1998	115	187
BASKET 1830BX, FERN, SAPPHIRE BLUE OPALESCENT, 5-1/2"	1990	37	65
BASKET 1830XC, PERSIAN BLUE FERN OPTIC, 5-1/2"	1989	37	76
BASKET 2033TP, HYDRANGEAS ON TOPAZ OPALESCENT, 8"	1997	80	129
BASKET 2039SF, FLORAL ON IRIDIZED GLASS, 10-1/2" (FAMILY SIGNATURE, SHELLEY FENTON)	1998	125	166
BASKET 2725XV, PERSIAN PEARL, 7"	1992	28	38
BASKET 2728XV, PERSIAN PEARL, 4"	1992	20	28
BASKET 2732CR, CRANBERRY HEART OPTIC, 7"	1993	59	71
BASKET 2735VF, BERRY & BUTTERFLY ON LOTUS MIST, 8-1/2"	2000	95	136
BASKET 2736CR CRANBERRY OPALESCENT 7"	1994	65	81
BASKET 2738, HAND-PAINTED LILACS, 7-1/2"	1994	65	76
BASKET 2745CR, CRANBERRY OPALESCENT MELON, 8"	1995	69	76
BASKET 2779RN, RUBY CARNIVAL, LION/LEAF, 8-1/2" (FAMILY SIGNATURE, TOM FENTON)	1994	65	77
BASKET 2787ST, STIEGEL GREEN STRETCH (FAMILY SIGNATURE, BILL FENTON)	1994	60	103
BASKET 2932UE, PURPLE PASSION FLOWERS ON BLUE BURMESE, 8"	*	100	164
BASKET 2932UL, BURMESE BUTTERFLY, 8" (90TH ANNIVERSARY)	1995	135	180
BASKET 2989Y8, MY FIRST PONY ON CRANBERRY, 7-1/2" (MARY GREGORY)	2004	140	153
BASKET 3076KT, MOUNTAIN BERRY ON GOLD OVERLAY, 8" (FAMILY SIGNATURE, DON FENTON)	1996	85	111
BASKET 3077XV, SPIRAL PERSIAN PEARL, 11"	1992	50	76
BASKET 3097QB, BLUE HYDRANGEAS ON BLACK, 10-1/2"	2004	80	87
BASKET 3127NG, STARFLOWERS ON CRANBERRY PEARL, 7" (FAMILY SIGNATURE, MIKE FENTON)	1996	95	134
BASKET 3132OT, IRIDESCENT CASED TEAL, MELON, 8-3/4" (CONNOISSEUR)	1988	65	181
BASKET 3133CR, CRANBERRY OPALESCENT SPIRAL OPTIC, 6"	1990	50	82
BASKET 3134PV, PLATED AMBERINA VELVET (CONNOISSEUR)	1984	85	188
BASKET 3138XC, PERSIAN BLUE OPALESCENT, RIBBED SPIRAL OPTIC, 7"	1989	40	78
BASKET 3281RQ, DANCING IN THE RAIN, 9-1/2" (MARY GREGORY)	2000	139	163
BASKET 3335GP, GOLD PEARL, LOOPED HANDLE	1992	35	76
BASKET 3337RV, ROSE MAGNOLIA IN HOBNAIL	1993	30	48
BASKET 3834RV, ROSE MAGNOLIA IN HOBNAIL, 4-1/2"	1993	25	48
BASKET 3834XC, PERSIAN BLUE OPALESCENT, 4-1/2"	1989	18	47
BASKET 4534CN, AMETHYST CARNIVAL, 9"	2004	60	65
BASKET 4634UN, PEACOCK, GOLDEN DAISY ON AMETHYST CARNIVAL, 8"	2004	90	101
BASKET 4647MD, ROSALENE, EMPRESS (CONNOISSEUR)	1991	64	163
BASKET 4648P9, SWEETBRIER ON PLUM OVERLAY, 9" (FAMILY SIGNATURE, LYNN FENTON)	1997	85	134
BASKET 4830DX, TRELLIS ON FRENCH OPALESCENT, 9-1/2" (FAMILY SIGNATURE, TOM FENTON)	1998	95	134
BASKET 4833TG, OPALINE DIAMOND LACE, 6"	1996	25	54

		Original price	Current price
BASKET 4838CP, DIAMOND LACE, EMPRESS ROSE, 5"	1997	$20	$28
BASKET 4979CR, HEART OPTIC IN CRANBERRY, 8-1/2"	2004	129	140
BASKET 5481GF, STAR FLOWERS ON GOLD PEARL, 9"	1992	49	71
BASKET 5483GF, STAR FLOWERS ON GOLD PEARL, 10-1/2"	1992	89	133
BASKET 5551SS, STIEGEL GREEN STRETCH, FOOTED, 9"	1994	40	56
BASKET 5555SS, STIEGEL GREEN STRETCH, FOOTED, 7"	1994	30	45
BASKET 5732MJ, LOTUS MIST BURMESE, 9" (FAMILY SIGNATURE, GEORGE FENTON)	2004	130	141
BASKET 5733BS, TULIP DELIGHT ON ROSEMILK OPALESCENT, 9"	2004	95	104
BASKET 5735JD, STRAWBERRIES IN APPLE GREEN, 7-1/2"	2004	40	43
BASKET 5735OQ, STRAWBERRIES IN VIOLET, 7-1/2"	2004	40	43
BASKET 5931ST, SUMMER, WISH UPON A STAR ON VIOLET, 9"	2004	110	122
(MARY GREGORY, SIGNED BY 10 FENTON FAMILY MEMBERS)			
BASKET 5937JQ, PANSY MORNING ON APPLE GREEN STRETCH, 10"	2004	85	93
BASKET 5937P2, PANELED, PERIWINKLE BLUE SLAG, 10"	2004	65	71
BASKET 5937TC, AUTUMN BEAUTY ON TOPAZ OPALESCENT, 10"	2004	90	98
BASKET 5977TT, CATCH ON COBALT BLUE, 9-1/2" (MARY GREGORY)	2004	100	108
BASKET 5995OE, PANEL DOT IN VIOLET	2004	60	65
BASKET 6335VQ, GRAPE ARBOR ON VIOLET, 9-1/2"	2004	90	98
BASKET 6335WS, FALL, HAPPY HALLOWEEN ON CRANBERRY (MARY GREGORY)	2004	110	121
BASKET 6432IM, VASA MURRHINA, MELON, 9" (CONNOISSEUR)	1983	75	195
BASKET 6567CR, CRANBERRY, 6"	1992	50	71
BASKET 6730PJ, PAISLEY, HAND-PAINTED LILACS (FAMILY SIGNATURE, BILL FENTON)	1993	65	104
BASKET 7122CR, CRANBERRY, MELON, 8"	1996	75	97
BASKET 7134SH, SPRING, BOUQUET FOR KITTY ON EMERALD GREEN (MARY GREGORY)	2004	100	112
BASKET 7139YN, MELON, WHISPERING WINGS ON LOTUS BURMESE, 7-1/2"	2004	100	112
BASKET 7237XA, CLYDESDALES ON CAMEO SATIN, 7" (MADE FOR BUDWEISER)	1983	14	167
BASKET 7438JD, RED FLORAL ON TEAL AND MILK OVERLAY (CONNOISSEUR)	1986	49	191
BASKET 7612VV, GRAPE ARBOR ON FRENCH OPALESCENT, 9-1/2"	2004	90	99
BASKET 7634EB, BUTTERFLY & FLOWERING BRANCH ON BURMESE, 8-1/2"	1985	95	191
BASKET 7731QH, BURMESE WITH RASPBERRIES, 7"	1990	75	184
BASKET 7732QD, BURMESE WITH TREES SCENE, 5-1/2"	1990	58	146
BASKET 8330XC, PERSIAN BLUE OPALESCENT, 7"	1989	25	48
BASKET 8437BX, LILY OF THE VALLEY, SAPPHIRE BLUE OPALESCENT	1990	27	59
BASKET 8637RG, "BUTTERFLY DELIGHT," RUBY, OVAL, 7-1/2" (MARY GREGORY)	1995	65	164
BASKET 8637RY, "HE LOVES ME, HE LOVES ME NOT," RUBY, OVAL, 7-1/2" (MARY GREGORY)	1994	59	163
BASKET 9234TO, BUTTERFLY & BERRY, TOPAZ OPALESCENT	1988	25	81
BASKET 9435TO, TOPAZ OPALESCENT, RIBBON CANDY EDGE, FOOTED	1988	30	81
BASKET 9435XV, PERSIAN PEARL, DRAPERY	1993	45	65
BASKET 9436IO, ROSE BOWL, AQUA BLUE CARNIVAL, LOOPED HANDLE, 8-1/2" (LEVAY)	1980	—	132
BASKET 9436TO, ROSE BOWL, TOPAZ OPALESCENT, FOOTED, LOOPED HANDLE	1988	—	82
BASKET 9535FO, FRENCH OPALESCENT	1986	—	34
BASKET 9536BQ, WINTERBERRY	1981	—	58
BASKET 9537DK, STRAWBERRIES, DUSTY ROSE, FOOTED	1990	—	33
BASKET 9537OC, STRAWBERRIES, TEAL ROYALE	1988	—	34
BASKET 9539PT, PEARLY SENTIMENTS (PINK PORCELAIN ROSE)	1989	—	34
BASKET 9544SR, VULCAN, SALEM BLUE	1990	—	38
BASKET 9635 DK, DUSTY ROSE, SWUNG, 7"	1984	—	34
BASKET 9637NK, LEAF WITH BUTTERFLY, COBALT MARIGOLD CARNIVAL	1985	—	56
BASKET 9638XC, GRAPE BASKET, PERSIAN BLUE, 3"	1989	23	49
BASKET 9639BQ, WINTERBERRY, PANELED	1987	—	56
BASKET 9639JU, MEADOW BLOOMS ON OPAL SATIN, 7-1/2"	1986	—	48
BASKET 9639VJ, VICTORIAN ROSES, PANELED	1987	—	49
BASKET A3335UO, PINK OPALESCENT HOBNAIL, LOOPED HANDLE	1988	23	82
BASKET A3830UO, PINK OPALESCENT HOBNAIL, 10" (COLLECTORS EXTRAVAGANZA)	1988	30	81
BASKET A3834UO, PINK OPALESCENT HOBNAIL, 6-1/2" (COLLECTORS EXTRAVAGANZA)	1988	16	49
BASKET C1868XN, OCEAN BLUE WITH COBALT CREST AND HANDLE, MELON	1990	—	76
BASKET C3538TC, SPANISH LACE, WHITE CARNIVAL WITH TEAL CREST (MADE FOR QVC)	1988	—	77
BASKET C5838LU, CORN SHOCK, LILAC CARNIVAL (MADE FOR QVC)	1989	—	82
BASKET C7244QX, ROSALENE WITH HAND-PAINTED ROSES, 8-1/2" (MADE FOR QVC)	1991	—	108
BASKET C8335XB, BASKETWEAVE, BLACK CARNIVAL (MADE FOR QVC)	1990	—	81
BASKET C9134DN, BUTTERFLY & BERRY, DUSTY ROSE CARNIVAL, MILK CREST (QVC)	1989	—	46
BASKET C9134OM, BUTTERFLY & BERRY, TEAL CARNIVAL, MILK-GLASS CREST (QVC)	1988	—	76
BASKET G1636AY, AMETHYST	2000	—	56
BASKET V8637FX, COUNTRY BOUQUET, OVAL, 7-1/2"	1986	—	49

BOWLS

BOWL 1726CR, DIAMOND OPTIC, CRANBERRY OPALESCENT, 10"	1990	—	92
BOWL 1825BX, FERN, SAPPHIRE BLUE OPALESCENT W/BRIDE'S BASKET, 10"	1990	125	192
BOWL 1826BX, FERN, SAPPHIRE BLUE OPALESCENT, 10"	1990	55	71
BOWL 2323XC, PERSIAN BLUE OPALESCENT, 10"	1989	50	65
BOWL 2624BI, BLUE RIDGE	1985	—	87
BOWL 2747RX, RUBY STRETCH WITH GOLD SCROLLS (CONNOISSEUR)	1993	95	190
BOWL 2754XV, SWAN IN PERSIAN PEARL	1993	45	61

Emerald Green basket with hand-painted shamrocks, one of 50 sold through Fenton gift shop, 2005, decorated by Susan Bryan, 10-1/2" h, **95+**.

Dave Fetty handmade bowl with a sand-carved stars-and-stripes motif (underside cobalt blue), 2006, 9-1/2" w, **$275**.

		Original price	Current price
BOWL 2909UK, VINTAGE BORDER IN BURMESE SATIN, 10-1/4"	1995	$150	$181
BOWL 3938PO, DEEP PLUM OPALESCENT HOBNAIL, 12" (MADE FOR LEVAY)	1984	—	217
BOWL 3938XV, PERSIAN PEARL, 12"	1992	35	54
BOWL 4619DT, LIGHT AMETHYST CARNIVAL, 10"	1991	—	48
BOWL 4627BO, GOOD LUCK, STIEGEL BLUE OPALESCENT, 10-1/4"	1991	—	56
BOWL 5150PI, ATLANTIS, PEACH OPALESCENT CARNIVAL (MADE FOR MLT GLASS)	1981	—	111
BOWL 5482GF, GRAY MIST, 9-1/2"	1992	65	81
BOWL 6320KL, FLOWER BAND ON FORGET-ME-NOT BLUE, 9"	1982	—	38
BOWL 6625UO, REFLECTIONS, PEACHES 'N CREAM OPALESCENT, 11"	1986	—	43
BOWL 6626UO, REFLECTIONS, PEACHES 'N CREAM OPALESCENT, 5-1/2"	1986	—	34
BOWL 7521IN, IRIS ON BONE WHITE, 6"	1982	—	49
BOWL 7523JA, ROLLED RIM, JADE GREEN	1980	—	38
BOWL 7523KP, ROLLED RIM, COPPER ROSES ON BLACK, 9-1/2"	1990	—	56
BOWL 7526VR, VELVA ROSE, 6-1/2"	1980	—	49
BOWL 7549PF, MELON, PETITE FLEUR ON OPALINE GLASS, 9"	1984	—	55
BOWL 7622RK, BERRIES & BLOSSOMS ON OPAL SATIN, 9"	1984	—	61
BOWL 7727AG, CASED JADE OPALINE, 14"	1990	—	73
BOWL 7727JC, CRANBERRY CAMEO, 14" (CONNOISSEUR)	1994	390	495
BOWL 7727KH, CRANBERRY OPALINE, 14"	1990	—	73
BOWL 8229BX, LILY OF THE VALLEY, SAPPHIRE BLUE OPALESCENT, 10"	1990	33	48
BOWL 8283OI, ORANGE TREE AND CHERRY IN TEAL MARIGOLD CARNIVAL, 10"	1989	—	49
BOWL 8289BR, ORANGE TREE AND CHERRY, PRESSED BURMESE	1986	—	72
BOWL 8289NK, ORANGE TREE AND CHERRY, COBALT MARIGOLD CARNIVAL	1986	—	49
BOWL 8321PW, BARRED OVAL, PERIWINKLE BLUE, 6-1/2"	1986	—	28
BOWL 8323OO, OPEN-EDGED, PROVINCIAL BLUE OPALESCENT	1987	—	34
BOWL 8428TO, FANTAIL FOOTED, TOPAZ OPALESCENT	1988	28	54
BOWL 8520BB, SCULPTURED ICE OPTIC, GLACIAL BLUE, 12"	1982	—	56
BOWL 8810EP, SHALLOW, PERIWINKLE, 9"	1985	—	122
BOWL 8810ER, SHALLOW, ROSE, 9"	1985	—	122
BOWL 8811EP, "V"-SHAPED, PERIWINKLE, 8"	1985	—	131
BOWL 8811ER, "V"-SHAPED, ROSE, 8"	1985	—	131
BOWL 9027XC, PERSIAN BLUE OPALESCENT	1989	30	43
BOWL 9059RN, GRAPE & CABLE, RED CARNIVAL, 10-1/2"	1990	—	59
BOWL 9425IO, RIBBON EDGE, AQUA BLUE CARNIVAL, 8" (MADE FOR LEVAY)	1980	—	94
BOWL 9425IP, RIBBON EDGE, IRIDIZED PLUM OPALESCENT, 8" (MADE FOR LEVAY)	1984	—	72
BOWL 9425TO, TOPAZ OPALESCENT	1988	23	55
BOWL 9442MG, JACQUELINE, MULBERRY, 9-1/2"	1989	—	104
BOWL 9627PW, BEAUTY, PERIWINKLE BLUE	1986	—	34
BOWL 9728NK, ACANTHUS, COBALT MARIGOLD CARNIVAL	1987	—	38
BOWL C3524TX, SPANISH LACE, TEAL WITH MILK-GLASS CREST (MADE FOR QVC)	1988	—	73
BOWL C3938DO, DUSTY ROSE CARNIVAL HOBNAIL, TEAL CREST (MADE FOR QVC)	1989	—	54
BOWL C8428XB, FOOTED, BUTTERFLY & BERRY IN BLACK CARNIVAL (MADE FOR QVC)	1989	—	68
BOWL G1625AY, OVAL, AMETHYST, 11"	1983	—	48
BOWL G1625FB, OVAL, FEDERAL BLUE, 11"	1983	—	49
BOWL K7722KN, MEDIUM FLARED BOWL, BANDED COLOR (KATJA)	1983	—	73
BOWL K7724KO, FLAME BAND, 9-3/4" (KATJA)	1983	—	82
BOWL R8430GS, FOOTED WATER LILY, GREEN (MADE FOR A.L. RANDALL CO.)	1982	—	33
BOWL R9426MI, RIBBED, MILK-GLASS HOBNAIL, 4-1/2" (MADE FOR A.L. RANDALL CO.)	1982	—	28
BOWL R9430GS, WATER LILY, GREEN, 6" (MADE FOR A.L. RANDALL CO.)	1982	—	39
BOWL R9430RU, FABERGE, RIBBED, RUBY, 6"	1982	—	39

BOXES

		Original price	Current price
BOX 1581BW, METAL COVER, FLORAL ON RUBINA VERDE	1997	—	182
BOX 1589CC, METAL COVER, COUNTRY CRANBERRY	1990	—	134
BOX 4600GP, GOLD PEARL	1992	85	135
BOX 4990CR, HEART OPTIC IN CRANBERRY	1998	125	163
BOX 5585DX, MELON, TRELLIS ON FRENCH OPALESCENT	1995	—	48
BOX 5585PF, PANSIES ON MILK-GLASS (FAMILY SIGNATURE SERIES, SHELLEY FENTON)	1996	—	93
BOX 6080RH, WAVE CREST WITH MARBLEIZED LUSTRE (CONNOISSEUR)	1992	—	164
BOX 6584CD, MELON, METAL COVER, MANDARIN RED (CONNOISSEUR)	1996	150	188
BOX 7603MD, FLORAL ON MULBERRY, METAL COVER	1996	75	143
(SHOWCASE DEALER EXCLUSIVE, SIGNED BY 11 FENTON FAMILY MEMBERS)			
BOX 7640PX, SQUARE, BEADED GRAPE IN PLUM CARNIVAL	1998	—	55
BOX 9080GE, SQUARE, FISH FINIAL, SEA GREEN SATIN, 4"	1998	—	49
BOX 9333JX, TWINING BERRIES (FAMILY SIGNATURE SERIES, TOM FENTON)	1999	—	147
BOX 9394FN, 3-PIECE OGEE, FAVRENE (CONNOISSEUR)	1991	—	171
BOX, CANDY 3786MI, OVAL, MILK-GLASS HOBNAIL	1984	—	32
BOX, CANDY 3886MI, MILK-GLASS HOBNAIL, 6-3/4"	1984	—	33
BOX, CANDY 4381ST, FLORAL ON STIEGEL GREEN STRETCH, 5-1/2"	1994	—	54
BOX, CANDY 6080ZX, CRANBERRY WAVE CREST (CONNOISSEUR)	1988	—	163
BOX, CANDY 6780EM, PAISLEY, ELIZABETH ON BLUE ROYALE	1990	—	56
BOX, CANDY 6780LX, PAISLEY IN LILAC	1990	—	48
BOX, CANDY 6780SR, PAISLEY IN SALEM BLUE	1990	—	49

		Original price	Current price
BOX, CANDY 7484BD, BLUE DOGWOOD ON CAMEO SATIN	1980	$—	$56
BOX, CANDY 7484BL, BLUE ROSES ON BLUE SATIN	1978	—	57
BOX, CANDY 7484DR, CHOCOLATE ROSES ON CAMEO SATIN (MADE FOR HERSHEY'S CHOCOLATE)	1979	—	72
BOX, CANDY 9280DK, BUTTERFLY FINIAL, DUSTY ROSE	1986	—	49
BOX, CANDY 9394FN, 3-PIECE OGEE, FAVRENE (CONNOISSEUR)	1991	90	163
BOX, CANDY 9394UE, 3-PIECE BLUE BURMESE SATIN (CONNOISSEUR)	1987		166
BOX, CANDY 9551EO, MINTED CREAM	1984	—	45
BOX, CANDY 9551UO, PEACHES 'N CREAM	1986	—	45
BOX, CANDY C9388RN, 3-TOED, RUBY CARNIVAL (MADE FOR QVC)	1991	—	62
BOX, CHESSIE CAT 9480GR, SEA GREEN SATIN (MADE IN REGULAR AND GLOSS, SOLD THROUGH THE FENTON GIFT SHOP)	1988	—	112
BOX, CHESSIE CAT 9480RE, ROSALENE	1990	—	381
BOX, CHESSIE CAT 9480RN, RED CARNIVAL	1977	—	92
BOX, CHESSIE CAT C9480DK, DUSTY ROSE CARNIVAL (MADE FOR QVC)	1991	—	91
BOX, HEART 4106XP, 3-TOED, FLORAL ON VIOLET SATIN	1999	—	72
BOX, HEART 5780AF, ANTIQUE ROSE	1997	—	34
BOX, HEART 5780KP, COPPER ROSES ON EBONY	1989	—	54
BOX, HEART 5780PT, PEARLY SENTIMENTS (WITH PORCELAIN ROSE)	1990	—	34
BOX, HEART 5780TH, ROSES ON VIOLET: "OPEN YOUR HEART"	2004	40	44
BOX, HEART 5780TL, TULIPS ON IRIDIZED OPAL	1988	—	33
BOX, HEART 5786DN, HUMMINGBIRD IN DUSTY ROSE	1993	—	43
BOX, PUFF 4950CR, HEART OPTIC IN CRANBERRY	1997	79	109
BOX, PUFF 6570RV, ROSE MAGNOLIA	1994	—	48
BOX, PUFF 7009WA, ROSEBUDS ON ROSALENE	1998	—	135
BOX, TRINKET 2740CR, CRANBERRY, 5"	1993	79	93
BOX, TRINKET 6506MI, MILK-GLASS BEAUTY	2004	25	27
BOX, TRINKET 6877SD, SUNSET ART NOUVEAU	2004	25	28
BOX, TRINKET 8384OO, VALENCIA, PROVINCIAL BLUE OPALESCENT	1987	—	48
BOX, TRINKET 9384MP, ROSE CORSAGE	1986	—	34
BOX, TRINKET 9384RN, FLORAL ON RED CARNIVAL	1989	—	39
BOX, TRINKET 9486PQ, CHAMPAGNE SATIN	1997	65	82
BOX, TRINKET 9589BQ, OVAL, BLUE ROSES ON CUSTARD SATIN	1990	—	49
BOX, TRINKET 9589BT, VICTORIAN BOUQUET ON BLACK	1995	—	48
BOX, TRINKET 9589DS, OVAL, PRIMROSE ON IRIDIZED OPAL	1994	—	32
BOX, TRINKET 9589FH, OVAL, HEARTS & FLOWERS	1981	—	34
BOX, TRINKET 9589PF, OVAL, WATERCOLORS ON PINK SATIN	1990	—	49

BOXES, ANIMAL COVERED

BUNNY ON NEST 4683/2A, SEA MIST SLAG	1994	—	56
BUNNY ON NEST 4683BT, HANDPAINTED ON PEARLIZED WHITE	1991	—	67
BUNNY ON NEST 4683C9, HANDPAINTED IN IRIDIZED OPAL	1992	—	71
BUNNY ON NEST 4683FG, FOLK ART	1998	—	93
BUNNY ON NEST 4683NB, FOLK ART	1996	—	92
BUNNY ON NEST 4683NU, FOLK ART	1997	—	91
BUNNY ON NEST 5380JX, SPRING FINERY, FOLK ART	2004	85	103
CHICK ON NEST 5185DN, ROSE PEARL	1993	—	45
CHICK ON NEST 5185OB, OCEAN BLUE	1993	—	44
DUCK BOX, SPRUCE CARNIVAL (U.S.)	1999	—	71
EAGLE BOX 4679DT, LIGHT AMETHYST CARNIVAL	1991	34	56
HEN ON NEST 5182BA, BLUE SATIN	1974	—	82
HEN ON NEST 5182CN, LARGE, ORIGINAL (AMETHYST) CARNIVAL	1970	—	105
HEN ON NEST 5182MB, LARGE, BLUE MARBLE	1971	—	136
HEN ON NEST 5182RN, LARGE, RED CARNIVAL	1996	—	56
HEN ON NEST 5186/2A, SEA MIST SLAG	1994	—	57
HEN ON NEST 5186EZ, JADE PEARL	1992	—	48
HEN ON NEST 5186FK, FOLK ART	1998	—	83
HEN ON NEST 5186FO, FRENCH CREAM	1986	—	49
HEN ON NEST 5186HZ, PINK PEARL	1992	—	48
HEN ON NEST 5186JX, SPRING FINERY, FOLK ART	2004	48	55
HEN ON NEST 5186LS, LIME SHERBET SATIN	1973	—	56
HEN ON NEST 5186NH, FOLK ART	1996	—	81
HEN ON NEST 5186PE, SHELL PINK	1991	—	49
HEN ON NEST 5186RX, RUBY SLAG (MADE FOR LEVAY)	1985	—	163
LION BOX 2799SS, STIEGEL GREEN STRETCH	1994	—	83
ROOSTER BOX 4680/8A, PLUM SLAG	1994	—	68
ROOSTER BOX 4680BT, HANDPAINTED ON PEARLIZED WHITE	1992	—	74
ROOSTER BOX 4680OB, OCEAN BLUE	1993	—	56
ROOSTER BOX 4680PE, SHELL PINK	1991	—	57
ROOSTER BOX 5265WG, BLUE TOILE (BLUE ON WHITE), 5-1/2"	2004	58	63
ROOSTER BOX 5292FV, FOLK ART	1998	—	133
ROOSTER BOX 6483WG, FOLK ART, RED DELICIOUS	2004	58	62
TURKEY ON NEST 6410AQ, AUTUMN GOLD	2003	40	58

Aubergine Overlay covered candy in Wave Crest, with hand-painted decoration and applied metal trim, 2005, 5" h, **$150**.

Price Guide

CANDLEHOLDERS/CANDLESTICKS

		Original price	Current price
CANDLEHOLDER, HURRICANE 8376DK, DUSTY ROSE	1987	$—	$44
CANDLEHOLDER, HURRICANE 8376HL, HOLLY BERRY	1988	—	49
CANDLEHOLDER, HURRICANE 8376MP, ROSE CORSAGE	1989	—	43
CANDLEHOLDER, HURRICANE 8376OC, TEAL ROYALE	1988	—	43
CANDLEHOLDER, HURRICANE 8376OO, VALENCIA, PROVINCIAL BLUE OPALESCENT	1987	—	43
CANDLEHOLDER, VOTIVE 7275RK, FOOTED, BERRIES & BLOSSOMS	1988	—	27
CANDLEHOLDER, VOTIVE 8294OO, FOOTED, PANELED DAISY IN PROVINCIAL BLUE OPALESCENT	1985	—	23
CANDLEHOLDER, VOTIVE 9555EO, MINTED CREAM	1986	—	23
CANDLEHOLDER, VOTIVE 9578AF, LEAF, 2-WAY, ANTIQUE ROSE	1990	—	23
CANDLEHOLDER, VOTIVE 9578PL, LEAF, 2-WAY, PLUM	1993	—	23
CANDLEHOLDERS, VIKING 7676PX, 2-ARMED, PLUM CARNIVAL	1998	—	97 Pr
CANDLELIGHT 9504FA, WITH SHADE, FROSTED ASTERS ON BLUE SATIN	1984	—	86
CANDLESTICKS 2911KA, CELESTE BLUE STRETCH, 3" (90TH ANNIVERSARY)	1995	—	55 Pr
CANDLESTICKS 3674XV, PERSIAN PEARL, 6"	1992	—	44 Pr
CANDLESTICKS 4672BO, STEIGEL BLUE OPALESCENT, 3-1/2"	1991	—	43 Pr
CANDLESTICKS 5172XV, SWAN, PERSIAN PEARL	1993	—	54 Pr
CANDLESTICKS 5526GF, STAR FLOWERS ON GOLD PEARL, 4"	1992	—	67 Pr
CANDLESTICKS 7475RK, BERRIES & BLOSSOMS ON OPAL SATIN	1984	—	67 Pr
CANDLESTICKS 9071AW, AUTUMN LEAVES ON BLACK	1994	—	67 Pr
CANDLESTICKS 9071EM, ELIZABETH ON BLUE ROYALE, 8-1/2"	1990	—	67 Pr
CANDLESTICKS 9071JX, TWINING BERRIES, 8-1/2"	1998	—	54 Pr
CANDLESTICKS 9071JY, PETAL PINK	1992	—	44 Pr
CANDLESTICKS 9071P2, PERIWINKLE BLUE SLAG, 8-1/2"	2004	—	88 Pr
CANDLESTICKS 9372KP, COPPER ROSES ON EBONY, 4-1/2"	1990	—	55 Pr
CANDLESTICKS G9071YL, CANDLEGLOW	1983	—	44 Pr

CLOCKS

CLOCK 8600BD, CHICKADEE BALLET ON OPAL SATIN, 6" (BIRDS OF WINTER)	1988	55	135
CLOCK 8600BL, DOWNY WOODPECKER-CHISELED SONG, 6" (BIRDS OF WINTER)	1990	60	136
CLOCK 8600HD, SLEIGH RIDE, 6"	1990	75	120
CLOCK 8600HJ, CHRISTMAS EVE, 6"	1991	75	120
CLOCK 8600HQ, FAMILY TRADITIONS, 6"	1992	75	120
CLOCK 8600HT, FAMILY HOLIDAY	1993	75	120
CLOCK 8600NB, BLUEBIRD IN SNOWFALL (BIRDS OF WINTER)	1990	60	135
CLOCK 8600PG, DEER SCENE	1989	—	163
CLOCK 8600X5, LET'S PLAY WITH MOM (MOTHER'S DAY, KITTIES)	1993	—	134
CLOCK 8600X7, DOE AND FAWN (MOTHER'S DAY)	1992	—	135
CLOCK 8600XS, LOVING PUPPY (MOTHER'S DAY)	1994	—	135
CLOCK 8691JV, FLORAL ON FAVRENE (CONNOISSEUR)	1994	—	320
CLOCK 8691LA, ALARM, IRISES ON MISTY BLUE SATIN	1997	—	81
CLOCK 8691LS, IRISES ON MISTY BLUE SATIN (FAMILY SIGNATURE SERIES, LYNN FENTON)	1998	95	134
CLOCK 8691PF, ALARM, WATERCOLORS ON PINK SATIN	1990	—	82
CLOCK 8691TL, ALARM, TULIPS ON IRIDIZED OPAL	1990	—	71

COMPORTS

COMPORT 1134KA, CELESTE BLUE STRETCH, 5-1/4"	1990	33	43
COMPORT 1269UB, RIBBED, BLUE BURMESE, 7"	1995	—	162
COMPORT 3522DV, FOOTED, SPANISH LACE, VIOLETS IN THE SNOW	1971	—	73
COMPORT 3522SC, SPANISH LACE IN SILVER CREST	1975	—	48
COMPORT 3522YB, FOOTED, SPANISH LACE, KRISTEN FLORAL ON OPAL SATIN, 7-1/2"	1984	—	59
COMPORT 3728CO, FOOTED, CAMEO OPALESCENT HOBNAIL	1995	—	44
COMPORT 3728PO, FOOTED, PLUM OPALESCENT	1959	—	92
COMPORT 3731GO, FOOTED, GREEN OPALESCENT HOBNAIL	1959	—	136
COMPORT 3731MB, FOOTED, BLUE MARBLE HOBNAIL, 10"	1978	—	81
COMPORT 3920GP, FOOTED, GREEN PASTEL HOBNAIL	1954	—	65
COMPORT 4693BO, STEIGEL BLUE OPALESCENT, 6-1/2"	1982	23	38
COMPORT 4854TG, OPALINE	1991	35	43
COMPORT 5554SS, STEIGEL GREEN STRETCH	1996	30	38
COMPORT 7153P2, DOLPHIN HANDLES, PERIWINKLE BLUE SLAG, 5-1/2"	2004	50	54
COMPORT, JEFFERSON 8476IB, COVERED W/EAGLE FINIAL, INDEPENDENCE BLUE (BICENTENNIAL)	1976	—	136
COMPORT, JEFFERSON 8476PR, COVERED W/EAGLE FINIAL, PATRIOT RED (BICENTENNIAL)	1976	—	145
COMPORT, JEFFERSON 8476VW, COVERED W/EAGLE FINIAL, VALLEY FORGE WHITE (BICENTENNIAL)	1976	—	110

CREAMERS

CREAMER 1461BO, BLUE OPALESCENT COIN DOT, 5"	1948	—	59
CREAMER 1461XC, COIN DOT IN PERSIAN BLUE OPALESCENT	1989	38	48
CREAMER 1924AC, AQUA CREST, 5"	1942	—	54
CREAMER 1924PC, PEACH CREST, 5"	1942	—	55
CREAMER 1924RC, ROSE CREST, 5"	1946	—	55
CREAMER 1924SC, SILVER CREST, 5"	1947	—	38
CREAMER 2726XV, BUTTON AND ARCH IN PERSIAN PEARL	1992	23	44
CREAMER 3901TO, TOPAZ OPALESCENT HOBNAIL	1941	—	55

		Original price	Current price
CREAMER AND COVERED SUGAR 3408RN, RED SUNSET CARNIVAL (MADE FOR LEVAY)	1982	$–	$43 Pr
CREAMER AND COVERED SUGAR 4403CA, COLONIAL AMBER THUMBPRINT	1963	–	33 Pr
CREAMER AND COVERED SUGAR 4403CB, COLONIAL BLUE THUMBPRINT	1963	–	56 Pr
CREAMER AND COVERED SUGAR 4403CP, COLONIAL PINK THUMBPRINT	1963	–	67 Pr
CREAMER AND OPEN SUGAR (#3) 3906BO, BLUE OPALESCENT HOBNAIL, STAR-CRIMP	1949	–	103 Pr
CREAMER AND OPEN SUGAR (#3) 3906CR, CRANBERRY OPALESCENT HOBNAIL, STAR-CRIMP	1949	–	218 Pr
CREAMER AND OPEN SUGAR 3900FO, FRENCH OPALESCENT	1942	–	33 Pr
CREAMER AND OPEN SUGAR 3901BO, BLUE OPALESCENT HOBNAIL	1940	–	87 Pr
CREAMER AND OPEN SUGAR 3901CR, CRANBERRY OPALESCENT HOBNAIL	1940	–	104 Pr
CREAMER AND OPEN SUGAR 5700SO, SPRUCE GREEN	1998	–	44 Pr
CREAMER AND OPEN SUGAR 6300CY, FOOTED REGENCY, FLOWER BAND IN CRYSTAL	1982	–	33 Pr
CREAMER AND OPEN SUGAR 8402CK, CHERRIES IN CHOCOLATE GLASS (LEVAY)	1976	–	103 Pr

CRUETS WITH STOPPERS

CRUET 1860BX, FLOWER AND FERN IN SAPPHIRE BLUE OPALESCENT, 7-1/2"	1990	49	104
CRUET 1865XC, FERN OPTIC IN PERSIAN BLUE OPALESCENT	1989	49	105
CRUET 3463TG, CACTUS IN OPALINE	1992	45	93
CRUET 3767MI, OIL (STRAIGHT SIDES), MILK-GLASS HOBNAIL	1956	–	48
CRUET 3863BO, ROUND, BLUE OPALESCENT HOBNAIL	1941	–	146
CRUET 3863CR, ROUND, CRANBERRY OPALESCENT HOBNAIL	1941	–	159
CRUET 3863GP, ROUND, GOLD PEARL HOBNAIL, 6-1/2"	1996	–	93
CRUET 3863RV, ROSE MAGNOLIA HOBNAIL, 6-1/2"	1992	48	93
CRUET 3869BO, OIL (STRAIGHT SIDES), BLUE OPALESCENT HOBNAIL	1942	–	71
CRUET 3869CR, OIL (STRAIGHT SIDES), CRANBERRY OPALESCENT HOBNAIL	1949	–	135
CRUET 3869FO, OIL (STRAIGHT SIDES), FRENCH OPALESCENT HOBNAIL	1942	–	43
CRUET 3869TO, OIL (STRAIGHT SIDES), TOPAZ OPALESCENT HOBNAIL	1942	–	103
CRUET 6462IM, SATINIZED VASA MURRHINA	1983	75	161
CRUET 7701OI, PETITE FLORAL ON BURMESE , 7" (85TH ANNIVERSARY)	1990	85	146
CRUET 7701TE, BLUSH ROSE ON OPALINE, 7"	1996	85	110
CRUET 7863CZ, CRANBERRY PEARL (CONNOISSEUR)	1986	75	163
CRUET CV120RB, DIAMOND OPTIC, ROSES ON BURMESE (MADE FOR QVC)	1996	–	171

EGGS

EGG 1642JM, BLUEBIRD ON CRANBERRY, 5"	1996	95	93
EGG 1642JO, BUTTERFLY FLORAL ON FRENCH OPALESCENT, 5"	1996	75	59
EGG 5030QB, MOTHER OF PEARL, 3 1/2"	1991	49	98
EGG 5031FU, ROSE, 5"	1994	75	98
EGG 5031FV, BLUE, 5"	1994	75	98
EGG 5031Q2, PETAL PINK IRIDESCENT, 5"	1992	65	98
EGG 5031Q3, BANDED FLORAL ON SEA MIST GREEN IRIDESCENT, 5"	1992	65	71
EGG 5031WD, MOTHER OF PEARL, 4-1/2"	1991	59	93
EGG 5031WE, PLUM, 5"	1993	69	93
EGG 5031WJ, OCEAN BLUE, 5"	1993	69	98
EGG 5031YW, FLOWERS ON SPRUCE, 5"	1995	75	98
EGG 5031YX, FLORAL ON GOLD, 5"	1995	75	54
EGG 5076JC, GREEN APPLE EGG, 2-1/2"	2004	23	26
EGG 5076NY, VIOLET EGG, 2-1/2"	2004	23	26
EGG 5076PV, CELESTE BLUE EGG, 2-1/2"	2004	23	26
EGG 51407U, GOLFER SILHOUETTE ON FRENCH OPAL IRIDESCENT	1992	30	54
EGG 51407V, PINK ROSE AND GOLD ON WHITE OPAL	1992	30	54
EGG 51407W, BUTTERFLIES ON BLACK	1992	30	54
EGG 51407X, PINK ROSES ON CUSTARD	1992	30	54
EGG 51407Y, IRIS	1992	30	54
EGG 51407Z, UNICORN ON COBALT	1992	30	48
EGG 5140A1, GOLD	1994	33	48
EGG 5140A2, TULIPS ON SEA MIST	1994	33	48
EGG 5140A3, VIOLETS ON MILK PEARL	1994	33	71
EGG 5140A5, SPRING LANDSCAPE ON OPAL SATIN	1994	33	55
EGG 5140A6, METALLIC FLORAL ON PLUM	1994	33	65
EGG 5140A7, ENAMELED FLOWERS ON BLUE	1994	38	43
EGG 5140C9, PATRIDGE	1991	30	43
EGG 5140D1, FUSCHIA FLORAL ON WHITE	1993	30	43
EGG 5140D2, SCROLLING FLORAL ON GREEN	1993	30	43
EGG 5140D3, GOLD ON RUBY	1993	30	43
EGG 5140D4, SEAGULL ON OCEAN BLUE	1993	30	54
EGG 5140D5, COTTAGE ON WHITE SATIN	1993	30	43
EGG 5140D8, GOLD ON PLUM	1993	$35	$49
EGG 5140E7, SKATER	1991	30	43
EGG 5140N9, POINSETTIAS	1991	30	43
EGG 5140Q9, GOLD DESIGN	1991	30	48
EGG 5140SD, MANGER SCENE ON RUBY, 3-1/2"	1992	30	48
EGG 5140SU, POINSETTIA ON CRYSTAL IRIDESCENT, 3-1/2"	1992	30	48
EGG 5140SW, ANGEL ON GREEN, 3-1/2"	1992	30	37
EGG 5140X9, SHELL	1991	35	43

Dave Fetty handmade Mosaic egg, 2006, 5" h, **$125**.

Price Guide

		Original price	Current price
EGG 5140ZN, SANDCARVED FAVRENE	1993	$35	$48
EGG 51457T, IRIS ON SEA MIST GREEN	1997	45	54
EGG 51457U, CARNATION ON BLUE IRIDESCENT	1997	45	54
EGG 51457W, LIGHTHOUSE ON WHITE OPAL	1997	45	48
EGG 51457X, SANDBLASTED ROSES ON CUSTARD	1997	39	53
EGG 51457Y, ROOSTER ON SPRUCE	1997	39	58
EGG 5145CH, HOLLY BERRIES ON GOLD, 3-1/2"	1996	38	49
EGG 5145F1, HONEYSUCKLE ON DUSTY ROSE	1996	38	55
EGG 5145F2, HUMMINGBIRD ON CRYSTAL IRIDIZED	1996	38	48
EGG 5145F3, BUTTERFLIES	1996	38	44
EGG 5145F4, MORNING GLORIES	1996	38	49
EGG 5145F5, LAKE SCENE ON IVORY SATIN	1996	38	43
EGG 5145F6, JEWELED	1996	38	48
EGG 5145F7, FISH ON SPRUCE GREEN	1996	38	48
EGG 5145QP, GOLDEN PATRIDGE ON SPRUCE, 3-1/2"	1996	35	48
EGG 5145QV, MOONLIT MEADOW ON RUBY, 3-1/2"	1996	40	75
EGG 5145RG, MARY GREGORY ON RUBY	1995	38	43
EGG 5145S2, SCROLLS ON BLACK	1995	33	43
EGG 5145S3, SCENIC ON WHITE OPAL IRIDESCENT	1995	33	43
EGG 5145S4, FLORAL ON WHITE	1995	33	43
EGG 5145S5, FLORAL ON GREEN	1995	33	43
EGG 5145S6, FLORAL ON BLUE	1995	33	43
EGG 5145S7, FLORAL ON GOLD	1995	33	49
EGG 5145S8, HUMMINGBIRD ON DUSTY ROSE	1995	35	59
EGG 5145TH, BOW & HOLLY ON IVORY, 3-1/2"	1996	45	48
EGG 5145TP, CHICKADEE ON GOLD, 3-1/2"	1995	35	43
EGG 5145VG, MAGNOLIA ON GOLD, 3-1/2"	1994	35	59
EGG 5145VK, PATRIDGE ON RUBY, 3-1/2"	1994	35	54
EGG 5146D1, FLORAL ON MISTY BLUE	1998	45	54
EGG 5146D2, FLORAL CHAMPAGNE	1998	45	72
EGG 5146D3, BERRIES ON ROSALENE	1998	55	54
EGG 5146D4, CLIPPER SHIP ON COBALT	1998	45	54
EGG 5146D5, BOUNTIFUL HARVEST ON SEA MIST	1998	45	65
EGG 5146D6, DRAGONFLY ON FRENCH OPALESCENT	1998	49	59
EGG 5146D7, FLORAL ON RUBY	1998	49	110
EGG 5146T5, RUBY CARNIVAL, 3-3/4"	2004	50	54
EGG 5146UL, BUTTERFLY ON BLACK, 5-3/4"	2004	50	54
EGG 5146VC, LOTUS MIST BURMESE, 5-3/4"	2004	50	54

EPERGNES

		Original price	Current price
EPERGNE 1522IC, 1-HORN, 4-PIECE (INCLUDES BASE), IVORY CREST	1940	—	190
EPERGNE 1948BO, 3-HORN, BLUE OPALESCENT WITH SILVER CREST, 12" BOWL	1948	—	245
EPERGNE 1948FO, 3-HORN, FRENCH OPALESCENT WITH AQUA CREST, 12" BOWL	1948	—	218
EPERGNE 3701PO, 3-HORN, DEEP PLUM OPALESCENT HOBNAIL (MADE FOR LEVAY)	1984	—	190
EPERGNE 3701RV, 3-HORN, ROSE MAGNOLIA OPALESCENT HOBNAIL, 10" BOWL	1993	99	163
EPERGNE 3701XV, 3-HORN, PERSIAN PEARL HOBNAIL	1992	99	135
EPERGNE 3800MI, 4-HORN, MILK-GLASS HOBNAIL	1954	—	163
EPERGNE 3801BO, 3-HORN, MINIATURE, BLUE OPALESCENT HOBNAIL	1949	—	158
EPERGNE 3801FO, 3-HORN, MINIATURE, FRENCH OPALESCENT HOBNAIL	1949	—	93
EPERGNE 3801GO, 3-HORN, MINIATURE, GREEN OPALESCENT HOBNAIL	1959	—	192
EPERGNE 3801GP, 3-HORN, MINIATURE, GREEN PASTEL HOBNAIL	1954	—	136
EPERGNE 3801MI, 3-HORN, MINIATURE, MILK-GLASS HOBNAIL	1950	—	59
EPERGNE 3801PO, 3-HORN, MINIATURE, PLUM OPALESCENT	1959	—	274
EPERGNE 3801XV, 3-HORN, MINIATURE, PERSIAN PEARL HOBNAIL	1993	50	136
EPERGNE 4401CA, 3-HORN, COLONIAL AMBER	1968	—	138
EPERGNE 4401CB, 3-HORN, COLONIAL BLUE	1968	—	191
EPERGNE 4801BO, 3-HORN, DIAMOND LACE, BLUE OPALESCENT, 10" BOWL	1948	—	214
EPERGNE 4801BX, 3-HORN, DIAMOND LACE, SAPPHIRE BLUE OPALESCENT	1990	75	191
EPERGNE 4801FO, 3-HORN, DIAMOND LACE, FRENCH OPALESCENT, 10" BOWL	1948	—	163
EPERGNE 4801GP, 3-HORN, DIAMOND LACE, GOLD PEARL	1992	99	191
EPERGNE 4801OI, 3-HORN, DIAMOND LACE, TEAL MARIGOLD	1989	—	245
EPERGNE 4801TO, 3-HORN, DIAMOND LACE, TOPAZ OPALESCENT (MADE FOR LEVAY)	1988	75	134
EPERGNE 4801XC, 3-HORN, DIAMOND LACE, PERSIAN BLUE OPALESCENT	1989	75	109
EPERGNE 4802SS, 1-HORN, DIAMOND LACE, STIEGEL GREEN STRETCH	1994	$65	$71
EPERGNE 4806TG, 1-HORN, MINIATURE, OPALINE, 4-1/2"	1996	35	245
EPERGNE 4808TG, 3-HORN, DIAMOND LACE, OPALINE, 10"	1996	115	595
EPERGNE 4809BR, 3-HORN, DIAMOND LACE, BURMESE	1986	—	191
EPERGNE 4809GO, 3-HORN, DIAMOND LACE, GREEN OPALESCENT (CONNOISSEUR)	1985	—	402
EPERGNE 6501RL, 1-HORN, RUBY AMBERINA STRETCH	2004	125	135
EPERGNE 6509VF, 1-HORN , BERRY & BUTTERFLY ON LOTUS BURMESE	2000	150	181
EPERGNE 7175TS, 1-HORN, TOPAZ OPALESCENT SWIRL	2004	110	120
EPERGNE 7200PC, 1-HORN, 3-PIECE, PEACH CREST	1956	—	163
EPERGNE 7202PC, 1-HORN, 2-PIECE, HIGH FOOTED BASE, PEACH CREST	1955		136

		Original price	Current price
EPERGNE 7305SC, 4-HORN, SILVER CREST	1956	$–	$180
EPERGNE 7308SC, 3-HORN, SILVER CREST	1956	–	146
EPERGNE 7601KA, 4-HORN, CELESTE BLUE STRETCH, 13" (90TH ANNIVERSARY)	1995	185	355
EPERGNE 7601SS, 4-HORN, STIEGEL GREEN STRETCH	1994	175	540
EPERGNE 7605BR, 4-HORN, BURMESE SATIN (CONNOISSEUR)	1983	200	545
EPERGNE 7605RE, 4-HORN, ROSALENE (CONNOISSEUR)	1989	250	245
EPERGNE A3701UO, 3-HORN, PINK OPALESCENT HOBNAIL, 10" (COLLECTORS EXTRAVAGANZA)	1985	55	163
EPERGNE A3801UO, MINIATURE, 3-HORN, PINK OPALESCENT HOBNAIL	1988	48	82

FAIRY LIGHTS

		Original price	Current price
FAIRY LIGHT 1505DW, MEADOW FLOWERS ON CRANBERRY	1997	79	191
FAIRY LIGHT 1610N4, 3-PIECE, COLONIAL SCROLL ON ROYAL PURPLE	1998	175	218
FAIRY LIGHT 1803XC, PERSIAN BLUE OPALESCENT	1989	85	163
FAIRY LIGHT 2040TP, HYDRANGEAS ON TOPAZ OPALESCENT	1997	125	166
FAIRY LIGHT 2903CR, HEART OPTIC IN CRANBERRY OPALESCENT	1986	135	171
FAIRY LIGHT 3608XC, PERSIAN BLUE OPALESCENT	1989	16	65
FAIRY LIGHT 4905CR, HEART OPTIC IN CRANBERRY	1998	65	104
FAIRY LIGHT 5405JQ, PANSY MORNING ON APPLE GREEN STRETCH	2004	55	59
FAIRY LIGHT 5980HB, LILY POND, APPLE GREEN STRETCH WITH COBALT BASE	2004	70	75
FAIRY LIGHT 5980YC, RAMBLING ROSES ON SUNSET IRIDIZED	2004	70	75
FAIRY LIGHT 73000C, COUNTRY CHRISTMAS	1982	35	65
FAIRY LIGHT 7300AI, ANTICIPATION	1987	35	64
FAIRY LIGHT 7300BC, CARDINAL IN THE CHURCHYARD (BIRDS OF WINTER)	1987	30	71
FAIRY LIGHT 7300BD, A CHICKADEE BALLET (BIRDS OF WINTER)	1988	30	71
FAIRY LIGHT 7300BL, DOWNY WOODPECKER - CHISELED SONG (BIRDS OF WINTER)	1990	30	71
FAIRY LIGHT 7300BS, TULIP DELIGHT ON ROSEMILK OPALESCENT, WITH STAND	2004	85	93
FAIRY LIGHT 7300CV, CHRISTMAS MORN	1978	25	70
FAIRY LIGHT 7300GE, EXPECTATION	1984	38	65
FAIRY LIGHT 7300GH, GOING HOME	1980	33	71
FAIRY LIGHT 7300HD, SLEIGH RIDE	1990	39	65
FAIRY LIGHT 7300HJ, CHRISTMAS EVE	1991	39	65
FAIRY LIGHT 7300HQ, FAMILY TRADITIONS	1992	39	65
FAIRY LIGHT 7300HT, FAMILY HOLIDAY	1993	39	65
FAIRY LIGHT 7300NB, A BLUEBIRD IN SNOWFALL (BIRDS OF WINTER)	1990	30	71
FAIRY LIGHT 7300SN, STAR OF WONDER	1996	48	65
FAIRY LIGHT 7300UQ, SWEET NECTAR, VIOLET ON MILK-GLASS	2004	63	70
FAIRY LIGHT 7300VS, SILENT NIGHT	1994	45	65
FAIRY LIGHT 7300VT, OUR HOME IS BLESSED	1995	45	65
FAIRY LIGHT 7300WP, HEART'S DESIRE ON CUSTARD SATIN	1985	38	65
FAIRY LIGHT 7300XA, CLYDESDALES (MADE FOR BUDWEISER)	1983	10	155
FAIRY LIGHT 7501TA, PERIWINKLE ON BLUE BURMESE (SHOWCASE DEALER EXCLUSIVE)	1999	–	325
FAIRY LIGHT 8405YZ, EASTER	1995	35	65
FAIRY LIGHT 8406BR, PRESSED BURMESE	1986	–	135
FAIRY LIGHT 9401N7, NATIVITY SCENE	1996	49	55
FAIRY LIGHT, SANTA 5080RU, RUBY	2003	40	48
FAIRY LIGHT, SANTA 5080XH, NATURAL FACE ON OPAL MIST	2003	60	90
FAIRY LIGHT, SNOWMAN 5080WX, "MELTON" (LET IT SNOW), 7-1/2"	2003	75	92

FIGURINES

		Original price	Current price
ANGEL 5014S3, INSPIRATIONS, STAR LIGHT, STAR BRIGHT ON COBALT	2004	43	49
ANGEL, GUARDIAN 5333DN, ROSE PEARL	1992	–	38
ANGEL, RADIANT 5542QB	1996	–	93
ANGEL, RADIANT 5542TA	1995	–	104
APPLE 5019OD, DUSTY ROSE OVERLAY	1984	$–	55
APPLE 5019OF, FEDERAL BLUE	1984	–	55
BALLERINA 5270PQ, CHAMPAGNE SATIN	1997	–	83
BALLERINA 5270WA, "NATALIE," ROSEBUDS ON ROSALENE	1998	–	135
BEAR, DAYDREAMING 5239EW, CRYSTAL W/RED HEART EYES	1989	–	59
BEAR, DAYDREAMING 5239NS, HAPPY SANTA	1990	–	71
BEAR, DAYDREAMING 5239NS, NATURAL SERIES	1985	–	81
BEAR, DAYDREAMING 5293BY, CRYSTAL W/RED HEART ON FANNY	1989	–	59
BEAR, PANDA RECLINING 5233PJ (NATURAL SERIES)	1985	–	110
BEAR, POLAR 5109FE, WOODLAND FROST	1999	–	48
BEAR, POLAR 5109KG, GOLDEN FLAX ON COBALT	1993	–	54
BEAR, POLAR 5109R1, BUTTERCUPS AND BERRIES ON RED CARNIVAL	1995	–	48
BEAR, POLAR 5109VC, GOLDEN PINE CONES	1994	–	49
BEAR, POLAR 5109VI, ICICLE KINGDOM (WITH RED VELVET RIBBON AND GOLD STAR)	2000	–	48
BEAR, POLAR 5109WX, "BLIZZARD" (LET IT SNOW)	2003	34	48
BEAR, RECLINING 5233DS, PRIMROSE ON IRIDIZED OPAL	1994	–	54
BEAR, RECLINING 5233FH, HEARTS & FLOWERS ON IRIDIZED OPAL	1988	–	55
BEAR, RECLINING 5233HL, HOLLY BERRY	1988	–	49
BEAR, RECLINING 5233NS, HAPPY SANTA	1990	–	59
BEAR, RECLINING 5233NS, NATURAL SERIES	1985	–	70

Leaves on Burmese fairy lamp, 1970s, 6" h, **$200+**.

237

Chocolate Cat, available exclusively to dealers, 2005, signed by George Fenton, 3-1/2" l, **$35+**.

		Original price	Current price
BEAR, RECLINING 5233RU, RUBY	1985	$—	$44
BEAR, SITTING 5151CC, COUNTRY CRANBERRY	1994	—	49
BEAR, SITTING 5151CY, CRYSTAL	1984	—	33
BEAR, SITTING 5151DX, TRELLIS ON FRENCH OPALESCENT	1995	—	43
BEAR, SITTING 5151ES, ELIZABETH ON MILK-GLASS	1990	—	48
BEAR, SITTING 5151EW, THISTLES & BOWS	1986	—	48
BEAR, SITTING 5151FA, FROSTED ASTERS ON BLUE SATIN	1984	—	54
BEAR, SITTING 5151FH, HEARTS & FLOWERS	1990	—	48
BEAR, SITTING 5151FO, FRENCH OPALESCENT (UNDECORATED)	1986	—	38
BEAR, SITTING 5151FS, PROVINCIAL BOUQUET	1987	—	49
BEAR, SITTING 5151FX, CRYSTAL W/RED HEART ON FOOT	1989	—	59
BEAR, SITTING 5151JB, IRISH TREASURES ON MILK-GLASS (WITH SWAROVSKI CRYSTALS)	2004	30	32
BEAR, SITTING 5151KP, COPPER ROSES ON BLACK	1990	—	48
BEAR, SITTING 5151LS, IRISES ON MISTY BLUE SATIN	1997	—	55
BEAR, SITTING 5151NC, "SCHWARTZ" HAND-PAINTED (OPERATION DESERT STORM)	1991	—	81
BEAR, SITTING 5151NK, COBALT MARIGOLD	1984	—	55
BEAR, SITTING 5151NS, "HAPPY SANTA"	1990	—	48
BEAR, SITTING 5151PJ, LILACS ON MILK-GLASS	1993	—	59
BEAR, SITTING 5151PT, PEARLY SENTIMENTS (WITH PINK PORCELAIN ROSE)	1988	—	48
BEAR, SITTING 5151PU, VIOLAS ON PETAL PINK	1994	—	48
BEAR, SITTING 5151PX, PLUM CARNIVAL	1998	—	48
BEAR, SITTING 5151RK, BERRIES & BLOSSOMS ON OPAL SATIN	1984	—	82
BEAR, SITTING 5151RN, RED CARNIVAL	1991	—	49
BEAR, SITTING 5151RX, RUBY SLAG (MADE FOR LEVAY)	1985	—	135
BEAR, SITTING 5151SR, SALEM BLUE	1990	—	43
BEAR, SITTING 5151UB, BLUE BURMESE	1983	—	135
BEAR, SITTING 5151VC, PASTEL VIOLETS ON CUSTARD	1988	—	54
BEAR, SITTING 5151XP, FLORAL ON VIOLET SATIN	1999	—	48
BEAR, SITTING 5151YB, KRISTEN'S FLORAL	1995	—	49
BIRD 5115HL, HOLLY BERRY	1988	—	27
BIRD 5115NG, ROSEMILK	2004	20	22
BIRD 5163AO, AUTUMN GOLD	1993	—	32
BIRD 5163BD, BLUE DOGWOOD ON CAMEO SATIN	1980	—	48
BIRD 5163EG, ROSE GARDEN ON OPAL SATIN	1995	—	59
BIRD 5163HV, GILDED STAR FLOWERS ON IRIDIZED OPAL	1993	—	48
BIRD 5163JA, JADE GREEN	1980	—	48
BIRD 5163LS, IRISES ON MISTY BLUE SATIN	1997	—	48
BIRD 5163NO, BIRD, RED BREAST (NATURAL SERIES)	1985	—	54
BIRD 5163PJ, LILACS ON MILK-GLASS	1993	—	48
BIRD 5163SF, STRAWBERRIES ON FRENCH OPALESCENT	1981	—	49
BIRD 5163TL, TULIPS ON IRIDIZED OPAL	1990	—	43
BIRD 5163VC, GOLDEN PINE CONES	1994	—	54
BIRD, BLUE JAY 5245L5, MISTY BLUE SATIN	1998	—	48
BIRD, CARDINAL 5245RU, RUBY	1997	20	38
BIRD, HAPPINESS 5197BA, BLUE SATIN	1978	—	49
BIRD, HAPPINESS 5197CA, COLONIAL AMBER	1987	—	38
BIRD, HAPPINESS 5197CD, DAISIES ON CAMEO SATIN	1980	—	49
BIRD, HAPPINESS 5197CW, CARDINAL IN WINTER	1977	—	55
BIRD, HAPPINESS 5197DK, DUSTY ROSE	1990	—	38
BIRD, HAPPINESS 5197FH, HEARTS & FLOWERS	1988	—	48
BIRD, HAPPINESS 5197GG, FLORAL INTERLUDE ON SEA GREEN SATIN	1998	—	54
BIRD, HAPPINESS 5197JE, BUTTERFLY ON GOLD IRIDESCENT (MILLENNIUM COLLECTION)	1999	—	71
BIRD, HAPPINESS 5197KP, COPPER ROSES ON BLACK	1989	—	54
BIRD, HAPPINESS 5197LX, LILAC	1990	—	48
BIRD, HAPPINESS 5197PS, PURPLE SLAG (MADE FOR LEVAY)	1981	—	55
BIRD, HAPPINESS 5197PT, PEARLY SENTIMENTS (W/PINK PORCELAIN ROSE)	1989	—	43
BIRD, HAPPINESS 5197RW, ROMANCE ON SPECKLED IRIDIZED IVORY	1997	—	54
BIRD, HAPPINESS 5197SR, SALEM BLUE	1990	—	43
BIRD, HAPPINESS 5197TP, HYDRANGEAS ON TOPAZ OPALESCENT	1997	35	59
BIRD, HAPPINESS 5197UO, PEACHES 'N CREAM	1987	—	48
BIRD, VASA MURRHINA, VARIOUS COLORS (STOWASSER)	1980	—	71 Ea
BUNNY 5162BD, BLUE DOGWOOD ON CAMEO SATIN	1980	—	59
BUNNY 5162BJ, PEKIN BLUE	1980	—	48
BUNNY 5162CD, DAISIES ON CUSTARD	1978	—	48
BUNNY 5162CY, CRYSTAL	1984	—	38
BUNNY 5162DR, CHOCOLATE ROSES ON CAMEO SATIN	1982	—	59
BUNNY 5162DV, VIOLETS IN THE SNOW	1978	—	82
BUNNY 5162JA, JADE GREEN	1980	—	55
BUNNY 5162JX, SPRING FINERY (FOLK ART COLLECTION)	2004	30	32
BUNNY 5162LN, LAVENDER SATIN	1977	—	71
BUNNY 5162LS, LIME SHERBET	1978	—	43
BUNNY 5162NS, NATURAL COLOR, BROWN or GRAY	1985	—	59
BUNNY 5162PS, PURPLE SLAG (MADE FOR LEVAY)	1981	—	71

		Original price $–	Current price $
BUNNY 5162RE, ROSALENE	1978	–	81
BUNNY 5162RX, RUBY SLAG (MADE FOR LEVAY)	1985	–	80
BUNNY 5162TL, TULIPS ON IRIDIZED OPAL	1980	–	48
BUNNY 5262/7S, WILLOW GREEN	2003	–	22
BUNNY 5262O5, VIOLET SATIN	2004	15	17
BUNNY 5262C3, ROSE	2003	–	22
BUNNY 5262C3, ROSEMILK SATIN	2004	15	17
BUNNY 5262J7, GREEN APPLE SATIN	2004	15	17
BUNNY, LOP-EARED 5283JX, SPRING FINERY (FOLK ART)	2004	30	32
BUNNY, LOP-EARED 5293EI, ROSE	2003	–	43
BUNNY, LOP-EARED 5293OI, VIOLET	2003	–	43
BUNNY, LOP-EARED 5293QR, LET'S BEE BURMESE	2003	39	54
BUTTERFLY ON STAND, WINGS OPEN 5171DK, DUSTY ROSE	1986	–	48
BUTTERFLY ON STAND, WINGS OPEN 5171LE, SEA MIST GREEN	1997	–	48
BUTTERFLY ON STAND, WINGS OPEN 5171PW, PERIWINKLE BLUE	1986	–	49
BUTTERFLY ON STAND, WINGS OPEN 5171TO, TOPAZ OPALESCENT	1988	15	48
BUTTERFLY ON STAND, WINGS OPEN 5171VR, VELVA ROSE	1980	–	38
BUTTERFLY, STYLIZED, WINGS UP 5271AA, AQUAMARINE	1999	–	54
BUTTERFLY, STYLIZED, WINGS UP 5271NX, VIOLETS ON ROSALENE	1999	–	54
BUTTERFLY, WINGS OPEN 5170CA, COLONIAL AMBER	1970	–	27
BUTTERFLY, WINGS OPEN 5170CB, COLONIAL BLUE	1970	–	27
BUTTERFLY, WINGS OPEN 5170CN, ORIGINAL AMETHYST CARNIVAL	1970	–	38
BUTTERFLY, WINGS OPEN 5170HG, HERITAGE GREEN	1970	–	27
BUTTERFLY, WINGS OPEN 5170OR, COLONIAL ORANGE	1970	–	49
BUTTERFLY, WINGS OPEN 5170RN, RUBY CARNIVAL (F.A.G.C.A.)	1989	–	27
CAT 5165AF, ANTIQUE ROSE ION IRIDIZED OPAL	1990	–	59
CAT 5165DC, DOGWOOD ON CAMEO SATIN	1980	–	54
CAT 5165DV, VIOLETS IN THE SNOW	1979	–	59
CAT 5165EG, ROSE GARDEN ON OPAL SATIN	1995	–	59
CAT 5165ES, ELIZABETH ON MILK-GLASS	1990	–	65
CAT 5165F5, PAINTED FLOWERS ON BURMESE	2002	37	53
CAT 5165FH, HEARTS & FLOWERS ON IRIDIZED OPAL	1990	–	54
CAT 5165GG, FLORAL INTERLUDE ON SEA GREEN SATIN	1998	–	54
CAT 5165HL, HOLLY BERRY	1988	–	93
CAT 5165IK, TRUE BLUE (IRIDIZED SLAG)	1986	–	48
CAT 5165JA, JADE GREEN	1980	–	65
CAT 5165KP, COPPER ROSES ON BLACK	1990	–	82
CAT 5165LX, LILAC	1990	–	43
CAT 5165NG, GRAY (NATURAL SERIES)	1985	–	54
CAT 5165OI, TEAL MARIGOLD CARNIVAL	1989	–	59
CAT 5165PF, WATERCOLORS ON PINK SATIN	1990	–	76
CAT 5165RK, BERRIES & BLOSSOMS	1984	–	54
CAT 5165SF, STRAWBERRIES ON FRENCH OPALESCENT	1981	–	48
CAT 5165SR, SALEM BLUE	1990	–	54
CAT 5165TO, TOPAZ OPALESCENT (MADE FOR ROSSO)	1991	–	54
CAT 5165TT, TULIPS ON TWILIGHT BLUE	1993	–	54
CAT 5165WS, WHITE SATIN	1971	–	59
CAT C5165EQ, BLUE FLORAL ON SHELL PINK (MADE FOR QVC)	1988	–	190
CAT, ALLEY 5177BN, ELECTRIC BLUE CARNIVAL (MADE FOR LEVAY)	1980	–	163
CAT, ALLEY 5177DK, DUSTY ROSE (MADE IN REGULAR AND SATIN GLASS) (SOLD THROUGH FENTON GIFT SHOP)	1992	–	191
CAT, ALLEY 5177OI, TEAL MARIGOLD	1988	–	103
CAT, ALLEY 5177P2, PERIWINKLE BLUE SLAG	2004	60	65
CAT, ALLEY 5177PS, PURPLE SLAG (MADE FOR LEVAY)	1981	–	180
CAT, ALLEY 5177RE, ROSALENE (MADE IN REGULAR AND SATIN FOR F.A.G.C.A.)	1997	–	190
CAT, ALLEY 5177RN, RED CARNIVAL (MADE FOR SINGLETON BAILEY)	1990	–	162
CAT, ALLEY 5177RX, RUBY SLAG (MADE FOR LEVAY)	1985	–	490
CAT, ALLEY 5177TS, TOPAZ SATIN (F.A.G.C.A.)	1997	–	162
CAT, ALLEY C5177BR, BURMESE SATIN (MADE FOR QVC)	1996	–	135
CAT, ALLEY Q5177DN, DUSTY ROSE CARNIVAL (MADE FOR QVC)	1992	–	104
CAT, CURIOUS 5193DW, VINING HEARTS ON ROSE PEARL	1993	–	54
CAT, CURIOUS 5243KN, FLORAL ON COBALT (MADE FOR QVC)	2000	–	54
CAT, CURIOUS 5243KP, COPPER ROSES ON BLACK (SOLD THROUGH FENTON GIFT SHOP)	1990	–	59
CAT, CURIOUS 5243P2, PERIWINKLE BLUE SLAG	2004	20	22
CAT, CURIOUS 5243SR, SALEM BLUE	1990	–	48
CAT, GROOMING 5074AV, LEAVES ON AUTUMN GOLD	2003	34	48
CAT, GROOMING 5074DC, "GLAMOUR QUEEN" (WITH SWAROVSKI CRYSTAL)	2004	30	33
CAT, HAPPY 5277BR, BURMESE (MADE IN BOTH SATIN AND GLOSS)	1966	–	103
CAT, HAPPY 5277RU, RUBY	1999	–	71
CAT, HAPPY 5277T2, TWILIGHT BLUE IRIDIZED	1996	–	72
CAT, HAPPY 5277T2, TWILIGHT BLUE SATIN	1994	–	72
CAT, SCAREDY 5291Y4, "MIDNIGHT" (HALLOWEEN)	2003	30	43
CAT, STYLIZED 5065EG, ROSE GARDEN ON OPAL SATIN	1999	–	71

Price Guide

		Original price $—	Current price $81
CAT, STYLIZED 5065IA, BLACK PANTHER (JUNGLE CATS)	2001		81
CAT, STYLIZED 5065IC, LEOPARD (JUNGLE CATS)	2001	—	81
CAT, STYLIZED 5065IU, TIGER (JUNGLE CATS)	2001	—	81
CAT, STYLIZED 5065JX, TWINING BERRIES	1999	—	54
CAT, STYLIZED 5065OE, VIOLET (MADE IN BOTH SATIN AND IRIDIZED)	1999	—	54
CAT, STYLIZED 5065QZ, HIBISCUS ON BLUE BURMESE	2000	—	71
CAT, STYLIZED 5065S3, HAND-PAINTED BURMESE (CATALOG EXCLUSIVE)	1999	—	71
CAT, STYLIZED 5065SB, HAND-PAINTED SPRUCE GREEN	1999	—	54
CAT, STYLIZED 5065UC, DAISY LANE ON CRYSTAL	2001	—	54
CLOWN 5111CW, FOOLS IN LOVE ON IRIDESCENT OPAL	1991	—	76
CLOWN 5111NE, BLUE CLOWN ON OPAL SATIN	1985	—	76
CLOWN 5111NL, BLUE CLOWN ON OPAL SATIN	1985	—	48
CLOWN BUST 5216HZ, WITH HEAD ON HAND, PINK PEARL	1991	—	59
CLOWN BUST 5217CW, WITH TOP HAT, FOOLS IN LOVE ON IRIDESCENT OPAL	1991	—	48
CLOWN BUST 5217HZ, WITH TOP HAT, PINK PEARL	1991	—	54
CLOWN BUST 5218FH, WITH HANDS UP, HEARTS & FLOWERS	1991	—	48
CLOWN BUST 5218HZ, WITH HANDS UP, PINK PEARL	1991	—	59
CLOWN BUST 5219HZ, WITH JESTER'S HAT, PINK PEARL	1991	—	81
COLT BALKING, ROSALENE (HEISEY MOLD FOR HEISEY COLLECTORS OF AMERICA)	1990	—	93
COLT KICKING, ROSALENE (HEISEY MOLD FOR HEISEY COLLECTORS OF AMERICA)	1990	—	103
COLT STANDING, ROSALENE (HEISEY MOLD FOR HEISEY COLLECTORS OF AMERICA)	1990	—	82
DOLL, "ALMOST HEAVEN" BLUE SLAG (SOLD THROUGH FENTON GIFT SHOP)	1985	—	70
DOLL, BRIDESMAID 5228EG, ROSE GARDEN ON OPAL SATIN	1995	—	81
DOLL, BRIDESMAID 5228ON, ROSES ON IRIDIZED FRENCH OPALESCENT (ROMANCE)	1997	—	71
DOLL, BRIDESMAID 5228US, FLORAL ON SPRUCE CARNIVAL	1999	—	59
DOLL, BRIDESMAID 5228WB, FLORAL DRESS W/BLUE TRIM	1996	—	76
DOLL, BRIDESMAID 5228YB, KRISTEN'S FLORAL	1996	—	76
DOLL, LITTLE SISTER 5328XP, FLORAL ON VIOLET SATIN (SHOWCASE DEALER'S EXCLUSIVE)	1999	—	54
DOLPHIN 5137AA, AQUAMARINE	1999	—	65
DONKEY 5125BA, BLUE SATIN	1972	—	135
DONKEY 5125BR, BURMESE	1986	—	218
DONKEY 5125DC, DAISIES ON CUSTARD	1978	—	163
DONKEY 5125RE, ROSALENE	1978	—	171
DONKEY 5125VE, CRYSTAL VELVET	1977	—	81
DONKEY 5125WS, WHITE SATIN	1972	—	110
DONKEY CART 5124BA, BLUE SATIN	1972	—	110
DONKEY CART 5124BR, BURMESE	1986	—	190
DONKEY CART 5124RE, ROSALENE	1978	—	136
DONKEY CART 5124VE, CRYSTAL VELVET	1977	—	71
DONKEY CART 5124WS, WHITE SATIN	1972	—	136
DUCK 5147AZ, MARTHA'S ROSE ON FRENCH OPALESCENT	1999	—	49
DUCK 5147FA, FROSTED ASTERS ON BLUE SATIN	1984	—	54
DUCK 5147IK, TRUE BLUE FRIENDS (IRIDIZED BLUE SLAG)	1986	—	59
DUCK 5147ND, CANVASBACK DUCK (NATURAL SERIES)	1985	—	54
DUCK 5147NM, DRAKE MALLARD (NATURAL SERIES)	1985	—	54
DUCK 5147NQ, BLUE WING TEAL (NATURAL SERIES)	1985	—	54
DUCK 5147RC, ROSES ON CUSTARD	1978	—	59
DUCK 5147RK, BERRIES & BLOSSOMS ON OPAL SATIN	1984	—	72
DUCKLING 5169BA, BLUE SATIN	1978	—	49
DUCKLING 5169BL, BLUE ROSES ON BLUE SATIN	1981	—	55
DUCKLING 5169CD, DAISIES ON CAMEO SATIN	1981	—	55
DUCKLING 5169JC, DECORATED GREEN APPLE	2004	30	32
DUCKLING 5169PY, PINK BLOSSOMS ON CUSTARD	1981	—	48
DUCKLING 5169RC, ROSES ON CUSTARD	1978	—	59
DUCKLING 5169TL, TULIPS ON IRIDIZED OPAL	1990	—	43
DUCKLING, MINI 5212/2A, SEA MIST SLAG	1999	—	22
DUCKLING, MINI 5212/8A, PLUM SLAG	1999	—	22
DUCKLING, MINI 5212PE, SHELL PINK	1991	—	22
EAGLE PAPERWEIGHT 8470IB, INDEPENDENCE BLUE CARNIVAL	1976	—	49
EAGLE PAPERWEIGHT 8470PR, PATRIOT RED	1976	—	49
ELEPHANT 5136DX, TRELLIS ON FRENCH OPALESCENT	1995	—	48
ELEPHANT 5136LE, SEA MIST GREEN	1996	—	48
ELEPHANT 5136LH, BELLFLOWERS ON MISTY BLUE SATIN	1999	—	48
ELEPHANT 5158P2, PERIWINKLE BLUE SLAG	2004	20	22
ELEPHANT 5158RK, BERRIES & BLOSSOMS ON OPAL SATIN	1984	—	69
ELEPHANT, ASSORTED VASA MURRHINA (STOWASSER)	1984	—	53 Ea
ELEPHANT, TRUNK DOWN 5108BA, BLUE SATIN	1972	—	181
ELEPHANT, TRUNK DOWN 5108WS, WHITE SATIN	1972	—	181
FAWN 5160BQ, WINTERBERRY	1987	—	69
FAWN 5160BR, BURMESE	1986	—	103
FAWN 5160CY, CRYSTAL	1986	—	37
FAWN 5160EW, THISTLES & BOWS	1984	—	58
FAWN 5160FA, FROSTED ASTERS ON BLUE SATIN	1984	—	81

	Year	Original price	Current price
FAWN 5160IK, TRUE BLUE FRIENDS (IRIDIZED BLUE SLAG)	1986	$–	$69
FAWN 5160LB, AUTUMN LEAVES ON OPAL SATIN	1985	–	69
FAWN 5160NF, FAWN (NATURAL SERIES)	1985	–	81
FAWN 5160NP, POINSETTIA ON MILK-GLASS	1997	–	48
FAWN 5160PT, PEARLY SENTIMENTS (WITH PINK PORCELAIN ROSE)	1988	–	43
FAWN 5160PZ, PEACH BLOOMS ON OPAL SATIN	1985	–	69
FAWN 5160RU, RUBY	1985	–	53
FAWN 5160RX, RUBY SLAG (MADE FOR LEVAY)	1985	–	103
FAWN 5160SE, MAGNOLIA & BERRY ON SPRUCE	1997	27	48
FAWN 5160UB, BLUE BURMESE	1984	–	131
FAWN 5160VE, CRYSTAL VELVET	1985	–	48
FAWN 5160VJ, VICTORIAN ROSES	1987	–	53
FAWN 5160Y3, GILDED HAND-PAINTING ON DARK GREEN (MEDALLION COLLECTION)	1996	40	58
FILLY, HEAD FORWARD, ROSALENE (HEISEY MOLD FOR HEISEY COLLECTORS OF AMERICA)	1991	–	81
FISH PAPERWEIGHT 5139CN, ORIGINAL (AMETHYST) CARNIVAL	1970	–	92
FISH PAPERWEIGHT 5193BA, BLUE SATIN	1990	–	132
FISH PAPERWEIGHT 5193RE, ROSALENE	1991	–	103
FISH PAPERWEIGHT 5193WS, WHITE SATIN	1991	–	81
FOX 5226AW, AUTUMN LEAVES ON BLACK	1994	–	69
FOX 5226NK, COBALT MARIGOLD	1987	–	58
FOX 5226RN, RED CARNIVAL	1994	–	58
FOX 5226Y6, GILDED DECORATION ON BLACK	1996	–	81
FROG 5166CD, DAISIES ON CAMEO	1980	–	59
FROG 5166DV, VIOLETS IN THE SNOW	1979	–	181
FROG 5166LS, LIME SHERBET	1979	–	69
FROG 5166RE, ROSALENE	1976	–	81
FROG 5166TO, TOPAZ OPALESCENT (MADE FOR ROSSO)	1998	–	53
FROG 5274I3, WILLOW GREEN	2003	–	27
FROG 5274JD, GREEN APPLE	2004	20	22
FROG 5274UI, SPOTS AND FLOWERS ON IRIDIZED CRYSTAL	2003	–	27
FROG 5274XJ, FLORAL ON BLUE	2003	–	27
GAZELLE, ROSALENE (HEISEY MOLD FOR HEISEY COLLECTORS OF AMERICA)	1994	–	102
GIRAFFF, ROSALENE (HEISEY MOLD FOR HEISEY COLLECTORS OF AMERICA)	1990	–	132
HEN, MINI 521-1/2A, SEA MIST SLAG	1990	–	22
HEN, MINI 5211/8A, PLUM SLAG	1994	–	22
HEN, MINI 5211OB, OCEAN BLUE	1993	–	22
HEN, ROSALENE (HEISEY MOLD FOR HEISEY COLLECTORS OF AMERICA)	1990	–	69
HOBBY HORSE 5135BQ, WINTERBERRY	1988	–	53
HOBBY HORSE 5135HY, BROWN (NATURAL SERIES)	1985	–	53
HOBBY HORSE 5135VJ, VICTORIAN ROSES ON SATIN	1987	–	53
HUMMINGBIRD 5066CN, AMETHYST CARNIVAL	2004	23	25
HUMMINGBIRD 5066OQ, VIOLET	2003	20	22
KISSING KIDS, BOY AND GIRL 5101CN, ORIGINAL (AMETHYST) CARNIVAL	1981	–	81 Pr
KISSING KIDS, BOY AND GIRL 5101HG, HERITAGE GREEN	1983	–	53 Pr
KISSING KIDS, BOY AND GIRL 5101VE, CRYSTAL VELVET	1985	–	42 Pr
KISSING KIDS, BOY AND GIRL 5101YL, CANDLEGLOW YELLOW	1983	–	53 Pr
KITTEN 5119FS, PROVINCIAL BOUQUET	1987	–	53
KITTEN 5119IK, TRUE BLUE FRIENDS (IRIDIZED SLAG GLASS)	1986	–	54
KITTEN 5119NK, COBALT MARIGOLD CARNIVAL	1986	–	42
KITTEN 5119PT, PEARLY SENTIMENTS (WITH PINK PORCELAIN ROSE)	1988	–	42
KITTEN 5119RK, BERRIES & BLOSSOMS	1984	–	81
KITTEN 5119VC, PASTEL VIOLETS ON CUSTARD	1987	–	48
KITTEN, MINI 5365CP, EMPRESS ROSE	2000	–	27
KITTEN, MINI 5365EO, VIOLET (MADE IN REGULAR AND SATIN)	2000	–	27
KITTEN, MINI 5365GE, SEA GREEN (MADE IN SATIN AND IRIDIZED, FENTON GIFT SHOP)	1999	–	27
KITTEN, SLEEPING 5064S3, INSPIRATIONS, STAR LIGHT, STAR BRIGHT ON BLUE COBALT	2004	30	37
KITTEN, SLEEPING 5064U4, BLUE FLOWERS ON MILK-GLASS (CATALOG EXCLUSIVE, SIGNED BY LYNN FENTON)	2003	30	42
KITTEN, SLEEPING 5064WX, "CUDDLES" (LET IT SNOW)	2003	34	69
KITTEN, SLEEPING 5064YN, WHISPERING WINGS ON LOTUS MIST BURMESE	2004	42	44
LION 5241KK, BLUE ROYALE	1990	–	37
LION 5241PE, SHELL PINK	1990	–	37
LION 5241RN, RED CARNIVAL	1990	–	58
LUV BUG 5149CY, CRYSTAL	1985	–	53
LUV BUG 5149NS, NATURAL SERIES	1985	–	47
LUV BUG 5149TO, TOPAZ OPALESCENT (MADE FOR ROSSO)	1999	–	53
MOUSE 5148DC, DAISIES ON CUSTARD	1978	–	42
MOUSE 5148DK, DUSTY ROSE	1997	–	53
MOUSE 5148EG, ROSE GARDEN ON OPAL SATIN	1995	–	58
MOUSE 5148FA, FROSTED ASTERS ON BLUE SATIN	1984	–	54
MOUSE 5148FH, HEARTS & FLOWERS ON IRIDIZED OPAL	1990	–	68
MOUSE 5148FO, FRENCH OPALESCENT	1986	–	69
MOUSE 5148NG, GRAY (NATURAL SERIES)	1985	–	43

		Original price	Current price
MOUSE 5148NS, HAPPY SANTA	1990	$—	$69
MOUSE 5148PF, PURPLE PANSIES ON MILK-GLASS	1996	—	68
MOUSE 5148QB, BLUE HYDRANGEAS ON BLACK	2004	30	32
MOUSE 5148RK, BERRIES & BLOSSOMS	1984	—	53
MOUSE 5148VC, GOLDEN PINE CONES	1987	—	53
MOUSE 5148VE, CRYSTAL VELVET	1984	—	38
MOUSE 5148WS, WHITE SATIN	1971	—	47
OWL 5158FN, FAVRENE, 6"	1993	95	131
OWL 5168BA, BLUE SATIN	1981	—	58
OWL 5168CU, CUSTARD	1981	—	53
OWL 5168JA, JADE GREEN	1980	—	42
OWL 5178BN, ELECTRIC BLUE CARNIVAL (MADE FOR LEVAY)	1980	—	91
OWL 5178CN, ORIGINAL (AMETHYST) CARNIVAL	1971	—	79
OWL 5252GP, GOLD PEARL, 7"	1992	—	53
OWL 5254DT, LIGHT AMETHYST CARNIVAL, 5-1/2"	1991	—	79
OWL 5258Y8, GILDED DECORATION ON BLACK	1996	65	102
OWL K5168TO, TOPAZ OPALESCENT	1998	—	48
PENGUIN 5267DD, "JASPER," HANDPAINTED OPAL SATIN	2000	—	42
PENGUIN 5267FJ, ROYAL LENTEN ROSE ON OPAL	2003	34	42
PENGUIN 5267WX, "PROFESSOR" (LET IT SNOW)	2003	34	48
PENGUIN C5667/8L, FLORAL ON FAVRENE (MADE FOR QVC)	2001	—	69
PIG 5220IK, TRUE BLUE FRIENDS (IRIDIZED BLUE SLAG)	1986	—	79
PIG 5220NK, COBALT MARIGOLD CARNIVAL	1985	—	69
PIG 5220QP, NATURAL COLORS	1985	—	53
PIG 5220SF, MEADOW BLOSSOMS ON OPAL SATIN	1991	—	53
PIG 5220WS, WHITE SATIN	1972	—	69
PLUG HORSE, ROSALENE (HEISEY MOLD FOR HEISEY COLLECTORS OF AMERICA)	1990	—	68
PRAYING CHILDREN, BOY AND GIRL 5100BA, BLUE SATIN	1981	—	53 Pr
PRAYING CHILDREN, BOY AND GIRL 5100BK, EBONY (DONE IN BOTH GLOSS AND SATIN)	1973	—	53 Pr
PRAYING CHILDREN, BOY AND GIRL 5100CN, ORIGINAL (AMETHYST) CARNIVAL	1977	—	64 Pr
PRAYING CHILDREN, BOY AND GIRL 5100CY, CRYSTAL	1972	—	32 Pr
PRAYING CHILDREN, BOY AND GIRL 5100JA, JADE GREEN	1980	—	64 Pr
PRAYING CHILDREN, BOY AND GIRL 5100LN, LAVENDER SATIN	1978	—	86 Pr
PRAYING CHILDREN, BOY AND GIRL 5100PK, PEKIN BLUE	1980	—	53 Pr
PRAYING CHILDREN, BOY AND GIRL 5100RE, ROSALENE	1978	—	85 Pr
PRAYING CHILDREN, BOY AND GIRL 5100VB, VELVA BLUE (BLUE VELVET)	1983	—	54 Pr
PRAYING CHILDREN, BOY AND GIRL 5100VR, VELVA ROSE (PINK VELVET)	1983	—	54 Pr
PRAYING CHILDREN, BOY AND GIRL 5100WS, WHITE SATIN	1981	—	42 Pr
PUPPIES, COCKER SPANIELS 5159NK, COBALT MARIGOLD	1985	—	53
PUPPIES, COCKER SPANIELS 5159SP, NATURAL SERIES	1985	—	68
PUPPIES, COCKER SPANIELS 5159VE, CRYSTAL VELVET	1985	—	42
PUPPY 5085DC, "PUPPY LOVE" (WITH SWAROVSKI CRYSTAL)	2004	30	32
PUPPY 5085UN, GOLDEN DAISY ON AMETHYST CARNIVAL	2004	35	37
PUPPY 5115VJ, VICTORIAN ROSES ON OPAL SATIN	1987	—	54
PUPPY 5225DX, TRELLIS	2000	—	48
PUPPY 5225FS, PROVINCIAL BOUQUET ON WHITE SATIN	1987	—	53
PUPPY 5225KY, BUTTERFLY GARDEN ON COBALT	2001	—	37
PUPPY 5225VC, PASTEL VIOLETS ON CUSTARD	1987	—	58
PUPPY C52254N, PINK FLORAL ON BURMESE (MADE FOR QVC)	1998	—	69
PUPPY, SCOTTIE 5214CY, CRYSTAL	1986	—	42
PUPPY, SCOTTIE 5214NH, GRAY (NATURAL SERIES)	1986	—	58
PUPPY, SCOTTIE 5214SI, SPRUCE CARNIVAL	1991	—	53
PUPPY, SCOTTIE 5214WH, WHITE (NATURAL SERIES)	1987	—	53
RABBIT 5178BN, ELECTRIC BLUE CARNIVAL (MADE FOR LEVAY)	1980	—	91
RABBIT PAPERWEIGHT, ROSALENE (HEISEY MOLD FOR HEISEY COLLECTORS OF AMERICA)	1990	—	58
RACCOON 5142FH, HEARTS & FLOWERS	1993	—	53
RACCOON 5142RN, RED CARNIVAL	1993	—	47
RACCOON 5142TT, TWILIGHT TULIPS	1993	—	53
REINDEER 5261FE, WOODLAND FROST	1999	—	102
REINDEER 5261FJ, ROYAL LENTEN ROSE	2003	90	102
REINDEER 5261JX, TWINING BERRIES	1999	—	103
ROOSTER 5077P2, PERIWINKLE BLUE SLAG, 10"	2004	159	170
ROOSTER 5257AA, AQUAMARINE	1999	—	58
ROOSTER 5257FV, NATURAL COLORS, 8-1/2" (FOLK ART COLLECTION)	1998	—	79
ROOSTER 5257NV, NATURAL COLORS ON SATIN, 8-1/2" (FOLK ART COLLECTION)	1997	—	181
ROOSTER 5257WG, BLUE TOILE, 8-1/2" (FOLK ART COLLECTION)	2004	155	159
ROOSTER 5257YJ, RED DELICIOUS, 8-1/2" (FOLK ART COLLECTION)	2004	155	159
ROOSTER 5292CB, NATURAL COLORS, 5-1/2" (FOLK ART COLLECTION)	1999	—	68
ROOSTER 5292FV, NATURAL COLORS, 5-1/2" (FOLK ART COLLECTION)	1998	—	68
ROOSTER 5292LR, MISTY BLUE SATIN, 5-1/2"	1997	—	47
ROOSTER 5292NO, NATURAL COLORS, 5-1/2" (FOLK ART COLLECTION)	1997	—	68
ROOSTER 5292PQ, CHAMPAGNE SATIN, 5-1/2"	1997	—	47
ROOSTER 5292WG, BLUE TOILE, 5-1/2" (FOLK ART COLLECTION)	2004	55	59

		Original price $	Current price
ROOSTER, MINI 5265AA, AQUAMARINE, 2-1/2"	1999	$—	$26
ROOSTER, MINI 5265CB, NATURAL COLORS, 2-1/2" (FOLK ART COLLECTION)	1999	—	53
ROOSTER, MINI 5265LK, MISTY BLUE IRIDESCENT	1997	—	27
SANTA 5249JN, GOLDEN AGE	1999	—	102
SANTA 5249VP, PATRIOTIC	1998	—	102
SANTA 5279JM, ENCHANTMENT	1999	—	107
SANTA 5299I2, OLDE WORLD	1997	—	107
SANTA 5299JO, BEJEWELED	1999	—	102
SANTA 5299JX, TWINING BERRIES	1999	—	79
SANTA 5299SJ, SPRUCE GREEN	1997	—	53
SANTA IN CHIMNEY 5235DS, HAND-PAINTED OPAL CARNIVAL	1988	—	48
SANTA, HUGGING 5294FJ, ROYAL LENTEN ROSE	2003	35	42
SANTA, HUGGING 5294WX, "NICK" (LET IT SNOW)	2003	35	42
SLEIGH 4695FE, WOODLAND FROST	1999	—	108
SLEIGH 4695FJ, ROYAL LENTEN ROSE	2003	80	88
SLEIGH 4695JX, TWINING BERRIES (SIGNED BY MIKE FENTON)	1999	—	108
SLEIGH 4695P7, POINSETTIA GLOW	1997	85	108
SLEIGH 4695RA, DECORATED RUBY	1997	75	89
SLEIGH 4695SD, GOLD FLORAL ON SPRUCE	1997	65	89
SLIPPER 1995AA, DAISY AND BUTTON, AQUAMARINE	1999	—	22
SLIPPER 1995BR, DAISY AND BUTTON, PRESSED BURMESE	1986	—	58
SLIPPER 1995CA, DAISY AND BUTTON, COLONIAL AMBER	1987	—	22
SLIPPER 1995CP, DAISY AND BUTTON, EMPRESS ROSE	1995	—	22
SLIPPER 1995DK, DAISY AND BUTTON, DUSTY ROSE	1995	—	28
SLIPPER 1995P2, DAISY AND BUTTON, PERIWINKLE BLUE SLAG	2004	17	19
SLIPPER 1995PW, DAISY AND BUTTON, PERIWINKLE BLUE	1986	—	22
SLIPPER 3700MI, MILK-GLASS HOBNAIL	1984	—	22
SLIPPER, CAT 3995BJ, PEKIN BLUE HOBNAIL	1968	—	27
SLIPPER, CAT 3995CG, COLONIAL GREEN HOBNAIL	1963	—	22
SLIPPER, CAT 3995MB, BLUE MARBLE HOBNAIL	1970	—	48
SLIPPER, CAT 3995MI, MILK-GLASS HOBNAIL	1984	—	22
SLIPPER, CAT 3995UB, BLUE BURMESE HOBNAIL	1983	—	69
SLIPPER, CAT 3995WT, WISTERIA HOBNAIL	1977	—	43
SLIPPER, CAT 5290CP, EMPRESS ROSE	1997	—	27
SLIPPER, CAT 5290LR, MISTY BLUE SATIN	1997	—	22
SLIPPER, ROSE 9259KP, COPPER ROSE ON BLACK	1990	—	27
SLIPPER, ROSE 9259LX, LILAC	1990	—	27
SLIPPER, ROSE 9259RN, RED CARNIVAL	1990	—	27
SLIPPER, ROSE 9259RU, RUBY	1990	—	32
SLIPPER, ROSE 9295DK, DUSTY ROSE	1990	—	22
SLIPPER, ROSE 9295ES, ELIZABETH	1990	—	27
SLIPPER, ROSE 9295WQ, LOVE BOUQUET ON BURMESE (MARY WALRATH)	1986	—	53
SNAIL 5134CY, CRYSTAL	1985	—	53
SNAIL 5134NK, COBALT MARIGOLD CARNIVAL	1985	—	64
SNAIL 5135NS, NATURAL SERIES	1985	—	79
SNAIL 5135RE, ROSALENE	1993	—	68
SOUTHERN GIRL 5141BG, DECORATED BURMESE	1997	—	131
SOUTHERN GIRL 5141NI, DECORATED WHITE OPAL SATIN	1992	49	78
SOUTHERN GIRL 5141NX, ROSE PEARL	1992	45	78
SOW, ROSALENE (HEISEY MOLD FOR HEISEY COLLECTORS OF AMERICA)	1990	—	131
SQUIRREL 5215DX, TRELLIS	1995	—	48
SQUIRREL 5215JU, MEADOW BLOSSOMS ON OPAL SATIN	1986	—	48
SQUIRREL 5215NS, NATURAL COLORS (MADE IN BOTH RED AND GRAY)	1985	—	53
SQUIRREL 5215RK, BERRIES & BLOSSOMS	1984	—	69
SQUIRREL 5215SD, SUNSET	2004	20	22
SQUIRREL 5215VE, CRYSTAL VELVET	1986	—	32
SUNFISH 5167GE, SEA GREEN SATIN	1999	—	37
SUNFISH 5167HZ, PINK PEARL	1991	—	32
SUNFISH 5167RN, RED CARNIVAL	1992	—	32
SWAN 5161CD, DAISIES ON CUSTARD	1978	—	53
SWAN 5161CY, CRYSTAL	1984	—	32
SWAN 5161DC, DAISIES ON CAMEO SATIN	1978	—	54
SWAN 5161LN, LAVENDER SATIN	1977	—	69
SWAN 5161PY, PINK BLOSSOM ON CUSTARD	1978	—	54
SWAN 5161RE, ROSALENE	1978	—	79
SWAN, OPEN 5127DK, DUSTY ROSE	1990	—	22
SWAN, OPEN 5127OC, TEAL ROYALE	1988	—	27
SWAN, OPEN 5127OI, TEAL MARIGOLD CARNIVAL	1989	—	27
SWAN, OPEN 5127OO, PROVINCIAL BLUE OPALESCENT	1987	—	27
SWAN, OPEN 5127XV, PERSIAN PEARL	1993	—	22
TREE 5535GL, GOLDEN GLOW, 6-1/2"	1993	—	37
TREE 5535P7, POINSETTIA GLOW, 6-1/2"	1997	39	48
TREE 5535R9, ICED RUBY, 6-1/2"	1994	—	37

Contemporary slippers, 1990s to 2000, each 6" l and **$35+** each, from left: Blue Topaz in Daisy Button pattern, Sea Green in Rose pattern, Champagne with hand-painted floral decoration in Rose pattern, and Golden Amber Carnival with hand-painted "ice gold and white daisies" in Daisy Button pattern. These were made for QVC in 1994.

Price Guide

		Original price	Current price
TREE 5535VU, ICED GREEN WITH GOLD CHIPMUNK, 6-1/2"	2003	$29	$37
TREE 5535XI, ROSE PEARL, 6-1/2"	1995	–	37
TREE 5535ZU, FROSTED GREEN WITH GOLD CARDINAL, 6-1/2"	1997	24	37
TREE 5556GL, GOLDEN GLOW, 4-1/2"	1993	–	27
TREE 5556R9, ICED RUBY, 4-1/2"	1994	–	27
TREE 5556XI, ROSE PEARL, 4-1/2"	1995	–	27
TREE 5556ZW, CRYSTAL IRIDIZED, 4"	1997	18	26
TREE 5557GL, GOLDEN GLOW, 3"	1993	–	27
TREE 5557R9, ICED RUBY, 3"	1994	–	27
TREE 5557XI, ROSE PEARL, 3"	1995	–	27
TREE 5563AQ, AUTUMN GOLD, 7"	2003	–	48
TREE 5563EA, GREEN, 7"	2003	30	42
TREE 5563FJ, ROYAL LENTEN ROSE, 7"	2003	40	48
TURTLE 5266GY, WHITE FLOWERS ON WILLOW GREEN	2002	–	27
TURTLE 5266UG, LAVENDER LILY ON BLUE BURMESE	2002	35	37
TURTLE 5266WJ, DECORATED VIOLET	2003	–	32
TURTLE 5266XJ, BLUE TOPAZ	2002	–	27
TURTLE 5266ZW, DECORATED BLUE	2003	–	32
UNICORN 5253AW, AUTUMN LEAVES ON BLACK	1994	–	58
UNICORN 5253BK, BLACK	1994	–	47
UNICORN 5253TB, TWILIGHT BLUE	1993	–	43
WHALE 5152RC, ROSES ON CUSTARD	1978	–	58
WHALE 5152DC, DAISIES ON CUSTARD	1978	–	58
WHALE 5152DN, DIANTHUS ON CUSTARD	1984	–	58
WHALE 5152FA, FROSTED ASTERS ON BLUE SATIN	1984	–	69
WHALE 5152KK, BLUE ROYALE	1998	–	42
WHALE 5152RE, ROSALENE	1978	–	78
WHALE 5152RK, BERRIES & BLOSSOMS ON OPAL SATIN	1984	–	78
WHALE 5152TP, PEARLY SENTIMENTS (WITH PORCELAIN ROSE)	1988	–	47
WOOD DUCKLING, ROSALENE (HEISEY MOLD FOR HEISEY COLLECTORS OF AMERICA)	1990	–	69

HATS

HAT 1137JE, CORALENE FLORAL ON CELESTE BLUE STRETCH (90TH ANNIVERSARY)	1995	–	69
HAT 1492XC, PERSIAN BLUE OPALESCENT	1989	25	37
HAT 1920BI, BLUE RIDGE (EARLY), 12"	1939	–	349
HAT 1920BO, STIEGEL BLUE SPIRAL OPTIC, 12"	1939	–	349
HAT 1920CR, CRANBERRY SPIRAL OPTIC, 12"	1938	–	420
HAT 1920FO, FRENCH OPALESCENT SPIRAL OPTIC, 12"	1939	–	161
HAT 1920GO, GREEN OPALESCENT SPIRAL OPTIC, 12"	1939	–	320
HAT 1920TO, TOPAZ OPALESCENT SPIRAL OPTIC, 12"	1940	–	340
HAT 1921BI, BLUE RIDGE (EARLY), 10"	1939	–	265
HAT 1921BO, STIEGEL BLUE SPIRAL OPTIC, 10"	1939	–	265
HAT 1921CR, CRANBERRY SPIRAL OPTIC, 10"	1938	–	365
HAT 1921GO, GREEN OPALESCENT SPIRAL OPTIC, 10"	1939	–	280
HAT 1922BI, BLUE RIDGE (EARLY), 8"	1939	–	185
HAT 1922BO, STIEGEL BLUE SPIRAL OPTIC, 9"	1939	–	160
HAT 1922CR, CRANBERRY SPIRAL OPTIC, 9"	1938	–	320
HAT 1922IC, IVORY CREST, 8"	1940	–	106
HAT 1922PC, PEACH CREST, 8"	1940	–	131
HAT 1923AC, AQUA CREST, 6"	1943	–	101
HAT 1923BI, BLUE RIDGE (EARLY), 6"	1939	–	106
HAT 1923CR, CRANBERRY SPIRAL OPTIC, 6"	1938	–	101
HAT 1923PC, PEACH CREST, 7"	1940	–	68
HAT 1924AC, AQUA CREST, 5"	1942	–	64
HAT 1924BI, BLUE RIDGE (EARLY), 4"	1939	–	68
HAT 1924BO, STIEGEL BLUE SPIRAL OPTIC, 4"	1939	–	57
HAT 1924CO, CRANBERRY SPIRAL OPTIC, 4"	1937	–	79
HAT 1924FO, FRENCH OPALESCENT SPIRAL OPTIC, 4"	1939	–	37
HAT 1924GC, GOLD CREST, 5"	1943	–	47
HAT 1924GO, GREEN OPALESCENT SPIRAL OPTIC, 4"	1939	–	58
HAT 1924RC, ROSE CREST, 5"	1946	–	47
HAT 1924SC, SILVER CREST, 5"	1943	–	37
HAT 3193PV, PLATED AMBERINA (RUBY CASED, CONNOISSEUR)	1984	–	159
HAT 3991MI, MINIATURE, MILK-GLASS HOBNAIL	1987	–	16
HAT 3992BO, BLUE OPALESCENT HOBNAIL	1941	–	37
HAT 3992FO, FRENCH OPALESCENT HOBNAIL	1941	–	16
HAT 3992TO, TOPAZ OPALESCENT HOBNAIL	1941	–	47
HAT 7292EC, EBONY CREST, 7"	1968	–	181
HAT 7292PC, PEACH CREST, 5"	1942	–	53
HAT 7292UB, BLUE BURMESE	1983	–	159
HAT 7293SC, SILVER CREST, 8"	1968	–	159
HAT 9495TO, BUTTERFLY & BERRY, TOPAZ OPALESCENT	1988	12	47

JARS

		Original price	Current price
CANDY, COVERED 3784RV, FOOTED, ROSE MAGNOLIA	1993	$38	$47
CANDY, COVERED 3784XV, PERSIAN PEARL	1992	38	47
CANDY, COVERED 7380AW, AUTUMN LEAVES ON BLACK, 9-1/2" (FAMILY SIGNATURE, DON FENTON)	1994	60	79
CANDY, COVERED 7380DC, FOOTED, DAISIES ON CUSTARD	1975	—	58
CANDY, COVERED 7380KD, FOOTED, GOLDEN FLAX ON COBALT BLUE	1993	—	79
CANDY, COVERED 7380VC, FOOTED, GOLDEN PINE CONES	1994	—	68
CANDY, COVERED 7380WD, FOOTED, WHITE DAISIES ON EBONY	1973	—	79
CANDY, COVERED 8489BX, SAPPHIRE BLUE OPALESCENT, 7"	1990	29	47
CANDY, COVERED 9185BR, DAISY IN PRESSED BURMESE, 8-3/4"	1986	—	89
CANDY, COVERED 9185PE, PANELED DAISY IN SHELL PINK	1989	—	53
CANDY, COVERED 9284NK, ROSES IN COBALT MARIGOLD	1987	—	58
CANDY, COVERED 9488KA, FOOTED, CELESTE BLUE STRETCH, 10-1/2" (90TH ANNIVERSARY)	1995	50	68
CANDY, COVERED 9488VB, FOOTED, VELVA BLUE	1987	—	64
COOKIE 3680MI, MILK-GLASS HOBNAIL	1981	—	53
CRACKER 3480CK, CACTUS IN CHOCOLATE GLASS (MADE FOR LEVAY)	1982	—	131
CRACKER 3480RN, RED SUNSET CARNIVAL (MADE FOR LEVAY)	1982	—	99
DOLPHIN HANDLE, COVERED 7580AY, SCULPTURED ICE OPTIC	1982	—	78
DOLPHIN HANDLE, COVERED C7580EQ, BLUE FLORAL ON SHELL PINK (MADE FOR QVC)	1990	—	78
GINGER 2950VN, 3-PIECE, FLORAL ON FAVRENE (CONNOISSEUR)	1978	—	160
GINGER 7288BL, 3-PIECE, BLUE ROSES ON BLUE CUSTARD	1995	—	370
GINGER 7288LC, 3-PIECE, LOG CABIN ON CUSTARD	1978	—	260
JAM, COVERED 3600MI, MILK-GLASS HOBNAIL	1984	—	32
TEMPLE JAR 7488BA, BLUE SATIN	1982	—	54
TEMPLE JAR 7488CD, DAISIES ON CAMEO SATIN	1979	—	79
TEMPLE JAR 7488DN, DIANTHUS ON CUSTARD	1980	—	64
TEMPLE JAR 7488FD, WILDFLOWER ON CAMEO	1982	—	79
TEMPLE JAR 7488IY, SANDCARVED IRIS ON AMETHYST	1987	—	91
TEMPLE JAR 7488LC, LOG CABIN ON CUSTARD	1979	—	91
TEMPLE JAR 7488PE, SILVER POPPIES ON BLACK	1981	—	68
TEMPLE JAR 7488SS, SUNSET ON CAMEO SATIN	1980	—	91
TEMPLE JAR 7488TT, DOWN BY THE STATION	1982	—	160
TEMPLE JAR 7488XA, CLYDESDALES ON CAMEO SATIN	1983	—	420
TEMPLE JAR 7488XZ, CLYDESDALES, SECOND ISSUE (MADE FOR BUDWEISER)	1984	—	420
TEMPLE JAR TALL 7588JA, JADE GREEN	1980	—	68
TEMPLE JAR TALL 7588PE, SILVER POPPIES ON BLACK	1982	—	79
TEMPLE JAR TALL 7708TC, AUTUMN BEAUTY ON TOPAZ OPALESCENT, 10-1/2" (SHOWCASE DEALER EXCLUSIVE)	2004	140	148
TOBACCO 9188DK, DUSTY ROSE (SOLD THROUGH THE FENTON GIFT SHOP)	1990	—	131
TOBACCO 9188P2, PERIWINKLE BLUE SLAG	2004	98	104
TOBACCO 9188RE, ROSALENE (SOLD THROUGH THE FENTON GIFT SHOP)	1990	—	158
TOBACCO 9188RN, GRAPE AND CABLE IN RED CARNIVAL	1996	—	131
TOBACCO 9188US, GRAPE AND CABLE IN SPRUCE CARNIVAL	1999	—	106
URN, COVERED 4602JU, GRAPES ON STIEGEL BLUE OPALESCENT	1991	—	131

LAMPS

LAMP 1413XC, COIN DOT, PERSIAN BLUE OPALESCENT WITH PRISMS, 21"	1989	250	318
LAMP 1509DW, STUDENT, MARY GREGORY ON CRANBERRY, 18"	2000	359	420
LAMP 1705TE, BLUSH ROSE ON OPALENE, 24"	1996	295	365
LAMP 1800BX, GONE WITH THE WIND, FERN, SAPPHIRE BLUE OPALESCENT, 24"	1990	250	420
LAMP 1801XV, PERSIAN PEARL WITH PRISMS, 21"	1992	295	365
LAMP 2780CX, REVERSE PAINTED, SPRING WOODS (CONNOISSEUR)	1993	590	685
LAMP 2940VT, STUDENT, OUR HOME IS BLESSED, 21"	1995	275	340
LAMP 3313GP, GOLD PEARL WITH PRISMS, 21"	1992	235	299
LAMP 3313RV, STUDENT, ROSE MAGNOLIA HOBNAIL WITH PRISMS, 21"	1993	250	341
LAMP 3313XC, STUDENT, PERSIAN BLUE OPALESCENT WITH PRISMS, 21"	1989	200	340
LAMP 4200BS, PETAL, TULIP DELIGHT ON ROSEMILK OPALESCENT, 21"	2004	260	272
LAMP 4603BO, STIEGEL BLUE OPALESCENT WITH PRISMS, 15"	1991	195	236
LAMP 4605JU, HAND-PAINTED GRAPES ON STIEGEL BLUE OPALESCENT, 20"	1991	215	365
LAMP 5486VU, BUTTERFLY AND FLORAL REVERSE PAINTED, 21" (CONNOISSEUR)	1995	595	680
LAMP 5581MD, EVENING BLOSSOM WITH LADYBUG ON MULBERRY, 21"	1996	495	555
LAMP 5582JB, HUMMINGBIRD REVERSE PAINTED (CONNOISSEUR)	1994	590	780
LAMP 6503VQ, STUDENT, GRAPE ARBOR ON VIOLET, 20"	2004	299	315
LAMP 6701RB, ROSES ON PAISLEY BURMESE, 20" (CONNOISSEUR)	1991	275	780
LAMP 6805EA, POPPIES REVERSE PAINTED (CONNOISSEUR)	1996	750	845
LAMP 7204AC, COLONIAL, ALL IS CALM, 16"	1981	175	290
LAMP 7204CV, CHRISTMAS MORN, 16"	1978	125	263
LAMP 7204GH, COLONIAL, GOING HOME, 16"	1980	165	318
LAMP 7204HD, SLEIGH RIDE, 16"	1990	250	320
LAMP 7204HJ, CHRISTMAS EVE	1991	250	320
LAMP 7204HT, FAMILY HOLIDAY	1993	250	320
LAMP 7204OC, COLONIAL, COUNTRY CHRISTMAS	1982	175	317
LAMP 7204SN, STUDENT, STAR OF WONDER, 21"	1996	275	340

West Virginia Woodland lamp, shade with sand-carved scene on Burmese, created for Fenton by Robert Bomkamp and Kelsey Murphy at their studio, Made in Heaven, in southern West Virginia, 2007, limited edition of 100, 17-1/2" h, **$1,000**.

Four decorated White Satin Christmas pieces, showing normal color variations: Mouse, Fenton Gift Shop exclusive, 2006, 3" h, **$35**; Poinsettia Glow bell, 1996, 7" h, **$35**; tree, Fenton Gift Shop exclusive, 2006, 6" h, **$55**; Bear Cub, Fenton Gift Shop exclusive, 2004, 3-3/4" h, **$45**.

		Original price	Current price
LAMP 7204XA, HAMMERED BRASS, CLYDESDALES, 16" (MADE FOR BUDWEISER)	1983	$—	$683
LAMP 7209BD, STUDENT, A CHICKADEE BALLET, 21" (BIRDS OF WINTER)	1988	—	290
LAMP 7209BL, STUDENT, BLUE ROSES ON BLUE SATIN, 20"	1978	—	320
LAMP 7209CD, STUDENT, DAISIES ON CAMEO SATIN, 21"	1978	—	320
LAMP 7209FV, DOWN HOME (DESIGNER SERIES)	1990	—	470
LAMP 7209LT, STUDENT, COUNTRY SCENE, 21"	1990	—	394
LAMP 7209NB, STUDENT, A BLUEBIRD IN SNOWFALL, 21" (BIRDS OF WINTER)	1990	275	394
LAMP 7215CD, HAMMERED COLONIAL, DAISIES ON CAMEO SATIN, 20-1/2"	1980	—	235
LAMP 7294NC, COLONIAL, NATURE'S CHRISTMAS, 16"	1979	150	235
LAMP 7294XS, BIRTH OF A SAVIOR, 16"	1994	195	262
LAMP 7311XA, ELECTRIFIED HURRICANE, CLYDESDALES, 11" (MADE FOR BUDWEISER)	1983	—	420
LAMP 7400DV, MARINER'S LAMP, VIOLETS IN THE SNOW	1970	—	740
LAMP 7400SB, MARINER'S LAMP, SHELLS ON BURMESE, 20" (CONNOISSEUR)	1986	350	790
LAMP 7410DC, STUDENT, DAISIES ON CUSTARD, 21"	1976	—	370
LAMP 7412LC, STUDENT, LOG CABIN ON CUSTARD, 21"	1976	—	630
LAMP 7412QH, RASPBERRIES ON BURMESE, 21" (CONNOISSEUR)	1990	295	845
LAMP 7412QH, STUDENT, RASPBERRY BURMESE, 21" (85TH ANNIVERSARY)	1990	295	530
LAMP 7502UQ, PILLAR, DAYBREAK ON BURMESE, 33" (90TH ANNIVERSARY)	1995	495	900
LAMP 7503CQ, STUDENT, CHICKADEES ON CAMEO SATIN, 23-1/2"	1982	—	530
LAMP 7503LT, STUDENT, LIGHTHOUSE POINT, 23-1/2" (DESIGNER SERIES)	1983	350	685
LAMP 7504CQ, PRINCESS, CHICKADEES ON CAMEO SATIN, 19"	1982	—	340
LAMP 7504YB, PRINCESS, KRISTEN'S FLORAL ON WHITE, 19"	1982	—	317
LAMP 7506MV, HANGING SWAG, MOUNTAIN REFLECTIONS	1982	—	500
LAMP 7506PD, HANGING SWAG, PINK DOGWOOD ON BURMESE	1981	—	530
LAMP 7507LT, LIGHTHOUSE POINT, 25-1/2" (DESIGNER SERIES)	1983	450	680
LAMP 7507YB, FRENCH PROVINCIAL, BRISTEN'S FLORAL, 25-1/2"	1982	—	575
LAMP 7508OW, FRENCH PROVINCIAL, OIL WELL SCENIC, 22"	1981	—	635
LAMP 75100C, STUDENT, COUNTRY CHRISTMAS, 21"	1982	225	320
LAMP 7510AC, STUDENT, ALL IS CALM, 20"	1981	225	320
LAMP 7510OW, OIL WELL SCENIC, 20"	1981	—	470
LAMP 7512GE, HURRICANE, EXPECTATION, 10-1/2"	1984	75	158
LAMP 7514B8, KNIGHTS OF THE SEA	1983	—	500
LAMP 7514TL, SMOKE 'N CINDERS, 23" (DESIGNER SERIES)	1984	—	680
LAMP 7514TP, JUPITER (TRAIN), 23"	1986	—	680
LAMP 7585VF, GONE WITH THE WIND, BERRY & BUTTERFLY ON LOTUS MIST	2000	450	575
LAMP 7602EB, BUTTERFLY & FLOWERING BRANCH ON BURMESE, 22" (CONNOISSEUR)	1985	300	620
LAMP 7802CZ, BOUDOIR, CRANBERRY PEARL (CONNOISSEUR)	1986	145	264
LAMP 9101BA, GONE WITH THE WIND, POPPIES IN BLUE SATIN, 24"	1974	—	420
LAMP 9101CS, GONE WITH THE WIND, POPPIES IN CUSTARD SATIN, 24"	1972	—	318
LAMP 9101LN, GONE WITH THE WIND, POPPIES IN LAVENDER SATIN, 24"	1977	—	845
LAMP 9101LS, GONE WITH THE WIND, POPPIES IN LIME SHERBET SATIN, 24"	1973	—	318
LAMP 9101TO, GONE WITH THE WIND, TOPAZ OPALESCENT, 24"	1988	200	365
LAMP 9101XV, GONE WITH THE WIND, POPPY IN PERSIAN PEARL	1993	225	342
LAMP 92190E, GONE WITH THE WIND, ROSES IN VIOLET, 23"	2004	265	279
LAMP 9301PD, COLUMN, PINK DOGWOOD ON BURMESE SATIN, 20"	1982	—	530
LAMP 9305SF, STUDENT, STRAWBERRIES ON FRENCH OPALESCENT, 20"	1981	—	320
LAMP 9308DV, STUDENT, VIOLETS IN THE SNOW, 19"	1973	—	420
LAMP 9308RB, ROSES ON BURMESE, 20" (CONNOISSEUR)	1990	250	785
LAMP 9308RW, STUDENT, RED ROSES ON MILK-GLASS HOBNAIL, 19-1/2"	1974	—	341
LAMP 9308TT, FLORAL ON ROSALENE SATIN, 21" (CONNOISSEUR)	1989	250	785
LAMP 9702BC, CARDINAL IN THE CHURCHYARD, 18-1/2" (BIRDS OF WINTER)	1987	250	366
LAMP 9830HQ, FAMILY TRADITIONS, 20"	1992	250	318
LAMP A3308UO, GONE WITH THE WIND, PINK OPALESCENT HOBNAIL, 25"	1988	200	366

MINIATURE SETS

		Original price	Current price
MINIATURE EPERGNE 4807PT, 1-HORN, CHAMPAGNE SATIN W/PLUM IRIDESCENT RING, 4-1/2"	1998	65	89
MINIATURE LEMONADE SET UNNUMBERED, 6-PIECE, CRANBERRY OPALESCENT HOBNAIL PITCHER AND CUPS ON FRENCH OPALESCENT TRAY (DORIS LECHTER)	1980	—	212
MINIATURE LEMONADE SET UNNUMBERED, 6-PIECE, LILY OF THE VALLEY PAINTED ON AMETHYST (DORIS LECHTER)	1980	—	263
MINIATURE LEMONADE SET UNNUMBERED, 8-PIECE, HOLLY ON CUSTARD (DORIS LECHTER)	1980	—	212
MINIATURE LEMONADE SET UNNUMBERED, 8-PIECE, PLAIN CUSTARD (DORIS LECHTER)	1980	—	158
MINIATURE LEMONADE SET, 6-PIECE, VIOLETS ON CUSTARD (DORIS LECHTER)	1980	—	212
MINIATURE LEMONADE SET, 8-PIECE, CASED COBALT HOBNAIL ON MILK-GLASS (DORIS LECHTER)	1980	—	236
MINIATURE PUNCH BOWL SET 6800DZ, 5-PIECE, DUSTY ROSE IRIDESCENT	1996	—	158
MINIATURE PUNCH BOWL SET UNNUMBERED, 7-PIECE, COBALT HOBNAIL (DORIS LECHTER)	1980	—	183
MINIATURE PUNCH BOWL SET 6800EZ, 5-PIECE, HOBSTAR AND FEATHER IN SPRUCE GREEN CARNIVAL)	1997	—	158
MINIATURE PUNCH BOWL SET 6801PT, 5-PIECE, DIAMOND LACE, CHAMPAGNE SATIN, 3-3/4"	1998	75	158
MINIATURE TABLE SET 8901N9, ENGLISH DAISY ON IRIDIZED CRYSTAL, WITH 10-1/2" TRAY	1999	—	131
MINIATURE TUMBLE UP UNNUMBERED, PLAIN CUSTARD (DORIS LECHTER)	1980	—	106
MINIATURE TUMBLE UP UNNUMBERED, VIOLETS ON CUSTARD (DORIS LECHTER)	1980	—	131

Price Guide

		Original price	Current price
MINIATURE WATER SET 6205S9, 5-PIECE DECORATED MILK-GLASS	2000	$69	$106
MINIATURE WATER SET UNNUMBERED, 6-PIECE, ROSES ON BURMESE (DORIS LECHTER)	1980	—	290

PITCHERS (AKA "JUGS")

		Original price	Current price
PITCHER 1211RW, EMPIRE, DECORATED CRANBERRY (CONNOISSEUR)	1992	—	235
PITCHER 1212PD, MEADOW BEAUTY ON FRENCH OPALESCENT	1997	95	131
PITCHER 1432CC, COIN DOT IN COUNTRY CRANBERRY, 32 OZ	1982	—	157
PITCHER 1432KB, COIN DOT IN COBALT BLUE, 32 OZ	1982	—	157
PITCHER 1562P9, SWEETBRIER ON PLUM OVERLAY, 9"	1997	—	99
PITCHER 1566FS, THISTLE, 9-1/2" (FAMILY SIGNATURE, DON FENTON)	1995	125	157
PITCHER 1568CW, PANSIES ON CRANBERRY, 6-1/2" (FAMILY SIGNATURE, FRANK FENTON)	1994	95	131
PITCHER 1671MD, EVENING BLOSSOM WITH LADYBUG ON MULBERRY, 7-1/2"	1996	—	131
PITCHER 1866CC, FERN IN CRANBERRY OPALESCENT, 16 OZ	1994	—	106
PITCHER 1875XV, PERSIAN PEARL, 8-1/2"	1992	75	94
PITCHER 2060CC, FEATHER IN COUNTRY CRANBERRY, 70 OZ	1982	—	157
PITCHER 2072TP, HYDRANGEAS ON TOPAZ OPALESCENT, 6-1/2"	1997	55	78
PITCHER 2167CR, HEART OPTIC IN CRANBERRY OPALESCENT, 6-1/2"	1997	89	131
PITCHER 2664BI, BLUE RIDGE, 9"	1985	—	152
PITCHER 2729JI, LATTICE ROSE ON BURMESE, 10" (CONNOISSEUR)	1995	165	235
PITCHER 2774CR, MELON, CRANBERRY, 5-1/2"	1995	69	78
PITCHER 2796AM, VICTORIAN ART GLASS (CONNOISSEUR)	1995	250	316
PITCHER 2960WQ, DRAGONFLY AND WATERLILY ON BURMESE, 8"	1996	165	235
PITCHER 2968UN, CHERRY BLOSSOM ON BURMESE, 10"	1995	175	209
PITCHER 2996V2, GOLDEN PINE CONES	1995	79	89
PITCHER 2997VF, BERRY & BUTTERFLY ON LOTUS MIST BURMESE, 7"	2000	99	131
PITCHER 2998YZ, BOUNTIFUL HARVEST ON BURMESE, 7" (CONNOISSEUR)	1998	—	209
PITCHER 3065DP, ASTERS ON ROSE OVERLAY, 6-1/2" (FAMILY SIGNATURE, LYNN FENTON)	1996	70	89
PITCHER 3265N4, COLONIAL SCROLL ON ROYAL PURPLE	1998	—	131
PITCHER 3275DM, MARY GREGORY ON CRANBERRY, 6-1/2"	1998	125	157
PITCHER 3664CR, WITH ICE LIP, CRANBERRY OPALESCENT HOBNAIL, 70 OZ	1965	—	290
PITCHER 3664MI, MILK-GLASS HOBNAIL, 70 OZ	1987	—	57
PITCHER 3664PO, PLUM OPALESCENT, WITH ICE LIP, 70 OZ (MADE FOR LEVAY)	1984	—	210
PITCHER 3762GO, SYRUP, GREEN OPALESCENT HOBNAIL	1959	—	89
PITCHER 3764BO, BLUE OPALESCENT HOBNAIL, 50 OZ	1993	59	89
PITCHER 3764RV, ROSE MAGNOLIA HOBNAIL, 54 OZ	1940	—	262
PITCHER 5367TE, BLUSH ROSE ON OPALINE	1996	75	89
PITCHER 5440LS, IRISES ON MISTY BLUE SATIN, 7-1/2" (FAMILY SIGNATURE, DON FENTON)	1997	85	105
PITCHER 5531QP, BERRIES ON BURMESE 4-1/2" (CONNOISSEUR)	1992	65	89
PITCHER 6063UN, GOLDEN DAISY ON AMETHYST CARNIVAL, 7-1/2"	2004	90	95
PITCHER 7060RE, DIAMOND OPTIC IN ROSALENE (CONNOISSEUR)	1989	55	131
PITCHER 9468QY, WHITE FLORAL ON ENAMELED AZURE (CONNOISSEUR)	1987	85	141
PITCHER 9666LX, SANDWICH IN LILAC	1990	—	52
PITCHER AND BOWL SET 3303PO, PLUM OPALESCENT (MADE FOR LEVAY)	1984	—	368
PITCHER AND BOWL SET A3000U0, PEACHES 'N CREAM , 52 OZ	1988	78	152
PITCHER C1866XN, FERN, OCEAN BLUE OPALESCENT WITH COBALT CREST AND HANDLE (MADE FOR QVC)	1990	—	68
PITCHER C3360DO, DUSTY ROSE CARNIVAL W/TEAL CREST AND HANDLE, HOBNAIL (MADE FOR QVC)	1989	—	131

PUNCH BOWL SETS

		Original price	Current price
PUNCH SET 3712GO, 14-PIECE, GREEN OPALESCENT HOBNAIL	1985	250	505
PUNCH SET 3712RV, 14-PIECE, ROSE MAGNOLIA HOBNAIL	1993	275	450
PUNCH SET 3712XC, 14-PIECE, PERSIAN BLUE OPALESCENT HOBNAIL	1989	275	450
PUNCH SET 4601DT, 14-PIECE, PANELED GRAPE IN LIGHT AMETHYST CARNIVAL	1991	300	355
PUNCH SET 4601XV, 14-PIECE, PERSIAN PEARL	1992	315	360
PUNCH SET 9750TS, HEART AND HOBSTAR IN TOPAZ OPALESCENT, WITH 8 CUPS AND METAL STAND	1997	350	450
PUNCH SET A3712UO, 14-PIECE, PEACHES 'N CREAM HOBNAIL	1988	275	360

ROSE BOWLS

		Original price	Current price
ROSE BOWL 2759JV, FLORAL ON GREEN APPLE STRETCH	2004	40	42
ROSE BOWL 2759PU, DECORATED FRENCH OPALESCENT	2004	40	42
ROSE BOWL 2759RK, FLORAL ON CELESTE BLUE STRETCH	2004	40	42
ROSE BOWL 2759SS, STIEGEL GREEN STRETCH	1994	25	32
ROSE BOWL 2759ST, WIND FLOWERS ON STIEGEL GREEN STRETCH	1994	30	37
ROSE BOWL 2759YZ, FLORAL ON ROSEMILK OPALESCENT	2004	40	42
ROSE BOWL 7424XE, HELLO FRIEND (FAWN) ON CRANBERRY (MARY GREGORY)	2004	95	99
ROSE BOWL 8223RN, ORANGE TREE IN RED CARNIVAL	1990	—	68
ROSE BOWL 8250VR, MINIATURE, VELVA ROSE	1980	—	37
ROSE BOWL 8429BA, WATER LILY IN BLUE SATIN	1977	—	53
ROSE BOWL 8429LS, WATER LILY IN LIME SHERBET	1977	—	48
ROSE BOWL 8429RN, WATER LILY IN RED CARNIVAL	1994	—	53
ROSE BOWL 8453BO, LILY OF THE VALLEY, BLUE OPALESCENT	1979	—	47
ROSE BOWL 8453BX, LILY OF THE VALLEY, SAPPHIRE BLUE OPALESCENT	1990	16	47
ROSE BOWL 8453FO, LILY OF THE VALLEY, CAMEO OPALESCENT	1979	—	42

Angelo Rossi tumbler in a swirl design, 2006, 5-3/4" h, **$85**.

Two free-hand vases by Dave Fetty and Angelo Rossi, 2006, 10-1/2" and 11" h, **$200** each.

		Original price	Current price
ROSE BOWL 8453TO, LILY OF THE VALLEY, TOPAZ OPALESCENT	1980	$—	$53
ROSE BOWL 8454CN, 3-TOED, CURTAIN, AMETHYST CARNIVAL	1978	—	47
ROSE BOWL 8454IO, 3-TOED, AQUA OPAL CARNIVAL (MADE FOR LEVAY)	1980	—	78
ROSE BOWL 8454IP, 3-TOED, IRIDIZED PLUM CARNIVAL (MADE FOR LEVAY)	1984	—	78
ROSE BOWL 8924TH, TURQUOISE HANGING HEART (ROBERT BARBER COLLECTION)	1975	—	89
ROSE BOWL 8925CI, CUSTARD HANGING HEART (ROBERT BARBER COLLECTION)	1976	—	106
ROSE BOWL 9126LS, POPPY IN LIME SHERBET	1977	—	42
ROSE BOWL 9436IO, 3-TOED, AQUA OPAL CARNIVAL, WITH LOOPED HANDLE (LEVAY)	1980	—	99
ROSE BOWL 9436IO, 3-TOED, IRIDIZED PLUM CARNIVAL, WITH LOOPED HANDLE (LEVAY)	1982	—	99
ROSE BOWL 9558WQ, LOVE BOUQUET ON BURMESE (MARY WALRATH)	1982	—	63
ROSE BOWL 9653NK, FABERGE, COBALT MARIGOLD CARNIVAL	1986	—	47
ROSE BOWL A3854UO, PINK OPALESCENT HOBNAIL	1988	12	37
ROSE BOWL C7424UI, FLORAL ON ROYAL PURPLE (MADE FOR QVC)	1998	—	99
ROSE BOWL, 7424DB, SCENE ON BURMESE	1973	—	99
ROSE BOWL, C1724, ROSES ON BURMESE DIAMOND OPTIC (MADE FOR QVC)	1999	—	106

SALT AND PEPPER SHAKERS

SHAKERS 2206CR, POLKA DOT IN CRANBERRY	1955	—	165 Pr
SHAKERS 3406MI, CACTUS IN MILK-GLASS	1959	—	33 Pr
SHAKERS 3406TO, CACTUS IN TOPAZ OPALESCENT	1959	—	110 Pr
SHAKERS 3806BO, BLUE OPALESCENT HOBNAIL	1949	—	55 Pr
SHAKERS 3806CA/AR, COLONIAL AMBER HOBNAIL	1959	—	33 Pr
SHAKERS 3806CR, CRANBERRY OPALESCENT HOBNAIL	1954	—	98 Pr
SHAKERS 3806FO, FRENCH OPALESCENT HOBNAIL	1949	—	44 Pr
SHAKERS 3806MI, MILK-GLASS HOBNAIL	1950	—	17 Pr
SHAKERS 4408CA, THUMBPRINT IN COLONIAL AMBER	1964	—	33 Pr
SHAKERS 4408CB, THUMBPRINT IN COLONIAL BLUE	1964	—	48 Pr
SHAKERS 4408CG, THUMBPRINT IN COLONIAL GREEN	1964	—	22 Pr
SHAKERS 4408CP, THUMBPRINT IN COLONIAL PINK	1964	—	65 Pr
SHAKERS 5606MI, BLOCK AND STAR IN MILK-GLASS	1955	—	44 Pr
SHAKERS 5606TU, BLOCK AND STAR IN TURQUOISE	1977	—	66 Pr
SHAKERS 6906MI, TEARDROP IN MILK-GLASS	1955	—	28 Pr
SHAKERS 6906TU, TEARDROP IN TURQUOISE	1955	—	44 Pr
SHAKERS 8606CY, REGENCY, CRYSTAL	1983	—	22 Pr
SHAKERS 9206CA, ROSES IN COLONIAL AMBER	1967	—	38 Pr
SHAKERS 9206CB, ROSES IN COLONIAL BLUE	1967	—	49 Pr
SHAKERS G1606AY, AMETHYST	1983	—	33 Pr
SHAKERS UNNUMBERED, BLUE OPALESCENT HOBNAIL, FOOTED	1940	—	81 Pr
SHAKERS UNNUMBERED, GREEN OPALESCENT HOBNAIL, FOOTED (RARE)	1940	—	220 Pr

TOOTHPICK HOLDERS

TOOTHPICK 3495RN, RED SUNSET CARNIVAL (MADE FOR LEVAY)	1982	—	32
TOOTHPICK 3795OR, FOOTED, COLONIAL ORANGE HOBNAIL	1963	—	21
TOOTHPICK 4644DT, LIGHT AMETHYST CARNIVAL	1991	10	26
TOOTHPICK 6688EO, PANELED DAISY IN MINTED CREAM	1986	—	21
TOOTHPICK 6688UO, PANELED DAISY IN PEACHES 'N CREAM	1987	—	21
TOOTHPICK 7590VY, PURPLE STRETCH (MADE FOR LEVAY)	1981	—	32
TOOTHPICK 8294BA, PANELED DAISY IN BLUE SATIN	1973	—	37
TOOTHPICK 8294BR, PANELED DAISY IN BURMESE	1986	—	68
TOOTHPICK 8294CU, PANELED DAISY IN CUSTARD SATIN	1973	—	26
TOOTHPICK 8294LS, PANELED DAISY IN LIME SHERBET SATIN	1973	—	32
TOOTHPICK 8294OC, PANELED DAISY IN TEAL ROYALE	1988	—	21
TOOTHPICK 8295BR, WILD STRAWBERRY IN BURMESE	1985	—	68
TOOTHPICK 8295CK, WILD STRAWBERRY IN CHOCOLATE GLASS (MADE FOR LEVAY)	1982	—	37
TOOTHPICK 8295CN, WILD STRAWBERRY IN ORIGINAL (AMETHYST) CARNIVAL	1971	—	37
TOOTHPICK 9572EO, MINTED CREAM	1986	—	21
TOOTHPICK 9572UO, PEACHES 'N CREAM	1987	—	21
TOOTHPICK 9592BQ, WINTERBERRY	1981	—	32
TOOTHPICK 9592WQ, LOVE BOUQUET ON BURMESE (MADE FOR MARY WALRATH)	1986	—	53

VASES

VASE 1136JE, FAN, CORALENE FLORAL ON CELESTE BLUE STRETCH, 6" (90TH ANNIVERSARY)	1995	50	63
VASE 1146TE, BLUSH ROSE ON OPALINE, 7"	1996	50	63
VASE 1216EH, SPIRAL, FUSCHIA, 10" (FAMILY SIGNATURE, GEORGE FENTON)	1994	95	131
VASE 1353XC, TULIP, FINE DOT OPTIC IN PERSIAN BLUE OPALESCENT, 10"	1989	38	78
VASE 1554RP, DAYDREAMING ON CRANBERRY, 9" (MARY GREGORY)	1996	135	157
VASE 1554S9, HEXAGONAL, SUMMER GARDEN ON SPRUCE, 9" (FAMILY SIGNATURE, DON FENTON)	1995	85	131
VASE 1559CW, PANSIES ON CRANBERRY, 9-1/2" (FAMILY SIGNATURE, BILL FENTON)	1994	95	158
VASE 1567CW, PANSIES ON CRANBERRY, 7" (FAMILY SIGNATURE, GEORGE FENTON)	1995	75	106
VASE 1577Z1, GARDEN TIME ON CRANBERRY, 8-1/2" (MARY GREGORY)	2004	129	135
VASE 1640C1, RIB, FLORAL ON CRANBERRY, 11" (FAMILY SIGNATURE, GEORGE FENTON)	1993	110	173
VASE 1649KG, GOLDEN FLAX ON COBALT, 9-1/2" (FAMILY SIGNATURE, SHELLEY FENTON)	1995	95	157
VASE 1684RP, TWINING FLORAL ON ROSALENE, 7" (CONNOISSEUR)	1992	110	183
VASE 1689MS, HUMMINGBIRD, 9-1/2"	1996	95	157

		Original price	Current price
VASE 1693GX, BUTTERFLY GARDEN ON GOLD, 8-1/2" (FAMILY SIGNATURE SERIES, NANCY FENTON)	2000	$95	$131
VASE 1786PV, VINTAGE ON PLUM, 10" (FAMILY SIGNATURE, DON FENTON)	1993	80	131
VASE 1795TE, BLUSH ROSE ON OPALENE, 11"	1996	85	106
VASE 1796BY, BLOSSOMS & BOWS ON CRANBERRY, 7-1/4" (CONNOISSEUR)	1987	95	131
VASE 1853BX, TULIP, FERN IN SAPPHIRE BLUE OPALESCENT	1990	40	53
VASE 2048TP, HYDRANGEAS ON TOPAZ OPALESCENT, 9-1/2"	1997	85	89
VASE 2056XV, PERSIAN PEARL, 5"	1992	40	53
VASE 2556Z1, TULIP, IRIDIZED CASED FRENCH OPALESCENT AND RUBY WITH TEAL RING (CONNOISSEUR)	1988	50	131
VASE 2743JP, CORALENE ON FAVRENE, 7" (CONNOISSEUR)	1994	—	210
VASE 2744JK, SCROLLWORK ON PLUM OPALESCENT, 8" (CONNOISSEUR)	1994	—	210
VASE 2748FW, AMPHORA, DECORATED FAVRENE WITH STAND (CONNOISSEUR)	1993	285	395
VASE 2750MS, MELON HERRINGBONE, HUMMINGBIRD AND WILD ROSE ON MULBERRY	1996	85	157
VASE 2752RN, ALPINE THISTLE IN RED CARNIVAL, 9" (FAMILY SIGNATURE, FRANK FENTON)	1993	105	210
VASE 2755CR, RIBBED CRANBERRY	1994	48	57
VASE 2767JE, FLORAL ON CELESTE BLUE STRETCH, 4-1/2" (90TH ANNIVERSARY)	1995	33	53
VASE 2782DD, WILD ROSE WITH BERRIES, 11" (CONNOISSEUR)	1996	195	270
VASE 2947US, AMPHORA , CHERRIES ON ROYAL PURPLE, WITH METAL STAND (CONNOISSEUR)	1995	195	290
VASE 2955UU, HUMMINGBIRD ON BURMESE, 9"	1995	150	235
VASE 2955VF, BERRY & BUTTERFLY ON LOTUS MIST BURMESE, 9-1/2"	2000	95	131
VASE 2988JB, IRISH TREASURES, 6": "MAY THE ROAD RISE UP TO MEET YOU	2004	60	63
VASE 3161OP, PERIWINKLE BLUE OVERLAY, 11"	1985	—	107
VASE 3183XV, TULIP, PERSIAN PEARL, 6-1/2"	1992	25	53
VASE 3190KF, HANDLED, FRENCH ROYALE, 7" (CONNOISSEUR)	1986	—	530
VASE 3194ZS, HANDLED URN, CRANBERRY SATIN	1986	—	240
VASE 3195FS, PROVINCIAL BOUQUET, 7"	1988	—	99
VASE 3196FS, PROVINCIAL BOUQUET, 13"	1988	—	157
VASE 3248R8, BOY FISHING, 5" (MARY GREGORY)	1999	—	131
VASE 3254QJ, QUEEN'S BIRD BURMESE, 11" (CONNOISSEUR)	1996	250	342
VASE 3292TC, AUTUMN BEAUTY ON TOPAZ OPALESCENT, 8-1/2" (SHOWCASE DEALER EXCLUSIVE)	2004	60	95
VASE 3355GP, GOLD PEARL, 6"	1992	27	47
VASE 3356RV, JACK IN THE PULPIT, ROSE MAGNOLIA, 7-1/2"	1993	28	47
VASE 3558CR, BUTTONS AND BRAIDS IN CRANBERRY OPALESCENT (SHOWCASE DEALER EXCLUSIVE, SIGNED BY GEORGE FENTON)	1995	—	210
VASE 3752BR, BURMESE HOBNAIL, 11"	1941	—	265
VASE 3752CR, CRANBERRY OPALESCENT HOBNAIL	1941	—	240
VASE 3759GO, SWUNG, GREEN OPALESCENT HOBNAIL, 18"	1959	—	210
VASE 3759MI, SWUNG, MILK-GLASS HOBNAIL, 18"	1959	—	53
VASE 3854RV, ROSE MAGNOLIA HOBNAIL, 4-1/2"	1993	—	47
VASE 3957BO, FAN, BLUE OPALESCENT HOBNAIL, 6-1/4"	1991	18	32
VASE 4651BO, STIEGEL BLUE OPALESCENT, 10"	1991	25	37
VASE 4653BO, TULIP, STIEGEL BLUE OPALESCENT, 9"	1997	25	37
VASE 4751PI, FIELD FLOWERS ON CHAMPAGNE SATIN (FAMILY SIGNATURE, SHELLEY FENTON)	1996	55	131
VASE 4759SE, MAGNOLIA & BERRY ON SPRUCE, 10" (FAMILY SIGNATURE, FRANK FENTON)	1991	80	131
VASE 4955CR, HEART OPTIC IN CRANBERRY, 5"	1998	40	68
VASE 5150PI, ATLANTIS, PEACH OPALESCENT CARNIVAL GLASS	1997	—	78
VASE 5150TS, ATLANTIS, TOPAZ OPALESCENT	1999	—	78
VASE 5153SI, MINIATURE HAND, SPRUCE CARNIVAL	1981	—	42
VASE 5153VY, MINIATURE HAND, PURPLE STRETCH (MADE FOR LEVAY)	1996	—	47
VASE 5355YN, MELON, WHISPERING WINGS ON LOTUS MIST BURMESE	2004	100	106
VASE 5357TE, BLUSH ROSE ON OPALINE, 8-1/2" (FAMILY SIGNATURE, GEORGE FENTON)	1992	75	131
VASE 5479GF, SEA GREEN SATIN, 6"	1992	35	47
VASE 5480GF, SEA GREEN SATIN, 12"	1992	45	63
VASE 5541QH, TULIP, RASPBERRIES ON BURMESE, 6-1/2" (CONNOISSEUR)	1994	45	89
VASE 5555SS, JACK IN THE PULPIT, STIEGEL GREEN STRETCH, 7"	1994	30	47
VASE 5559SS, HANDKERCHIEF, STIEGEL GREEN STRETCH, 8"	1994	30	47
VASE 5559ST, HANDKERCHIEF, WIND FLOWERS ON STIEGEL GREEN STRETCH, 8"	1990	30	53
VASE 5750DK, DUSTY ROSE, 9"	1982	—	32
VASE 5858CC, WHEAT, COUNTRY CRANBERRY, 8"	1982	—	53
VASE 5858KB, WHEAT, COBALT BLUE, 8"	1985	—	53
VASE 5858OP, WHEAT, PERIWINKLE BLUE OVERLAY, 8"	1990	—	53
VASE 5956P2, PLUME, PERIWINKLE BLUE SLAG (FAMILY SIGNATURE, SHELLEY FENTON)	2004	60	64
VASE 6056CR, WAVE CREST IN CRANBERRY	1981	—	47
VASE 6056SF, STRAWBERRIES ON FRENCH OPALESCENT, 6"	1989	—	47
VASE 6453RG, PINCH VASE, VASA MURRHINA, ROSE WITH AVENTURINE GREEN, 8" (CONNOISSEUR)	1999	65	131
VASE 6470N4, COLONIAL SCROLL ON ROYAL PURPLE, 6-1/2"	2000	—	183
VASE 6533R9, PILLAR VASE, BUTTERFLY CHASING (MARY GREGORY SERIES)	1992	139	158
VASE 6548UQ, PERIWINKLE ON BLUE BURMESE, 11"	1986	—	184
VASE 6568CR, CRANBERRY, 4"	1986	35	42
VASE 6650U0, BUD, PEACHES 'N CREAM OPALESCENT, 6"	1998	—	32

Pink Dogwood on Burmese vases, 1980s, 6-3/4" and 6" h, **$100+** and **$60+**.

Three Atlantis vases, with form variations and found in more than a dozen colors, in Periwinkle Blue Iridized (2004 for QVC), Peach Opalescent Carnival (1981) and Ruby Carnival (mid-1990s), 5-1/2" to 6-1/2" h, **$75 to $85** each.

Off-hand overlay vase in a swirl pattern with clear ovals by Dave Fetty, 2005, 7-1/2" h, **$225+**.

West Virginia Woodland vase with sand-carved scene on Burmese, created for Fenton by Robert Bomkamp and Kelsey Murphy at their studio, Made in Heaven, in southern West Virginia, 2007, limited edition of 375, 8-3/4" h, **$600**.

Price Guide

		Original price	Current price
VASE 6854IU, AURORA, AMERICANA WITH BLUE CREST, 7-1/2" (FAMILY SIGNATURE, MIKE FENTON)	1982	$90	$95
VASE 7051WA, SPIRAL RIBBED, ROSEBUDS ON ROSALENE, 6"	1982	—	131
VASE 7241BA, BLUE SATIN, 4-1/2"	1982	—	26
VASE 7241VI, VINTAGE ON CAMEO SATIN, 4-1/2"	1980	—	32
VASE 7252BD, BLUE DOGWOOD ON CAMEO SATIN, 7"	1976	—	47
VASE 7252LC, LOG CABIN ON CUSTARD, 7"	1991	—	78
VASE 7252QH, RASPBERRY BURMESE, 7-1/2" (CONNOISSEUR)	1983	65	183
VASE 7252XA, CLYDESDALES, 7" (MADE FOR BUDWEISER)	1977	14	318
VASE 7254SS, SUNSET ON CAMEO SATIN, 4"	1988	—	52
VASE 7254VC, PASTEL VIOLETS ON CUSTARD, 4-1/2"	1983	—	42
VASE 7254XA, CLYDESDALES, 4-1/2" (MADE FOR BUDWEISER)	1998	10	183
VASE 7255GG, TULIP, FLORAL INTERLUDE ON SEA GREEN SATIN, 11"	1982	99	131
VASE 7255PD, TULIP, PINK DOGWOOD ON BURMESE, 10-1/2"	1980	—	131
VASE 7255SS, TULIP, SUNSET ON CAMEO SATIN, 10-3/4"	1980	—	131
VASE 7255UZ, TULIP, MORNING GLORIES ON BURMESE, 10" (GLASS MESSENGER EXCLUSIVE)	1998	—	157
VASE 7257BC, BLUEBIRDS ON CUSTARD, 10"	1977	—	78
VASE 7257MV, MOUNTAIN REFLECTIONS, 10"	1982	—	158
VASE 7542FJ, OVAL, SCULPTURED ROSE QUARTZ, 4-1/2" (CONNOISSEUR)	1983	33	106
VASE 7544PF, PETITE FLEUR, 5"	1984	—	37
VASE 7547PD, PINK DOGWOOD ON BURMESE, 5-1/2"	1981	—	79
VASE 7550IN, IRIS ON BONE WHITE, 6-1/2"	1982	—	58
VASE 7550KP, COPPER ROSES, 6-1/2"	1982	—	53
VASE 7551VR, FAN WITH DOLPHIN HANDLES, VELVA ROSE	1980	—	63
VASE 7551VY, FAN WITH DOLPHIN HANDLES, PURPLE STRETCH (MADE FOR LEVAY)	1981	—	68
VASE 7552PD, SMALL TULIP, PINK DOGWOOD ON BURMESE, 6-3/4"	1982	—	89
VASE 7554BQ, BLUE ROSES ON CUSTARD SATIN, 5"	1981	—	47
VASE 7557IN, IRIS ON BONE WHITE, 9"	1982	—	68
VASE 7557JA, JADE, 10"	1980	—	53
VASE 7558PD, BUD, PINK DOGWOOD ON BURMESE, 6"	1981	—	53
VASE 7558PE, SILVER POPPIES ON EBONY, 6"	1982	—	32
VASE 7559IN, IRIS ON BONE WHITE, 7-1/2"	1982	—	53
VASE 7559IY, SAND-BLASTED IRIS ON AMETHYST, 7-1/2"	1982	—	89
VASE 7655SX, SPHERE, SOPHISTICATED LADIES	1982	—	157
VASE 7659GJ, SCULPTURED ROSE QUARTZ, 7" (CONNOISSEUR)	1983	50	142
VASE 7660RN, RIBBED, BERRIES & BLOSSOMS, 7-1/2"	1984	—	131
VASE 7660VC, RIBBED, PASTEL VIOLETS ON CUSTARD, 7-1/2"	1988	—	57
VASE 7661LJ, ROSE QUARTZ, 9" (CONNOISSEUR)	1986	75	320
VASE 7661MD, MOTHER AND CHILD, SCULPTURED ROSE VELVET, 9" (CONNOISSEUR)	1984	125	340
VASE 7661P4, GOLD LEAVES SAND-CARVED ON PLUM IRIDESCENT, 9" (CONNOISSEUR)	1993	175	235
VASE 7661Z8, COTTAGE SCENE, 9" (FAMILY SIGNATURE, SHELLEY FENTON)	1993	90	157
VASE 7688QB, BLUE HYDRANGEAS ON BLACK, 5-1/2"	2004	58	61
VASE 7691MP, AURORA, ROSE CORSAGE, 7"	1989	—	37
VASE 7691WF, AURORA, WILD ROSE (CONNOISSEUR)	1995	125	235
VASE 7693ES, BEADED MELON, ELIZABETH ON SILVER CREST, 6"	1990	—	53
VASE 7696KP, COPPER ROSES ON BLACK, 7-1/2"	1983	—	47
VASE 7754KE, SMALL BLOWN WITH AQUAMARINE RIM (KATJA)	1889	—	53
VASE 7790RB, ROSES ON BURMESE, 6" (85TH ANNIVERSARY)	1990	—	99
VASE 7791RB, ROSES ON BURMESE, 6-1/2" (85TH ANNIVERSARY)	1990	45	106
VASE 7792QD, TREES SCENE ON BURMESE, 9" (85TH ANNIVERSARY)	1990	75	142
VASE 8251GE, MANDARIN, SEA GREEN SATIN	1998	90	131
VASE 8251HU, MANDARIN, BLUE ON CAMEO SATIN, 9"	1982	—	157
VASE 8251JA, MANDARIN, JADE GREEN	1980	—	78
VASE 8252HU, EMPRESS, BLUE ON CAMEO SATIN	1982	—	89
VASE 8252VE, EMPRESS, CRYSTAL VELVET	1987	—	89
VASE 8257BR, PEACOCK, PRESSED BURMESE, 8"	1986	—	183
VASE 8351PW, BUD, BARRED OVAL, PERIWINKLE BLUE, 8-1/2"	1986	—	26
VASE 8354AG, BASKETWEAVE, CASED JADE OPALINE, 9"	1990	—	53
VASE 8354CR, BASKETWEAVE, CRANBERRY OPALESCENT, 9"	1991	—	131
VASE 8354KH, BASKETWEAVE, CRANBERRY OPALINE, 9"	1990	—	68
VASE 8354RE, BASKETWEAVE, ROSALENE, 9" (CONNOISSEUR)	1989	45	131
VASE 8458BX, BUD, SAPPHIRE BLUE OPALESCENT, 10"	1990	17	26
VASE 8528CC, SPHERE, COUNTRY CRANBERRY, 8"	1982	—	68
VASE 8550AY, AMETHYST, 10"	1982	—	47
VASE 8551AY, CYLINDER, AMETHYST, 10-1/2"	1982	25	53
VASE 8551BB, CYLINDER, GLACIAL BLUE, 10-1/2"	1982	—	47
VASE 8551CC, CYLINDER, COUNTRY CRANBERRY, 10-1/2"	1982	—	53
VASE 8552AY, AMETHYST, 9-1/2"	1982	—	47
VASE 8553AY, AMETHYST, 6-1/2"	1990	18	37
VASE 8651BX, SAPPHIRE BLUE OPALESCENT, 3-1/2"	1990	14	26
VASE 8801ER, OVAL, ETCHED GEOMETRIC, ROSE (ARTISAN SERIES)	1985	—	173
VASE 8801NV, OVAL, BLUE AND WHITE GEOMETRIC (ARTISAN SERIES)	1985	—	235
VASE 8802ER, OVAL, ETCHED GEOMETRIC, ROSE, 12" (ARTISAN SERIES)	1985	—	173
VASE 8802LY, GABRIELLE, SAND-CARVED COBALT BLUE CASED (CONNOISSEUR)	1985	150	320

		Original price	Current price
VASE 8805X3, SAND-CARVED LEAVES OF GOLD ON IRIDIZED PLUM, 9" (CONNOISSEUR)	1993	$125	$183
VASE 8806ER, ETCHED GEOMETRIC, ROSE, 7-1/2" (ARTISAN SERIES)	1985	—	131
VASE 8807EP, ETCHED GEOMETRIC, PERIWINKLE, 9" (ARTISAN SERIES)	1985	—	131
VASE 8808SB, BURMESE SHELLS, 7-1/2" (CONNOISSEUR)	1985	135	318
VASE 8812EK, SILHOUETTES, 10-1/2"	1986	—	157
VASE 8812ET, MISTY MORNING, 10-1/2" (CONNOISSEUR)	1986	95	194
VASE 8812FQ, FLORAL ON FAVRENE, 10-1/2" (CONNOISSEUR)	1991	125	173
VASE 8812G1, FRUIT ON FAVRENE, 10-1/2" (CONNOISSEUR)	1991	125	178
VASE 8812JY, DANIELLE, 10-1/2" (CONNOISSEUR)	1986	95	211
VASE 8817KP, COPPER ROSES ON BLACK, 8-1/2"	1990	—	78
VASE 8817QZ, SEASCAPE ON BURMESE, 8" (CONNOISSEUR)	1992	150	290
VASE 9458AV, SWAN IN GOLDEN AZURE, 8" (CONNOISSEUR)	1984	65	157
VASE 9550DC, FLORAL ON CHAMPAGNE SATIN (SHOWCASE DEALER EXCLUSIVE, SIGNED BY BILL FENTON)	1996	75	106
VASE 9556PY, BUD, PINK BLOSSOMS ON CUSTARD SATIN, 8-1/2"	1981	—	32
VASE 9650OP, DOGWOOD IN PERIWINKLE BLUE OVERLAY, 11"	1985	—	68
VASE 9651HD, FLORAL ON ROSE VELVET, 9"	1984	75	158
VASE 9658OP, DOGWOOD IN PERIWINKLE BLUE OVERLAY, 8"	1985	—	57
VASE 9659DK, DUSTY ROSE, 7-1/2"	1986	—	37
VASE 9752RN, DAFFODIL IN RED CARNIVAL	1990	—	63
VASE 9754LX, LILAC WITH BOW, 6-1/4"	1990	—	42
VASE 9758PN, PETAL PINK, 8"	1990	—	42
VASE 9855EV, CUTBACK LILIES ON FAVRENE (CONNOISSEUR)	1996	195	235
VASE 9866TR, TROUT, 8" (CONNOISSEUR)	1996	135	183
VASE 9869VF, BERRY & BUTTERFLY ON LOTUS MIST BURMESE, 5"	2000	65	89
VASE K7751KN, CRYSTAL WITH HICKORY FADE, 3-1/2" (KATJA)	1983	20	47
VASE K7753KN, CRYSTAL WITH HICKORY FADE, 7" (KATJA)	1983	—	68
VASE K7754KE, CRYSTAL WITH AQUAMARINE RIM, 3-1/2" (KATJA)	1983	20	47
VASE UNNUMBERED, BLUE BUBBLE OPTIC (F.A.G.C.A.)	1992	—	63
VASE UNNUMBERED, MELON, BUBBLE OPTIC (F.A.G.C.A.)	1985	—	131

WATER SETS (PITCHERS WITH GLASSES)

WATER SET 1404XC, 7-PIECE, COIN DOT IN PERSIAN BLUE OPALESCENT	1989	200	318
WATER SET 1802BX, 7-PIECE, FERN IN SAPPHIRE BLUE OPALESCENT	1990	200	288
WATER SET 1870XV, 5-PIECE, FERN IN PERSIAN PEARL	1992	175	210
WATER SET 3407IO, 7-PIECE, CACTUS IN AQUA OPAL CARNIVAL (MADE FOR LEVAY)	1980	—	430
WATER SET 3407RN, 7-PIECE WITH GOBLETS, RED SUNSET CARNIVAL (MADE FOR LEVAY)	1982	—	380
WATER SET 3407TO, 7-PIECE , CACTUS IN TOPAZ OPALESCENT	1988	140	270
WATER SET 3908GP, 5-PIECE, HOBNAIL IN GOLD PEARL	1992	99	160
WATER SET 3908RV, 5-PIECE , HOBNAIL IN ROSE MAGNOLIA	1993	109	145
WATER SET 3908XC, 7-PIECE, COIN DOT IN PERSIAN BLUE OPALESCENT	1989	100	160
WATER SET 5560SS, 5-PIECE, STIEGEL GREEN STRETCH WITH GOBLETS	1994	150	185
WATER SET 5906DG, 3-PIECE, PUPPY LOVE ON CRANBERRY (MARY GREGORY)	2004	295	335
WATER SET 6555C1, 5 PIECE, APPLE IN AMETHYST CARNIVAL	2004	199	215
WATER SET 6555RN, 5-PIECE, APPLE TREE IN RED CARNIVAL	1995	—	290
WATER SET 7509VV, 7-PIECE, PURPLE STRETCH (MADE FOR LEVAY)	1981	—	380
WATER SET 7700QH, 7-PIECE, RASPBERRIES ON BURMESE (CONNOISSEUR)	1990	275	480
WATER SET 9001KA, LINCOLN INN IN CELESTE BLUE STRETCH (90TH ANNIVERSARY)	1995	—	350
WATER SET 9003CK, 7-PIECE, LINCOLN INN IN CHOCOLATE GLASS (MADE FOR LEVAY)	1982	—	430
WATER SET A3908UO, 7-PIECE, PINK OPALESCENT HOBNAIL	1988	99	235

ORNAMENTS

BIRDS OF WINTER SERIES

ORNAMENT 1714BC, CARDINAL IN THE CHURCHYARD, 3-1/2"	1990	—	26
ORNAMENT 1714BD, A CHICKADEE BALLET, 3-1/2"	1990	—	26
ORNAMENT 1714BL, DOWNY WOODPECKER-CHISELED SONG, 3-1/2"	1990	—	26
ORNAMENT 1714NB, A BLUEBIRD IN SNOWFALL, 3-1/2"	1990	—	26

GENERAL ISSUES

ORNAMENT 1714AC, GOLDEN WINGED ANGEL ORNAMENT	1996	28	37
ORNAMENT 1714CY, CRYSTAL	1982	—	16
ORNAMENT 1714DH, HOLLY ON MILK-GLASS	1982	—	21
ORNAMENT 1714JW, BABY'S FIRST CHRISTMAS (TEDDY BEAR), IRIDESCENT, 3-1/2"	1991	—	21
ORNAMENT 1714KE, SNOWMAN ON COBALT BLUE, 3-1/2"	1999	—	21
ORNAMENT 1714KG, KELLY GREEN	1982	—	16
ORNAMENT 1714QQ, ANGEL WITH HARP AND PUPPY, IRIDESCENT, 3-1/2"	1991	—	21
ORNAMENT 1714QR, ANGEL WITH FLUTE AND FAWN, IRIDESCENT, 3-1/2"	1991	—	21
ORNAMENT 1714QV, ANGEL WITH GUITAR AND KITTEN, IRIDESCENT, 3-1/2"	1991	—	21
ORNAMENT 1714QY, ANGEL WITH HORN AND LAMB, IRIDESCENT, 3-1/2"	1991	—	21
ORNAMENT 1714RU, RUBY	1982	—	16
ORNAMENT 5242WU, RENAISSANCE ANGEL, 4-1/2"	1999	—	47
ORNAMENT 9414FL, FLORENTINE NATIVITY	1982	—	26
ORNAMENT 9414TD, NATIVITY ON ANTIQUE BROWN	1982	—	26

Blue Ridge 80th Anniversary water set, 1985: jug, 10" h; and four tumblers, 5" h each, **$300+** set.

Dave Fetty handmade ornament with pulled ovals, sold with stand, 3-3/4" diameter, 2006, **$95**.

Price Guide

		Original price	Current price
MADE FOR QVC			
ORNAMENT C1059, FAMILY TRADITIONS (HOUSE IN SNOW) ON OPAL IRIDESCENT, 3-1/2"	1992	$—	$26
ORNAMENT C15302, CARDINAL ON IVORY SATIN, 3-1/2"	1994	—	32
ORNAMENT C8556, CHRISTMAS EVE (MAILBOX) ON IVORY SATIN, 3-1/2"	1991	—	26
ORNAMENT C95526, SNOWMAN ON FRENCH OPALESCENT, 3-1/2"	1999	—	26
PLATES			
BICENTENNIAL			
PLATE 9419CH, EAGLE IN BICENTENNIAL CHOCOLATE	1976	—	47
PLATE 9419IB, EAGLE IN INDEPENDENCE BLUE	1976	—	47
PLATE 9419PR, LAFAYETTE IN PATRIOT RED	1975	—	47
PLATE 9419VW, VALLEY FORGE WHITE	1974	—	37
PLATE NO. 1, "THE SEEDS ARE SOWN" IN ANTIQUE AMERICAN MILK-GLASS SATIN (G.F.W.C.)	1973	—	16
PLATE NO. 1, "THE SEEDS ARE SOWN" IN ANTIQUE POWDER BLUE SATIN (MADE FOR GENERAL FEDERATION OF WOMEN'S CLUBS - G.F.W.C.)	1973	—	21
PLATE NO. 2, "INDEPENDENCE IS DECLARED" IN ANTIQUE AMERICAN MILK GLASS SATIN (G.F.W.C.)	1974	—	16
PLATE NO. 3, "A TEST OF COURAGE" IN ANTIQUE AMERICAN MILK-GLASS SATIN (G.F.W.C.)	1975	—	16
PLATE NO. 3, "A TEST OF COURAGE" IN ANTIQUE POWDER BLUE SATIN (G.F.W.C.)	1975	—	21
PLATE NO. 4, "LIBERTY IS PROCLAIMED" IN ANTIQUE AMERICAN MILK-GLASS SATIN (G.F.W.C.)	1976	—	16
BIRDS OF WINTER			
PLATE 7418BC, CARDINAL IN THE CHURCHYARD IN OPAL SATIN, 8"	1987	40	48
PLATE 7418BD, A CHICKADEE BALLET ON OPAL SATIN, 8"	1988	40	47
PLATE 7418BL, DOWNY WOODPECKER-CHISELED SONG, 8"	1989	40	47
PLATE 7418NB, A BLUEBIRD IN SNOWFALL, 8"	1990	40	47
CHRISTMAS			
PLATE 7418AI, ANTICIPATION (BOY AND GIRL LOOKING OUT SNOWY WINDOW), 8"	1983	45	54
PLATE 7418CV, SHARING THE SPIRIT	1987	50	53
PLATE 7418GE, EXPECTATION (CHILD LOOKING UP CHIMNEY), 8"	1984	50	54
PLATE 7418HT, FAMILY HOLIDAY ON WHITE SATIN, 8"	1993	49	53
PLATE 7418NA, COUNTRY CHRISTMAS, 8"	1982	43	47
PLATE 7418NC, NATURE'S CHRISTMAS, 8"	1979	35	43
PLATE 7418OC, COUNTRY CHRISTMAS (MAN AND BOY BRINGING HOME TREE), 8"	1982	—	48
PLATE 7418RX, THE WAY HOME ON RED SATIN, 8"	1997	—	79
PLATE 7418SN, STAR OF WONDER ON GOLD SATIN, 8"	1996	65	79
PLATE 7418VS, SILENT NIGHT (DEER) ON COBALT SATIN, 8"	1994	—	68
PLATE 7418WP, HEART'S DESIRE (BOY LOOKING AT PUPPY IN WINDOW), 8"	1985	50	53
PLATE 7610KP, THE ANNOUNCEMENT IN COBALT SATIN (BIRTH OF A SAVIOR)	1999	—	52
PLATE 7610QP, THE JOURNEY IN SPRUCE GREEN SATIN (BIRTH OF A SAVIOR)	2000	—	52
PLATE 7610XS, THE ARRIVAL ON GREEN SATIN, OPEN EDGE, 9" (BIRTH OF A SAVIOR)	1998	—	52
PLATE 7618AC, ALL IS CALM, 8"	1981	—	53
PLATE 8270CN, THE LITTLE BROWN CHURCH IN THE VALE IN ORIGINAL CARNIVAL	1971	—	27
PLATE 8270WS, THE LITTLE BROWN CHURCH IN THE VALE IN WHITE SATIN	1971	—	22
PLATE 8276BA, THE OLD NORTH CHURCH IN BLUE SATIN (CHRISTMAS IN AMERICA)	1976	—	27
PLATE 8276CN, THE OLD NORTH CHURCH IN ORIGINAL CARNIVAL	1976	—	27
PLATE 8276WS, THE OLD NORTH CHURCH IN WHITE SATIN	1976	—	22
PLATE 8280BA, CHRIST CHURCH IN BLUE SATIN (CHRISTMAS IN AMERICA)	1980	17	27
PLATE 8280BA, SAN XAVIER DEL BAC CHURCH IN BLUE SATIN (CHRISTMAS IN AMERICA, LAST IN SERIES)	1981	17	27
PLATE 8280CN, CHRIST CHURCH IN ORIGINAL CARNIVAL	1980	17	27
PLATE 8280CN, SAN XAVIER DEL BAC CHURCH IN ORIGINAL CARNIVAL	1981	19	27
PLATE 8280FL, SAN XAVIER DEL BAC CHURCH, HANDPAINTED FLORENTINE, SIGNED	1981	25	38
PLATE 8280WS, CHRIST CHURCH IN WHITE SATIN	1980	17	22
PLATE 8280WS, SAN XAVIER DEL BAC CHURCH IN WHITE SATIN	1981	19	22
CRAFTSMAN PLATES			
PLATE 9170CN, GLASSMAKER IN ORIGINAL (AMETHYST) CARNIVAL	1970	50	27
PLATE 9171CN, PRINTER IN ORIGINAL CARNIVAL	1971	55	33
PLATE 9172CN, BLACKSMITH IN ORIGINAL CARNIVAL	1972	100	38
PLATE 9173CN, SHOEMAKER IN ORIGINAL CARNIVAL	1973	55	34
PLATE 9174CN, COOPER IN ORIGINAL CARNIVAL	1974	40	27
PLATE 9175CN, SILVERSMITH IN ORIGINAL CARNIVAL	1975	45	27
PLATE 9176CN, GUNSMITH IN ORIGINAL CARNIVAL	1976	30	28
PLATE 9177CN, POTTER IN ORIGINAL CARNIVAL	1977	20	27
PLATE 9178CN, WHEELWRIGHT IN ORIGINAL CARNIVAL	1978	20	27
GENERAL ISSUES			
PLATE 4611DT, PANELED GRAPE IN AMETHYST CARNIVAL WITH "GOOD LUCK" INTERIOR	1991	35	43
PLATE 7418LT, COUNTRY SCENE ON WHITE SATIN, 8"	1989	—	69
PLATE 7418SS, SUNSET ON CAMEO SATIN, 8"	1981	—	54
PLATE 7418SU, STUDEBAKER-GARFORD, 8"	1986	—	103
PLATE 7418TP, JUPITER (TRAIN), 8"	1986	—	103
PLATE 8415TB, THE OLD HOMESTEAD IN ANTIQUE BLUE (CURRIER & IVES)	1981	—	44
PLATE 8417TN, HARVEST IN ANTIQUE BROWN (CURRIER & IVES)	1981	—	44

Fenton Resources

The Fenton Art Glass Co.: www.fentonartglass.com

The Fenton Art Glass Collectors of America, Inc. is an independent association dedicated to learning more about Fenton glass. The office of this non-profit, educational collectors' club is located in Williamstown, W.Va. The FAGCA is run by a Board of Trustees elected by its membership: http://fagcainc.wirefire.com

Formed in 1990, the National Fenton Glass Society is a not-for-profit corporation. The Society's purpose is to promote the study, understanding, and enjoyment of handmade glass, the handmade glass industry and especially glass made by the Fenton: http://www.fentonglasssociety.org

The Early American Pattern Glass Society has a comprehensive listing of museum glass holdings in the U.S. and U.K.; http://www.eapgs.org/eapgsmuseum.html

Entomologist David Shetlar, Ph.D., of Ohio State University, has put together a Web site on American stretch glass, and includes a detailed overview of Fenton pieces, at: http://bugs.osu.edu~bugdoc/Shetlar/StretchGlass/Sgopenpage.htm

Fenton Finders

Fenton Finders of Illiana (Illinois and Indiana). Meets four times year, members' homes. Info: D. Nielsen, 1101 Maple Ave., La Porte, IN 46350; (219) 362-7205.

Fenton Finders of Michigan. Meets fourth Tuesday every month except July and August, 7:30 p.m., Riley Junior High School, 15555 Henry Ruff, Room 7, Livonia, MI. Info: D. Frazee, (313) 427-6929.

Fenton Finders of Northern California. Meets fourth Tuesday, 7:30 p.m., January, March, May, July, September, November. Info: L. Parker; (415) 523-4870.

Fenton Finders of Tampa Bay. Meets first Saturday, St. Paul's Lutheran Church, Second Floor, Education Building, Clearwater, Fla.

Fenton Finders of the Buckeye State. Meets different locations. Info: (419) 738-6512

Fenton Finders of Twin Cities area (Minnesota). Meets monthly. Info: Randy (651) 639-1841 after 6 p.m.

Fenton Finders of Southeastern Wisconsin. Meets five times each year. Info: Mel (262) 242-3273.

Collector Contacts

Alan and Sharon Fenner
Browerville, MN
(320) 594-2752
fennersa@rea-alp.com

Randy's Antiques & Gifts
867 Grand Ave.
St. Paul, MN 55105
(651) 312-0303
(877) 924-2400
www.randys-antiques.com
Rabbitmpls@aol.com

Tom and Diane Rohow
St. Paul, MN 55105

Dick and Marilyn Trierweiler
North St. Paul, MN
(651) 770-9388
dmtrier@visi.com

Kill Creek Antiques
Steve and Connie Duncan
P.O. Box 46
De Soto, KS 66018

Bob Grissom (Carnival Glass)
Raytown, Mo.
(816) 356-5320
Bobimocg@aol.com

Chuck Bingham
Altoona, Wis.
Torchaven@aol.com

Jim Langer and Doug Horton
612-623-0134

Other Glass Clubs

Arizona Depression Glass Club
Contact: Anne
623-872-9020
E-mail: epserbus@worldnet.att.net

Arkansas Glasshoppers
Contact: E. Mitchell
2507 Howard St.
Little Rock, AR 72206
501-375-0435.
E-mail: EstherMitchell@msn.com

Big D Depression Glass Club (Texas)
Contact: Ellen Evans
972-530-9907
E-mail: elleneva@attbi.com

Central Florida Glassaholics
Contact: Cheryl Cantrall
P.O. Box 2319
Lakeland, FL 33806
Web site: www.glassaholics.com
E-mail: information@glassaholics.com

City of Five Flags Depression Glass Club (Florida)
Contact: Madelynn Deason
904-433-7722

Crescent City Depression Glass Society (Louisiana)
Web site: www.crescentcityglass.org
E-mail: glass55981@yahoo.com

Depression Era Glass Society of Wisconsin
Contact: Carol Jarosz
1534 S. Wisconsin Ave.
Racine, WI, 53403
414-637-5054 or 715-854-2278

DG Club of Northeast Florida
Contact: Joel Holley
904-221-0478
E-mail: KWPEWP@aol.com

Gateway Depressioneers Glass Club of Greater St. Louis (Missouri)
Contact: Don Baker
314-839-2874

Greater Tulsa Depression Era Glass Club (Oklahoma)
Contact: Mike Thompson
918-291-5817
E-mail: Finis Riggs; 4489@mindspring.com

Heart of America Glass Collectors (Missouri)
Contact: 816-461-8016 or 816-246-4421
Web site: www.hoagc.org

Houston Glass Club (Texas)
Contact: 281-342-4876 or 713-461-6049
Web site: www.houstonglassclub.org

Hudson Valley Depression Glass Club
Contact: Diane Seawall
5 Croft Hill Rd., Rd. 2
Poughkeepsie, NY 12603
914-473-3898

Illinois-Missouri Glass & China Club
Contact: 1203 No. Yale
O'Fallon, IL 62269
618-632-9067

Illinois Valley Depression Glass Club
Contact: C. Bartlett
RR 1, Box 52
Rushville, IL 62681
217-322-3989

Iowa Depression Glass Club
Contact: B. Ballantyne; 515-225-8157
J. Settell; 515-223-9364
E-mail: Jeff_wdms@earthlink.net

Kansas City Depression Glass Club
Contact: 816-322-8289
Web site: www.kcdepressionglassclub.com

Lincoln Land Depression Glass Club (Illinois)
Contact: J. Maher
217- 793-2182
E-mail: lots1@earthlink.net

Old Dominion Depression Glass Club (Virginia)
Contact: K. Nenstiel
703-256-0090
Web site: www.mnsinc.com/cornucopia/oddgc.htm

Peach State Depression Glass Club
Contact: J. Newsome
2249 Bridle Ct.
Norcross, GA 30071-3337
770-368-9790

Permian Basin Depression Glass Club
Contact: P. Terrell
2205 E. 12th
Odessa, TX 79761
915-332-0851

Pikes Peak Depression Glass Club (Colorado)
Contact: Les Stewart
719-598-1424
Web site: www.ppdgc.com
E-mail: Les.Stewart@iwantglass.com

Portland's Rain of Glass Club (Oregon)
Contact: 503-282-3838

Prairie Land Depression Era Glass Club (Kansas)
Contact: Pres. Cathy Fisher
785-272-0955

Queen City Glass Club (Maryland)
Contact: Mary Lou Brookley
310-689-8629

Rocky Mountain Depression Glass Society
Contact: 303-973-5287
Web site: www.rmdgs.com
E-mail: Martie Grubenhoff
martieg1215@comcast.net

South Florida Depression Glass Club
Contact: Robin Rhea
954-572-6049
E-mail: robbier@mindspring.com or sfdgc@aol.com

Tarheel Depression Glass Club (North Carolina)
Contact: 919-563-1004 or 336-227-3331
Web site: members.tripod.com/~wwantiques/tdgc.html
E-mail: ncglassclub@hotmail.com

Tidewater Depression Glass Club (Virginia)
Contact: Doug Mills
757-467-0229
E-mail: vabeach_tdgc@hotmail.com

Wichita Glass Gazers Club (Kansas)
Contact: 316-684-6019
E-mail: LEE1JEAN@aol.com

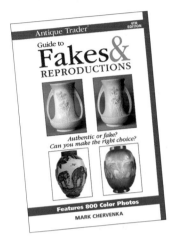

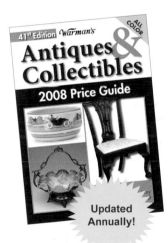

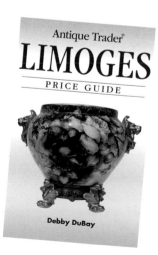